Jurisdictional Battlefields

Political Culture, Theatricality, and Spanish Expeditions in
Charcas in the Second Half of the Sixteenth Century

Liverpool Latin American Studies

Series Editor: Matthew Brown, University of Bristol
Emeritus Series Editor: Professor John Fisher

Liverpool Latin American Studies, New Series 32

Jurisdictional Battlefields
Political Culture, Theatricality, and Spanish Expeditions in Charcas in the Second Half of the Sixteenth Century

Mario Graña Taborelli

LIVERPOOL UNIVERSITY PRESS

First published 2024 by
Liverpool University Press
4 Cambridge Street
Liverpool
L69 7ZU

British Library Cataloguing-in-Publication data
A British Library CIP record is available

ISBN 978-1-83553-709-1

Typeset by Carnegie Book Production, Lancaster

Contents

Illustrations

Acknowledgements

Over the years of research behind this book, I grew indebted to organisations and individuals across various countries. In Argentina, a fees-free and state-run university education enabled someone like me to undertake and complete, first his qualification as a high-school history teacher at the Instituto de Formación Docente 41 in Adrogué in Buenos Aires province, and subsequently his degree as a historian, or Licenciado en Historia, at the Universidad Nacional de Luján. After a long hiatus, of nearly two decades, I was able to resume my studies and, here in the UK, at the University of London, my PhD supervisor Dr Linda Newson's support, time, patience, and expertise in the field of Spanish America were invaluable. My co-supervisor and long-time friend, Dr Ana María Presta, was of immense help with her knowledge of sixteenth-century Charcas and Latin American history. A member of CONICET and the Programa de Historia de América (PROHAL) at the Instituto de Historia Argentina y Americana 'Dr Emilio Ravignani', part of the Facultad de Filosofía y Letras of the Universidad de Buenos Aires (UBA), Dr Presta contributed for many years with her inquisitiveness, honesty, and experience.

This book also owes a great deal to a legion of archivists and librarians who, many times under difficult, almost impossible, circumstances because of a global pandemic, helped me with materials. My full admiration goes to them. In Bolivia, at the Archivo y Biblioteca Nacionales de Bolivia (ABNB) archive and library, Nelva Celia Delgadillo Hurtado has always been ready to step in and help with document searches and reproductions. The work that archivists and staff in general do at ABNB to preserve Bolivia's heritage is priceless. I am also thankful to staff at the Archivo General de Indias (AGI) in Seville, the Archivo Histórico Nacional (AHN) in Madrid, and the Biblioteca de la Real Academia de la Historia in the same city. Librarians at DeGolyer Library at the Southern Methodist University in the USA, and the Biblioteca Nacional del Perú, were also extremely helpful. Finally, I must express my gratitude to staff at the British Library and, at Senate House, in the University of London, and my special thanks to Julio Cazzasa, who has always provided support and a friendly and familiar voice every time we engaged in conversations and discussed my projects.

My gratitude also extends to colleagues, and friends, with whom I exchanged views and materials over the years, including Adrian Masters, Kris Lane, Lia Guillermina Oliveto, Mauricio Onetto, Nathan Weaver Olson, Carlos Piccone Camere, Juan José Ponce, Tatiana Suárez, Paola Revilla Orias, Virginia Ghelarducci, Ainhoa Montoya, Felipe Ruan, Francisco Quijano, Carolina Jurado, Guillaume Candela, Sergio Angeli, Domingo Centenero de Arce, and the late Luis Córdoba Ochoa. Many of you are probably unaware of how much I appreciate your comments, most of them given informally and at times over webcams, social media, phone calls, or emails. I have also benefited greatly from the study group created by José Sovarzo in Colegio de México and the seminar organised by UNAM, CONICET, and the Universidad Nacional de Rosario on 'Integration and Fragmentation of the Iberian Worlds'. I have cherished the opportunities I was given to present preliminary versions of this work in virtual discussions held at the Institute of Latin American Studies (ILAS), now Centre for Latin American and Caribbean Studies (CLACS), housed at the Institute of Modern Languages Research (IMLR), now Institute of Languages, Cultures and Societies (ILCS), in London; the Universidad de Salamanca; and the Cambridge Legal and Social History Workshop at the University of Cambridge. I am also thankful to Federico García Blaya for all his help with this book's maps. I have also benefited greatly from the comments by my *viva voce* examiners Dr Fernando Cervantes and Dr Christine Matthias, and the two anonymous reviewers of Liverpool University Press. My thanks also go to the Society for Latin American Studies (SLAS) as I have been the recipient of a SLAS Postgraduate & Postdoctoral Research Support Award; and the Institute of Historical Research at the University of London for the Scoloudi award. Both covered some of the costs associated with my fieldwork. Finally, this book owes a great deal to the internet. At a time of social distancing and lockdowns, the World Wide Web brought home books and documents that complemented my previous years of research at the Archivo General de la Nación Argentina (AGNA) and the libraries of the Museo Etnográfico 'Juan B. Ambrosetti' and the Instituto de Historia Argentina y Americana 'Dr Emilio Ravignani' in Argentina.

At a more personal level, I am thankful to my family and friends, especially my husband, Andrew Graña Taborelli, who have patiently and supportively accompanied this work. Thanks to you all.

Abbreviations

ABNB	Archivo y Biblioteca Nacionales de Bolivia
AGI	Archivo General de Indias
AGNA	Archivo General de la Nación Argentina
AHN	Archivo Histórico Nacional, Paraguay
AHP	Archivo Histórico de Potosí
BL	British Library
BNE	Biblioteca Nacional de España
BNF	Bibliothèque Nationale de France
CBC	Centro Bartolomé de las Casas
IEP	Instituto de Estudios Peruanos
IFEA	Instituto Francés de Estudios Andinos

Introduction

'O mundo nâo se nos dá em espetáculo; o mundo é o espetáculo
que as sociedades constroem, organizando-o e impondon-lhe
uma narrativa.'

'The world is not displayed in front of us as a show; the world
is a show that societies build, organising it and imposing a
narrative on it.'

António Hespanha[1]

At the peak of their careers, three Spanish men of high social status—the
holder of a grant of indigenous peoples or *encomendero*, Martín de Almendras;
the fifth viceroy of Peru, don Francisco de Toledo (1569–1581); and the royal
official Juan Lozano Machuca—left the comforts of their late sixteenth-
century urban lives behind, to travel to remote areas in the company of
relatives, soldiers, priests, and hundreds of indigenous peoples and their
chiefs, not in search of El Dorado and its promising wealth, but looking to
strengthen something less tangible yet still relevant to their future and that
of the Spanish monarchy: their political authority. This book describes their
journeys, as well as the historical journey of the process of implementation,
settlement, and consolidation of the jurisdiction of the Spanish Crown on the
borders of Charcas, in present-day Bolivia and the northwest of Argentina, a
region that was at the time the jewel in the crown because of its silver mines
in Potosí.

Based on the early modern political culture that saw justice as the ultimate
purpose of rule, both divine and on earth, jurisdiction is here understood

---

1 António Manuel Hespanha, *A ordem do mundo e o saber dos juristas: Imaginários do
antigo direito europeu* (Lisbon: independently published, 2017), p. 365. (Translation
by this book's author.)

not in a territorial sense, but as *iurisdictio*, or the authority to establish law and deliver justice.[2] This had to be fought and negotiated in battlefields and courtrooms, through consensus as well as coercion and violence. For the Spanish monarchy, which spanned from the Philippines to Mexico and from Peru to Spain, long distances and communication hurdles meant that such authority had to be shared with individuals and groups who were appointed royal agents. Through this process of sharing and creating jurisdiction, the Crown localised its power, in a manner that gave it a presence across its vast domains; and its agents and their networks, scope for action.[3]

Global in a geographical sense, the Spanish monarchy was a localised polity, where laws were collaboratively produced, scrutinised, adapted, and open to interpretation, ignored if needed.[4] A pragmatic polity, it expanded either by dynastic union, or succession/annexation, or conquest; by aggregating or incorporating territories, kingdoms, and realms, which meant that these entities were able to preserve a large degree of autonomy.[5] This made it a composite polity of multiple local centres, or polycentric, as the Catholic

2 Pietro Costa, *Iurisdictio. Semantica del potere politico nella pubblicistica medievale (1100–1433)* (Milan: Giuffrè, 2002 [1969]), Ch. III; Jesús Vallejo, 'Power Hierarchies in Medieval Juridical Thought: An Essay in Reinterpretation', *Ius Commune* 19 (1992): pp. 1–29; António Manuel Hespanha, *La gracia del derecho. Economía de la cultura en la Edad Moderna* (Madrid: Centro de Estudios Constitucionales, 1993), p. 66; Bartolomé Clavero, 'Justicia y gobierno. Economía y gracia', in *Real Chancillería de Granada: V Centenario 1505–2005* (Granada: Junta de Andalucía, Consejería de Cultura, 2006), pp. 122, 125; Alejandro Agüero, 'Las categorías básicas de la cultura jurisdiccional', in *De justicia de jueces a justicia de leyes: Hacia la España de 1870*, Vol. VI, Cuadernos de Derecho Judicial (Madrid: Consejo General del Poder Judicial, 2006), pp. 31–32; Carlos Garriga, 'Orden jurídico y poder político en el Antiguo Régimen', *Revista de Historia Internacional* 16 (2004): p. 30; Javier Barrientos Grandón, *El gobierno de las Indias* (Madrid: Marcial Pons, 2004), p. 45; Colin MacLachlan, *Spain's Empire in the New World: The Role of Ideas in Institutional and Social Change* (Berkeley: University of California Press, 1991), p. 38; John Owens, *'By My Absolute Royal Authority': Justice and the Castilian Commonwealth at the Beginning of the First Global Age* (Rochester, NY: University of Rochester Press, 2005), p. 1.
3 Hespanha, *La gracia del derecho*, p. 100.
4 Alejandro Agüero, 'Local Law and Localization of Law: Hispanic Legal Tradition and Colonial Culture (16th–18th Centuries)', in *Spatial and Temporal Dimensions for Legal History Research: Experiences and Itineraries* (Frankfurt am Main: Max Planck Institute for European Legal History, 2016), pp. 101–29; Richard Ross and Philip Stern, 'Reconstructing Early Modern Notions of Legal Pluralism', in *Legal Pluralism and Empires, 1500–1850* (New York, London: New York University Press, 2013), pp. 109–43; Lauren Benton, *Law and Colonial Cultures: Legal Regimes in World History, 1400–1900* (Cambridge, New York: Cambridge University Press, 2002), pp. 7–15; Adrian Masters, *We, the King: Creating Royal Legislation in the Sixteenth-Century Spanish New World* (Cambridge: Cambridge University Press, 2023).
5 Oscar Mazín Gómez, 'Architect of the New World: Juan Solórzano Pereyra and the Status of the Americas', in *Polycentric Monarchies: How Did Early Modern Spain and*

monarch was king in each of his domains in a different manner, showing a great degree of respect for local political cultures.[6] This shifts the discussion on the character of the monarchy away from the periphery–centre dichotomy and challenges the idea that this polity was centralised and centralising in a manner that prepared the ground for the creation of the nation-states prevalent in Latin America from the nineteenth century onwards. The early modern Spanish monarchy did not anticipate these developments, which were only one of the many possible futures at the time.[7]

To the distant Crown, without royal armies to command and exclusively relying on locals for the defence of its realm, delegation of authority and localisation were indispensable government tools. However, in a society made of dense and extended networks of patronage that saw royal posts and the missions associated with them as rewards worth fighting for, the downscaling of authority also bolstered intense competition. It caused tension as jurisdictions frequently overlapped, creating a 'legal patchwork' or an 'orderly disorder' where multiple authorities and a variety of legal regimes co-existed.[8] Subject to compromises on the ground and tenuous in character, jurisdiction had to be confirmed and reconfirmed and was regularly staged through 'ceremonies of possession' which gave it a theatrical character.[9] With the imprint of Catholicism, such rituals were great displays of political imagery, pomp, and circumstance, constituting a theatre of royal presence

---

    Portugal Achieve and Maintain a Global Hegemony? (Eastbourne: Sussex Academic Press, 2012), pp. 27–42.

6 'Composite monarchy' was a concept originally developed by historian Helmut Georg Koenigsberger. John Elliott, 'A Europe of Composite Monarchies', *Past and Present*, no. 137 (1992): p. 50; 'polycentrism' as a concept was coined by Hespanha. Hespanha, *La gracia del derecho*, p. 112; Pedro Cardim, Tamar Herzog, José Javier Ruiz Ibañez, and Gaetano Sabatini, eds, *Polycentric Monarchies*, pp. 3–4; Bartolomé Yun-Casalilla, *Iberian World Empires and the Globalization of Europe 1415–1668* (Puchong, Selangor: Springer Singapore, 2018), p. 148.

7 Examples of this teleological approach could be found in: José María Ots Capdequí, *El estado español en las Indias* (México: El Colegio de México, 1941), pp. 17, 47, 49; Richard Konetzke, *América Latina*, Vol. II, *La época colonial*, trans. Pedro Scaron (México: Siglo Veintiuno, 1977), Ch. 5; Horst Pietschmann, *El estado y su evolución al principio de la colonización española de América* (México: Fondo de Cultura Económica, 1989); and Clarence Henry Haring, *The Spanish Empire in America* (New York and Burlingame, CA: First Harbinger Books, 1963), p. 4.

8 António Manuel Hespanha, 'The Legal Patchwork of Empires', review of *Legal Pluralism and Empires, 1500–1850*, by Lauren Benton and Richard J. Ross, *Rechtsgeschichte* 22 (2014), pp. 303–14; MacLachlan, *Spain's Empire in the New World*, p. 40; Benton refers to this situation as an 'orderly disorder'. Lauren Benton, 'Making Order out of Trouble: Jurisdictional Politics in the Spanish Colonial Borderlands', *Law & Social Inquiry* 26, no. 2 (2001): p. 373.

9 Patricia Seed, *Ceremonies of Possession in Europe's Conquest of the New World, 1492–1640* (Cambridge, New York: Cambridge University Press, 1995).

and invocation, through spectacles designed to bring the body politics of the realm together, in communion with their absent monarch, fostering loyalty and obedience.[10] They reproduced chivalric tropes at a time of revival of courtly literature.[11] In the political culture of the time, government and justice had to be paraded and displayed, so that the audience could experience it as something real and tangible.[12] This book frames the expeditions to the Charcas borders as one of such occasions.

In this same culture, borders were understood as devoid of jurisdiction—this is without justice, law, and Catholic religion—and their indigenous populations were reinvented using stereotypes that reflected such beliefs. Built upon 'hegemonic knowledges' that saw such peoples as perpetual minors and in need of guardianship, classing those who rejected and resisted Spanish jurisdiction by refusing to live under its law and religion as 'savages and cannibals', these stereotypes were reworked, shared, and conveyed by local elites as 'strategic narratives'.[13] They were widely manipulated in the discourse and conversations between these elites and the Crown and were used to justify punitive action against indigenous groups, who also learned to use those same stereotypes to their advantage, when possible. The expeditions are a testament to the presence of such stereotypes and their widespread political use.[14]

The expeditions were also a way for the authorities to 'tie' Spanish men and their clients and relatives 'to the land' and settle them in towns and farms. They were frequently perceived as 'loose soldiers', prone to crime and fights, and these events were expected to transform them into loyal vassals, ready to defend the monarch and his religion and help with the expansion of royal jurisdiction into remote areas. Following the medieval concept of *auxilium*, which established the obligation of a lord's vassals to defend him, they would be recruited under banners and the influence of promises and propaganda,

---

10 William Egginton, *How the World Became a Stage: Presence, Theatricality, and the Question of Modernity* (Albany: State University of New York Press, 2003), pp. 35, 53–54.

11 Teofilo Ruiz, *A King Travels: Festive Traditions in Late Medieval and Early Modern Spain* (Princeton, NJ: Princeton University Press, 2012), p. 70.

12 Antje Flüchter, 'Structures on the Move: Appropriating Technologies of Governance in a Transcultural Encounter', in *Structures on the Move: Technologies of Governance in a Transcultural Encounter* (Heidelberg, New York, London, Dordrecht: Springer, 2012), p. 10.

13 Germán Morong Reyes, *Saberes hegemónicos y dominio colonial. Los indios en el Gobierno del Perú de Juan de Matienzo (1567)* (Rosario, Argentina: Prohistoria Ediciones, 2016); Alister Miskimmon, Ben O'Loughlin, and Laura Roselle, *Strategic Narratives: Communication Power and the New World Order* (New York, London: Routledge, 2013), p. 3.

14 Luis Miguel Córdoba Ochoa, 'Guerra, imperio, y violencia en la Audiencia de Santa Fe, Nuevo Reino de Granada 1580–1620', PhD dissertation, Universidad Pablo de Olavide, 2013.

from sermons to speeches, and visual displays, that portrayed the expeditions as part of the monarchy's mission to extend its view of Catholicism across the globe.[15] Through their involvement, they would supposedly learn obedience and serve, upholding knightly values, in the face of adversity. The borders were thus perceived as fields of learning where men would mature, adopt a more pragmatic approach to life, and serve a just cause. They would learn and put into practice transferable skills that many of them had accumulated in battlefronts across the globe, from Flanders to Chile. Their victories, or defeats, would be reflected in the prose of books and theatre works, verses of poems, and in their own reports of merits and services.

Borders are frequently seen as places of *mestizaje*, a process of cultural and social mixing that involved indigenous peoples and the Spanish as its main participants, though not the only ones.[16] They are also seen as spaces where coloniality and subalternity were constructed.[17] Borders, thus, are commonly conceived as zones of alterity and identity making, with an emphasis on classification, resistance, permanence, and their legacy. However, classificatory practices, such as the stereotyping of natives, and to

---

15 This was underpinned by the ideology of a 'Christian citizenship' which took coherent form in the wake of the Council of Trent (1545–1563), a major Catholic reform effort in Europe, the successful culmination of which was tied to a wave of ecclesiastical legislation in church synods and councils, as suggested by Max Deardorff. Max Deardorff, *A Tale of Two Granadas: Custom, Community, and Citizenship in the Spanish Empire, 1568–1668* (Cambridge: Cambridge University Press, 2023), p. 7; Anon., *Las Siete Partidas del Sabio Rey don Alonso El Nono, Nuevamente Glosadas por el Licenciado Gregorio López del Consejo Real de Indias de Su Magestad*, Vol. 1 (Salamanca: Andrea de Portonari, 1555), Segunda Partida, Título XXIII, Ley II, p. 79; Barrientos Grandón, *El gobierno de las Indias*, pp. 197, 199.

16 Fabricio Prado, 'The Fringes of Empires: Recent Scholarship on Colonial Frontiers and Borderlands in Latin America', *History Compass* 10, no. 4 (2012): pp. 318–33; Danna Levin Rojo and Cynthia Radding Murrieta, eds, *The Oxford Handbook of Borderlands of the Iberian World*, Oxford Handbooks (New York: Oxford University Press, 2019); Guillaume Boccara, 'Génesis y estructura de los complejos fronterizos euro-indígenas. Repensando los márgenes americanos a partir (y más allá) de la obra de Nathan Wachtel', *Memoria Americana* 13 (2005): pp. 21–52; Christophe Giudicelli, 'Encasillar la frontera. Clasificaciones coloniales y disciplinamiento del espacio en el área diaguito-calchaquí. Siglos XVI–XVII', *Anuario IEHS*, no. 22 (2007): pp. 161–211; Shawn Michael Austin, *Colonial Kinship: Guaraní, Spaniards, and Africans in Paraguay* (Albuquerque: University of New Mexico Press, 2020); Susana Truchuelo and Emir Reitano, *Fronteras en el mundo atlántico (siglos XVI–XIX)* (Universidad Nacional de La Plata. Facultad de Humanidades y Ciencias de la Educación, 2017).

17 José Rabasa, *Writing Violence on the Northern Frontier: The Historiography of Sixteenth Century New Mexico and Florida and the Legacy of Conquest* (Durham, NC: Duke University Press, 2000), p. 6; Susan M. Deeds, *Defiance and Deference in Mexico's Colonial North: Indians under Spanish Rule in Nueva Vizcaya* (Austin: University of Texas Press, 2003).

that effect identities and alterities, were contested fields, relational in nature, and highly dependent on context. Indigenous peoples who were one day classed as friends, were the next day and under different circumstances seen as enemies.[18] One set of Spaniards and their allies saw them as 'cannibals', and others as ideal partners. If the argument is shifted and the focus placed upon agency and claim making, as is suggested in this book, borders are perceived as constructed through 'complex processes of appropriation that were carried out by hundreds of individuals in thousands of daily interactions'.[19] Alterities and identities become thus fields defined by political agency which was limited by jurisdiction. It is argued here that it was in relation to those able to establish law and deliver justice—those with jurisdiction—and in line with their concepts of status, race, and religion that agents defined themselves, negotiating and contesting identities and labels. Along these borders of possession, where life was precarious, agency and political posturing, more than identity and continuity, provided means for political and social survival.[20]

The expeditions discussed here cover three crucial decades in the history of Peru and Charcas that saw the establishment of this district's body of royal justice and regional seat of power or Real Audiencia de Charcas in La Plata—present-day Sucre—and the transformations that came with this, after decades of civil war and unrest. The Audiencia and the viceroys were at the centre of the distribution of royal rewards and privileges and therefore played a key role in how jurisdiction was shared, who should be recompensed, and who should not.[21] They were able to favour certain individuals and their networks over others, or even manipulate some characters against others, yet at the same time they were also exposed to power games played by local elite groups. It was within this context that the expeditions discussed in this book were negotiated and arranged.

Sometimes the expeditions were arranged with individuals prepared to establish towns to engage with indigenous peoples, clearing the way to their evangelisation, the exchange of goods, and eventually, their transformation into the monarch's vassals, becoming subject to taxation and work drafts. At other times, the purpose of such expeditions was punitive, in a political culture that understood justice as essential to government and saw border natives in a paternalistic manner. Despite the Crown's intentions, because of jurisdictional politics the southeast borders of Charcas were unstable and

---

18 Joanne Rappaport, *The Disappearing Mestizo: Configuring Difference in the Colonial New Kingdom of Granada* (Durham, NC: Duke University Press, 2014), p. 5.

19 Tamar Herzog, *Frontiers of Possession: Spain and Portugal in Europe and the Americas* (Cambridge, MA: Harvard University Press, 2015), p. 8.

20 Or 'logics of subsistence'. David Martín Marcos, *People of the Iberian Borderlands: Community and Conflict between Spain and Portugal, 1640–1715* (New York, London: Routledge, 2023), p. 1.

21 Clavero, 'Justicia y gobierno. Economía y gracia', pp. 121–48.

life there precarious. The power to establish law and deliver justice on the edges of the realm, where checks were sporadic and the political balance was fragile, weighed more in favour of the recipients of such power, in this case Spanish colonists and their indigenous allies, and their agendas.

This study approaches the expeditions through a wide array of documentary sources, including published and unpublished reports and letters. Because of the military nature of the events, reports on merits and services, also known as *Probanzas*, of those who travelled as expedition members, represent a large part of the documents analysed. Drafted with the help of notaries and lawyers, involving witnesses to past events, the aim of these documents was to secure favours and grants from the monarch.[22] *Probanzas* involved a large degree of self-fashioning and self-promotion and scholars have analysed them from this perspective.[23] The documents have also been approached from the perspective of indigenous and *mestizo* identities and how these were negotiated in Spanish America.[24] The focus here is to situate such records, with help from other documentary evidence, in their wider social and political context, reading them as part of an extended archive made of thousands of documents interconnected with each other. This approach will enable a better appreciation of the cacophony of voices that can be elicited from these records. The information they provide can also be matched with that of other documents. Through *probanzas* it is possible to reconstruct backgrounds, social networks, and compare narratives of different agents in the same events, in a manner that very few other sources can match.[25]

---

22 Through such documents merits and services were commodified, meaning that they could be passed down from one generation to the next and be integrated into an 'economy' of rewards and privileges. Javier Barrientos Grandón, '"Méritos y servicios": Su patrimonialización en una cultura jurisdiccional (s. XVI–XVII)', *Revista de Estudios Histórico-Jurídicos* XL (2018): pp. 589–615.

23 Murdo McLeod, 'Self-Promotion: The *Relaciones de Méritos y Servicios* and Their Historical and Political Interpretation', *CLAHR* 7, no. 1 (1998): pp. 25–42; Robert Folger, *Writing as Poaching: Interpellation and Self-Fashioning in Colonial Relaciones de Méritos y Servicios* (Leiden, Boston, MA: Brill, 2011).

24 Mario Julio Graña, 'La verdad asediada. Discursos de y para el poder. Escritura, institucionalización y élites indígenas surandinas. Charcas, siglo XVI', *Andes. Antropología e Historia*, no. 12 (2001): pp. 123–39; María Carolina Jurado, '"Descendientes de los primeros." Las probanzas de méritos y servicios y la genealogía cacical. Audiencia de Charcas, 1574–1719', *Revista de Indias* 74, no. 261 (2014): pp. 387–422; Ximena Medinaceli, 'La ambigüedad del discurso político de las autoridades étnicas en el siglo XVI. Una propuesta de lectura de la probanza de los Colque Guarachi de Quillacas', *Revista Andina* 38 (2004): pp. 87–104; Felipe Ruan, 'The *Probanza* and Shaping a Contesting *Mestizo* Record in Early Colonial Peru', *Bulletin of Spanish Studies* 94, no. 5 (2017): pp. 843–69; and Gabriela Ramos, 'El rastro de la discriminación. Litigios y probanzas de caciques en el Perú colonial temprano', *Fronteras de La Historia*, 21, no. 1 (2016): pp. 66–90.

25 Roxana Nakashima and Lia Guillermina Oliveto, 'Las informaciones de méritos

The around 140 probanzas examined for this book offer a unique glimpse, sometimes very intimate, difficult to find in other documents.[26]

The choice of expeditions discussed here provides scope for a diverse approach to events, as they took place in three very distinctive moments of early Charcas history. The 1564–1565 expeditions discussed in Chapter Two were undertaken by Captain Almendras at a crucial time, just after the Real Audiencia de Charcas was settled in 1561, when its judges and president were trying to negotiate the extension of its jurisdiction.[27] From its onset, this body understood that communications across the Audiencia's vast geography were key to enforcing and sustaining its jurisdictional pretentions. This was particularly so along the southern route to Tucumán, which was seen as a potential route to deliver silver from Potosí, and alternative to the Pacific Ocean–Lima–Panama–Atlantic Ocean route that was time-consuming and expensive. However, because the Tucumán route was regularly blocked by native unrest, but probably more importantly due to a unique opportunity to reconfirm the Audiencia's jurisdiction in Tucumán, two expeditions were mounted. These expeditions arranged by Almendras show an *encomendero* group allied to a new Audiencia working together to settle, consolidate, and expand royal jurisdiction in remote settings. The final expedition would see Captain Almendras' demise, yet it would also be the Audiencia's opportunity to finally instal its political presence in Tucumán and secure the Atlantic route, a move that shifted the whole of the area known today as northwest Argentina away from the influence of Chile for good.

Ten years later, as described in Chapter Three, the stage was totally different, as Peru's most famous viceroy, don Francisco de Toledo, mounted

y servicios y el imperio global de Felipe II a través de la trayectoria de Francisco Arias de Herrera', *Revista Electrónica de Fuentes y Archivos*, no. 5 (2014): pp. 120–28; and Antonio Jiménez Estrella, 'Las relaciones de servicios y la capitalización de la memoria de los antepasados y familiares de los militares de la monarquía hispánica en el siglo XVII', *Tiempos Modernos*, no. 47 (2023): pp. 314–37.

26 These *probanzas* date between the 1560s and the mid-seventeenth century. They are complex documents, sometimes of just a few folios and sometimes hundreds of them, that often include copies of sections, or entire documents, from previous times, known as *traslados*, frequently used as evidence of merits and services. *Probanzas* have a starting date, but they were an unfinished work as more merits and services could be added at any time. *Probanzas* were to a degree archives within larger archives. Together, they were the collective memory of the services of vassals to their monarch and thus were a key element in the economy of rewards and privileges.

27 See Map in Figure 0.1 with routes of all three expeditions. Unfortunately, the maps of the expeditions from the time, if they ever existed, have not been found. The author has reconstructed the routes from the sources consulted for the analysis of the expeditions. Normally, Spanish expeditions followed the Capac Ñam or Inca Road to Charcas and further south (see Figure 1.2). I have interpreted those sources as indicating that this was also the route followed, either in full or partly, by the expeditions described in this book.

the largest expedition ever to the borders of Charcas. The historiography on Toledo's period, owing to its emphasis on state construction based on the national states of the nineteenth century, has focused on his character as organiser, strategist, and law maker. However, the approach adopted in this book shows his role as leader of an expedition, bringing a different image of him, one of defeat, which has not received the required attention. With royal instructions that urged him to settle and evangelise the indigenous peoples of southeast Charcas, leaving violence as a last resort, and against a backdrop of uncooperative *encomenderos*, Peru's fifth viceroy launched an expedition largely funded by a windfall of silver generated by the introduction to Potosí of the amalgamation process for treating the mineral. Viceroy Toledo, who was prone to an arbitrary approach to rule, wanted to confirm and instal royal jurisdiction along the border. The official took with him 'the best of Peru', as Jesuit priest and author José de Acosta referred to those who followed the viceroy in an almost religious procession to the dense Andean slopes inhabited by the lowland natives known as Chiriguanaes.[28] The 'King's living image', as viceroys were seen, returned from the expedition in poor health.[29] In the wake of his defeat, the Chiriguanaes and the Audiencia emerged as the main winners,[30] the former because of how they humiliated Toledo, the latter because it had only limited involvement with the event.

The final expedition, discussed in Chapter Four, took place at a challenging time for the Charcas borders caused by Toledo's defeat and the establishment of two new Spanish towns. The book moves from the highly embellished journey of the viceroy to the expedition of one of his protégés, Juan Lozano Machuca. Following Toledo's departure from Peru, and the passing of his successor, Martín Enríquez de Almanza y Ulloa (1581–1583), Peru was left without its head. It was the opportunity for a strong and consolidated Real Audiencia de Charcas to show that, apart from providing advice, as it had done under Toledo, it could be more involved in the government of its district and organise and command large-scale punitive expeditions to border areas. This would effectively make the monarchy present there, with less expense and loss of lives than viceregal expeditions. This expedition of 1584–1585 provides a glimpse into a Real Audiencia de Charcas increasingly aware of the importance of keeping the border in peace by negotiating concessions with those Spanish and *mestizo* captains and their networks who were already present there. It shows that the Audiencia's officials understood the

---

28 'La flor del Perú' was the expression used by the Jesuit. José de Acosta, *Historia natural y moral de las Indias* (Sevilla: Casa de Juan León, 1590), p. 590.

29 Alejandro Cañeque, *The King's Living Image: The Culture and Politics of Viceregal Power in Colonial Mexico*, New World in the Atlantic World (New York: Routledge, 2004).

30 This book uses the names of indigenous peoples as they appear in sixteenth-century documents to make it easier for readers and scholars to identify these groups in the historical record.

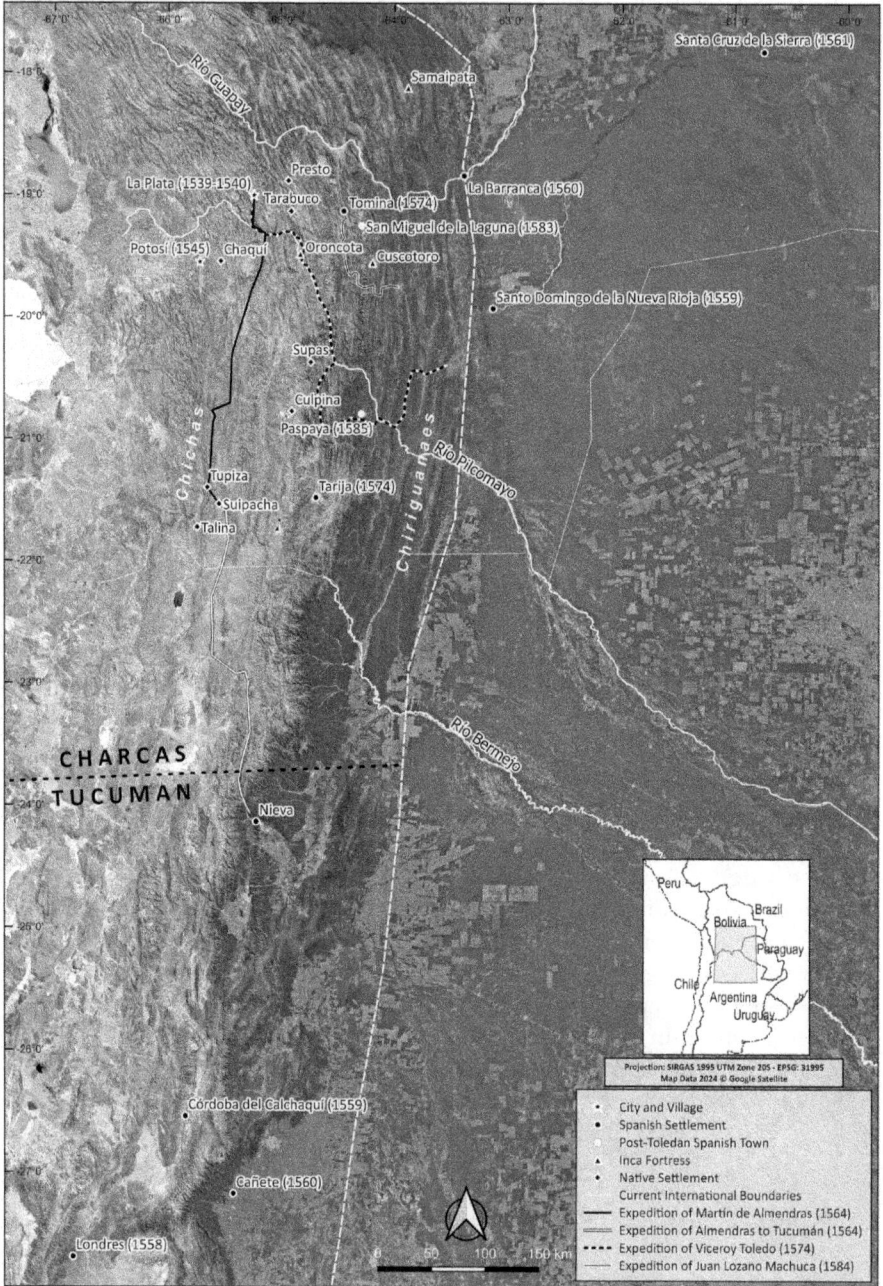

Figure 0.1   Physical map showing the routes of the three expeditions
examined in this book

downscaling of politics as the best way to expand jurisdiction with little cost and few responsibilities to bear. The idea was to leave behind the era of costly expeditions of 'feathers, silks, and trappings' as a witness of the period stressed.[31] It was now time for the 'practical men', as another witness stated, who were able to handle matters using local manners.[32]

These three chapters are preceded by Chapter One, which sets the background for the expeditions and analyses the transformations experienced by these borders first under the Inca and then in the early years of the Spanish conquest. This book concludes with a discussion of the political culture of the Spanish monarchy, Charcas, and its borders. It includes three annexes: a chronology of Charcas (1438–1585) with the main events mentioned in this book; another giving the names of those who went on the expeditions; and, finally, a third with some documents representing a selection of their voices.

---

31 Letter by Lope Diez de Armendariz to the King, 25 September 1576, in Roberto Levillier, *La Audiencia de Charcas. Correspondencia de presidentes y oidores. 1561–1579*, Vol. 1 (Madrid: Colección de Publicaciones Históricas de la Biblioteca del Congreso Argentino, 1918), p. 371.
32 AGI, Patronato, 125. R4, [1582] Probanza de Pedro de Segura.

CHAPTER ONE

A Background to the Expeditions

The Southeast Charcas Borders Between the Inca and the Spanish

1. Introduction

This first chapter sets the background for the expeditions. Beginning with a description of the geography and the peoples of the southeastern borders of the region the Spanish called Charcas, which includes parts of present-day Bolivia and the northwest of Argentina, the aim is to discuss the incorporation of these borders first into the Inca realm, a largely diverse and sophisticated polity historians mainly know through documents written after its collapse, and the subsequent transition these border zones experienced during the early Spanish period. The chapter then addresses the beginnings of the process of installation, consolidation, and expansion of the Crown's jurisdiction in Charcas through *encomiendas* and expeditions. This was a process that relied on the political organisation and legacy of the Inca. The Spanish inherited these borders from that polity and addressed the challenges these presented them with the religious and ideological tools they had at their disposal. After a brief analysis of the incorporation of native peoples into the Spanish monarchy, the chapter moves on to consider the construction of stereotypes around one of such indigenous groups: the Chiriguanaes. Finally, it reflects on how borders and their inhabitants were invented through a process that mirrored politics under both the Inca and the first decades of Spanish presence.

2. A diverse geography

The landscapes of this book run along the edges of the southern Andes, north to south, through the territories of present Bolivia and Argentina. This section of the *cordillera* is made of different mountain ranges known in Bolivia under names such as Azanaques, Chocaya, San Vicente, Central, de los Chichas, de Lípez, and de Los Frailes; and in Argentina as Sierra de Santa Victoria in Jujuy and Salta provinces. In Bolivia, these ranges are separated by valleys with altitudes between 2,000 and 3,000 metres above sea level. Crossed by mountain rivers having variable flow-rates—such as

San Juan Mayo or San Juan del Oro, Tupiza, Grande de Tarija, Pilaya, and Cotagaita in Bolivia; and Santa Victoria, El Pescado, Nazareno, Iruya, and San Francisco in Argentina—these fertile valleys are ideal for agriculture. The rivers are tributaries of larger rivers such as Pilcomayo, Bermejo, and Paraguay. To the east of these valleys lie the *yungas*, ideal for coca cultivation; and the Andean foothills, the sub-Andean zone, with altitudes between 1,000 and 2,000 metres above sea level and a dense vegetation of low and thorny trees. Beyond, below 1,000 metres above sea level, lie the Gran Chaco lowlands with their savanna vegetation of palm and quebracho trees and tropical high-grass areas.[1] In the northwest of Argentina, in Jujuy, the *puna* habitat presents a terrain with average heights of 6,000 metres above sea level and average lows of 3,800 metres above sea level, crossed by a narrow mountain valley known as Quebrada de Humahuaca, having a north–south orientation and extending for around 150 kilometres.

Along with such vast geography comes a wide array of climatic zones that vary in line with altitude, from the dry and cold high plateau, or *altiplano*, to the more benign mesothermic valleys, followed by the torrid and arid conditions of the Andean foothills and the humid and tropical climate of the Gran Chaco savanna or Chaco plain. Argentina's *puna* shares its climate with Bolivia's high plateau, and so great temperature contrasts between day and night. Such geographic and climatic diversity is mirrored by a diverse fauna and flora, and soil conditions that made possible the domestication of certain animals (camelids such as llamas and alpacas in the high plateau), and plants (corn, quinoa, potatoes, peppers, and chillies, to name a few), by societies which either had dispersed settlement patterns to be able to maximise their access to multiple resources (in the Andean area) or moved around with seasonal changes (in the foothills and Gran Chaco areas).

2.1 A diverse human landscape

What scholars know about the societies that inhabited this vast space mainly comes from two sources. One is archaeological findings; the other, an immense *corpus* of records written during the Spanish era that echoes concepts and prejudices not only among the Spanish but also among the Inca. Researchers are thus faced with a double filter, posed by both polities, which makes understanding of such groups a complicated and confusing task. Names like *Chichas, Quillacas, Asanaques, Charcas, Caracara, Moyos-Moyos, Juríes, Atacamas, Omaguacas, Tomatas, Chanés,* Chiriguanaes or *Guaraní,* refer to different groups and/or locations—in some cases, as they could be ethnonyms, toponyms, or both—yet very little is known about how these groups interacted with each other, if they did; or why and how they were named, or by whom. To complicate matters further, many groups did not

---

1 Rodolfo Raffino, Diego Gobbo, and Anahí Iácona, 'De Potosí y Tarija a la frontera chiriguana', *Folia Histórica del Nordeste,* no. 16 (2006): p. 85; Herbert S. Klein, *Historia de Bolivia* (La Paz: Libreria Editorial 'Juventud', 1997), pp. 22–24.

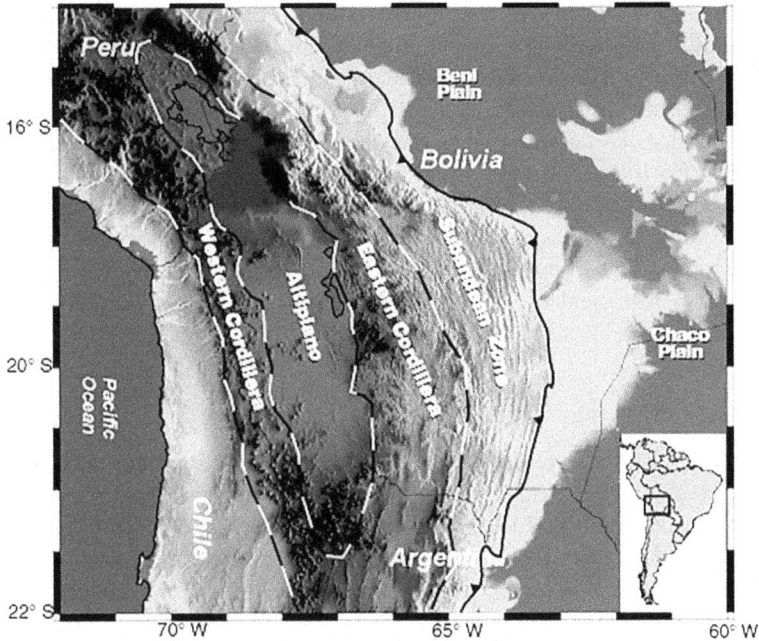

Figure 1.1 Map showing the regional topographies of the areas examined in
this book
Source: Adapted from B. P. Murray et al., 'Oligocene–Miocene Basin
Evolution in the Northern Altiplano, Bolivia: Implications for Evolution of
the Central Andean Backthrust Belt and High Plateau', *Geological Society of
America Bulletin* 122, nos 9–10 (2010): p. 1444. Used with permission of the
Geological Society of America.

originate from the areas where they were found by the Spanish, as they had
been moved as part of the Inca's expansionist policies. In summary, this
means that the first human map of these areas is one that reflects the final
period of Inca rule in Charcas.

Based on this first and (for the time) only picture of the human landscape
that we have, the indigenous populations present in the area under study
in this book could be divided into three groups, depending on their level
of integration within the Inca realm, or complete lack of it. A first group is
made up of Andean peoples, also called *naciones de Charcas* in the *Memorial
de Charcas*, a long letter allegedly written to the Spanish monarch by their
chiefs between 1582 and 1591.[2] These *naciones de Charcas* were largely part of

2 The *naciones* in question were Charca, Caracara, Quillaca, Caranga, Soras, Chichas,
and Chuys. The names are quoted here as they appear in the documentary evidence.
The *Memorial*, a long letter supposedly submitted by their leaders between 1582 and
1591, is in the Archivo General de Indias (from here on AGI), in Charcas 45, and

the Inca polity at the beginning of the sixteenth century. At the opposite end of the scale, there were the inhabitants of the lowlands beyond the Andean foothills, mainly Guaraní/Chiriguanaes and Chanés, who were geographically and culturally a world apart from the Inca and the Andeans under Incan influence. In between were indigenous peoples who had been recently moved by the Inca to border areas to defend these from the Chiriguanaes and the other lowland inhabitants; this was where the Spanish would eventually find them. They include the Churumatas, Juríes, Ocloyas, Omaguacas, Moyos-Moyos, Casabindos, Lacaxas, Cotas, and Tomatas, who are more elusive in the historical record, despite intense research by scholars in recent decades.[3]

3. Inca expansion into Charcas

To understand how the Inca turned geographical barriers into the first cultural, social, and political borders available in the historical record, differentiating peoples who had been incorporated into the polity in Charcas from those who had not, it is best to approach first the political organisation of those *naciones de Charcas*, as the *Memorial* labelled them, since they would play a significant role in the creation of these boundaries. The existence of

has been published: Tristán Platt, Thérèse Bouysse-Cassagne, and Olivia Harris, eds, *Qaraqara–Charka: Mallku, Inka y rey en la provincia de Charcas (siglos XV–XVII): Historia antropológica de una confederación aymara* (Lima, La Paz: Instituto Francés de Estudios Andinos (IFEA); Plural Editores; University of London; University of St Andrews; Fundación Cultural del Banco Central de Bolivia; Inter-American Foundation, 2006).

3 Ana María Presta, *Espacio, etnias, frontera. Atenuaciones políticas en el sur del Tawantinsuyu. Siglos XV–XVIII* (Sucre: ASUR, 1995); Carlos Zanolli, 'Los chichas como mitimaes del inca', *Relaciones de la Sociedad Argentina de Antropología* XXVIII (2003): pp. 45–60; Rodolfo Raffino, Christian Vitty, and Diego Gobbo, 'Inkas y chichas: identidad, transformación y una cuestión fronteriza', *Boletín de Arqueología PUCP*, no. 8 (2004): pp. 247–65; Silvia Palomeque, 'Casabindos, cochinocas y chichas en el siglo XVI. Avances de investigación', in *Las tierras altas del área Centro Sur Andina entre el 1000 y el 1600 D.C.*, pp. 233–63; Lia Guillermina Oliveto and Paula Zagalsky, 'De nominaciones y estereotipos: los chiriguanos y los moyos moyos, Dos casos de la frontera oriental de Charcas en el siglo XVI', *Bibliographica Americana*, no. 6 (2010); Ana María Presta, 'Los valles mesotérmicos de Chuquisaca entre la fragmentación territorial yampara y la ocupación de los migrantes qaraqara y charka en la temprana colonia', in *Aportes multidisciplinarios al estudio de los colectivos étnicos surandinos, reflexiones sobre qaraqara-charka tres años después* (La Paz: Plural-IFEA, 2013): pp. 27–60; Carlos Zanolli, 'Tierra, encomienda e identidad: Omaguaca (1540–1638)', colección tesis doctorales (Buenos Aires: Sociedad Argentina de Antropología, 2005); Lia Guillermina Oliveto, 'De mitmaqkuna incaicos en Tarija a reducidos en La Plata. Tras las huellas de los moyos moyos y su derrotero colonial', *Anuario de Estudios Bolivianos. Archivísticos y Bibliográficos* 17 (2011): pp. 463–90.

identity markers that separated them in line with the weapons of hunting and war that they favoured—with those using bows and arrows classed as lowland natives and those using clubs and slings classed as indigenous peoples from high-altitude areas—could suggest that all *naciones de Charcas* were tied together into some macropolitical organisation or confederation based on such divisions, yet their level of unification remains a subject of academic discussion. Scholars find it difficult to establish when these groups were tied together and whether this pre-dated the Inca or was a consequence of the polity's expansion into the region.[4] Based on the fact that the *Memorial* was only written at the end of the sixteenth century and that it largely reflects the interests of Andean leaders to self-legitimise their roles in the colonial context, it is argued here that these *naciones* were only grouped in the wake of the Spanish conquest and that any alliance between them was extremely loose and easy to break as a result. This may well explain how, after an initial resistance, the Spaniards were able to speedily negotiate their expansion into the area with the elites of these *naciones*. It is fitting to highlight here that these were polities connected with one another in ways still difficult to ascertain and that such links, rather than any clear lack of them, facilitated first their incorporation into the Inca realm and then, in the early sixteenth century, the establishment, settlement, and expansion of the Spanish monarchy's jurisdiction over Charcas. Both the Inca and the Spanish benefited from these early connections.

In contrast, for indigenous groups with a high degree of political fragmentation, who inhabited the Andean foothills, lowlands, or the territory the Spanish called Tucumán—which roughly covered the northwest of present-day Argentina, incorporation into the Inca polity and the expansion of the Spanish were more challenging. Not only was integration into the Inca realm highly contested and superficial, if it happened at all, but the incorporation of these groups into the Spanish monarchy was a process full of setbacks and never completed, as this book explores.

Inca incorporation of Charcas began with Inca Pachacuti (1438–1471) and was slow, not uniform, with advances and retreats, and followed how reciprocities and dynastic succession were understood by the parties

---

4 According to archaeologist Martti Pärssinen, there is some evidence that political and military units larger than provinces existed in Tahuantinsuyu, which he calls 'Hatun Apocazgos' from 'Hatun: The Great; Apo: The King—both in Quechua'. This should translate as Great Kingdoms. Martti Pärssinen, *Tawantinsuyu: The Inca State and Its Political Organization* (Helsinki: Societas Historicas Finlandiae, 1992), pp. 261–69. In the Coya area, Elizabeth Arkush suggests a fractured or loosely confederated political landscape: *Hillforts of the Ancient Andes: Colla Warfare, Society, and Landscape* (Gainesville: University Press of Florida, 2011); Jonathan Scholl, 'At the Limits of Empire: Incas, Spaniards, and the Ava-Guarani (Chiriguanaes) on the Charcas-Chiriguana Frontier, Southeastern Andes (1450s–1620s)', PhD dissertation, University of Florida, 2015, p. 221.

involved.[5] It was also highly ritualised and in this regard the region's further aggregation to the Spanish Crown would not be different. When not fiercely opposed, the Inca expanded through a complex set of alliances that had to be periodically nurtured and were renegotiated between every new Inca ruler and local lords.[6] Thus, the succession of a new Inca resulted in unrest, which was always followed by expeditions into the rebellious areas. Such alliances were based on the principle of large-scale redistribution of any imperial surplus through an institutionalised 'generosity policy' that provided gifts to local chiefs in exchange for indirect control of labour and natural resources. They involved mobilisation of colonists—*mitimaes*—who were transferred from their settlements; the construction of a highly sophisticated road network—Capac Ñam; and the organisation of an elaborate warehouse system.[7] In Charcas Inca rule was therefore a negotiated matter that required the agreement of local elites, a situation that would be repeated when the first Spanish conquistadors arrived, as they would rely on material support, auxiliary natives, and logistics that Andean lords could supply. On the ground, expansion of jurisdiction would require a collective effort not only from the Spanish but also their indigenous allies.

Returning to Inca expansionism, its first test in Charcas took place after Inca Pachacuti's death and was faced by his successor, Topa Inca Yupanqui (1471–1493), as unrest gathered pace across the region. This culminated with a siege of the fortress of Oroncota, located at the eastern border, where the local populations had gathered to battle Inca armies (see Figure 1.2).[8] This was a decisive moment that revitalised the ties between local indigenous elites and the Incas. Under Topa Inca Yupanqui's successor, Huayna Capac (1493–1525), imperial presence in the region was strengthened thanks to a system of fortresses along the southeastern border attended by *mitimaes* and *mitayos*.[9] These indigenous peoples were fed by agriculturalists transferred from their original settlements, as happened in the valley of Cochabamba. With support from regional elites, Huayna Capac reorganised the space,

---

5 For a full chronology of the events described in this book, see Appendix 1.

6 AGI, Charcas 53, [1574–1576] Información de méritos y servicios de don Juan Colque Guarache, fol. 28; Platt, Bouysse-Cassagne, and Harris, eds, *Qaraqara–Charka*, pp. 884, 898–99, 928, 932, 938.

7 Figure 1.2 shows the section of the Capac Ñam used to travel south of Charcas. John V. Murra, *La organización económica del estado inca*, trans. Daniel R. Wagner (México: Siglo Veintiuno, 1978); Terence N. D'Altroy, *The Incas* (Malden, MA: Blackwell, 2002); María Rostworowski de Diez Canseco, *History of the Inca Realm*, trans. Harry B. Iceland (Cambridge, New York: Cambridge University Press, 1999); Craig Morris and Adriana Von Hagen, *The Incas: Lords of the Four Quarters* (London: Thames & Hudson, 2011); Pärssinen, *Tawantinsuyu*.

8 Pedro Sarmiento de Gamboa, *Historia de los incas* (Madrid: Miraguano, 2001 [1572]), p. 114; John Rowe, 'Probanza de los incas nietos de conquistadores', *Histórica* IX, no. 2 (1985): p. 226.

9 A *mitayo* was a male adult compulsorily serving by turn in different labour levies.

mobilising peoples and resources. During this period the southeastern borders of the Inca realm took the shape that continued until the first Spaniards arrived.

3.1 The invention of the Inca's borders

After the initial resistance to the new Inca ruler in Oroncota, the Chichas, who would actively participate in the extension of Spanish jurisdiction in the southeast border area, as this book shows, were given an important role in the new phase of Inca expansion. Those who sided with the invaders were given the status 'Warriors of the Inca'.[10] Under this privilege, several polities located in pre-Hispanic Charcas were responsible for patrolling the southeastern border from newly built fortresses in Pocona, Samaipata, and Cuscotoro, among other sites, that were located in the lowlands between Cochabamba and Tarija (see Figure 0.1).[11] Economically, they contributed labour for the large-scale maize production centre that Huayna Capac set up in Cochabamba to feed his vast armies.[12] They were also deployed to control other groups and suppress any rebellions that might spring up.[13] This policy extended well beyond the eastern slopes of the Andes into the northwest of present-day Argentina.[14] Such roles were a practical approach to integrating newly conquered groups into the Inca polity's structure and one that gave both sides the opportunity to maximise the pool of skills and resources coming from the conquered peoples and their lands. They also gave the Andean elites involved a 'badge of honour' that they would use in accounts of their merits and services, submitted to demand similar privileges from the Spanish monarchy in the late sixteenth century.[15] Moved to new locations, many of those who had served the Inca would struggle after the

10 AGI, Charcas 45. *Memorial de Charcas*, in Platt, Bouysse-Cassagne, and Harris, eds, *Qaraqara–Charka*, pp. 842–43.
11 Ana María Presta, 'La población de los valles de Tarija, Siglo XVI. Aportes para la solución de un enigma etnohistórico en una frontera incaica', in *Espacio, etnías, frontera*, p. 240; Raffino, Vitty, and Gobbo, 'Inkas y chichas', p. 252; Rowe, 'Probanza de los incas nietos de conquistadores', p. 226.
12 Nathan Wachtel, 'Los mitimaes del valle de Cochabamba: La política colonizadora de Wayna Capac', *Historia Boliviana* I, no. I (1981): pp. 21–57.
13 Scholl, 'At the Limits of Empire', p. 183; Zanolli, 'Los chichas como mitimaes del inca', p. 54.
14 Gustavo Paz and Gabriela Sica, 'La frontera oriental del Tucumán en el Río de la Plata (siglos XVI–XVIII)', in *Las fronteras en el mundo atlántico (siglos XVI–XVIII)* (La Plata: Universidad Nacional de La Plata. Facultad de Humanidades y Ciencias de la Educación, 2017), pp. 295–96.
15 María Carolina Jurado, '"Descendientes de los primeros". Las probanzas de méritos y servicios y la genealogía cacical. Audiencia de Charcas, 1574–1719', *Revista de Indias* 74, no. 261 (2014): pp. 387–422; Mario Julio Graña, 'Autoridad y memoria entre los killakas. Las estrategias discursivas de don Juan Colque Guarache en el sur andino. S. XVI', *Historica* XXIV, no. I (2000): pp. 23–47; AGI, Charcas, 79,

fall of that polity. These indigenous peoples found themselves occupying geographies from which they had not originated, surrounded by other peoples they had been trying to subject in the name of the Inca, who were hostile to their presence; finally, they had to face Spanish conquistadors. Many would return to their original settlements, but others would remain to either adapt or fight the Spanish.

Although the system of Inca alliances worked reasonably well among Andeans, that was not the case with other natives. The Incas failed to conquer the unruly and fierce Guaraní/Chiriguanaes and Chanés, and the only alternative left was to follow a 'defence-in-depth border strategy' using Huayna Capac's fortress system.[16] The sites were used largely to contain any potential threat and their purpose was not solely warlike but to facilitate other forms of exchange, such as feasts and limited trade, in a cycle of alliances and conflict.[17] Far from impregnable, they were porous military borders that brought together Andeans and lowland peoples.[18] The former received exotic feathers and animals, honey, timber, and river fish; the latter, silver, gold, and fine Inca clothing and textiles. This well-structured and organised system would be of invaluable help when the Inca confronted the advance of one of these lowland groups: the Chiriguanaes.

3.2   The Inca under threat from lowland natives

In the final years of the Inca realm, a group of lowland natives that came to be known as Chiriguanaes, also referred to in some Spanish sources as Guaraní, started moving westward towards the Andes.[19] They were not permanent nomads, as they lived in large dwellings called *malocas*, each measuring around 50–60 metres in length and 20–25 metres in width, and each able to accommodate up to 250 people. The Chiriguanaes grew their own maize and complemented their diet with wild game and foraged items.[20] Although frequently seen as independent and egalitarian, this politically fragmented people were organised around strict hierarchies of nobles or *ava*

N22, [1592–1593] Informaciones de oficio y parte: Francisco Aymozo [*sic*], cacique principal y gobernador de los indios yamparaes de Yotala y Quilaquila.

16 Scholl, 'At the Limits of Empire', p. 199.

17 Sonia Alconini Mujica, *Southeast Inka Frontiers: Boundaries and Interactions* (Gainesville: University Press of Florida, 2016), p. 179.

18 Lia Guillermina Oliveto, 'Ocupación territorial y relaciones interétnicas en los Andes Meridionales. Tarija, entre los desafíos prehispánicos y temprano coloniales', Universidad de Buenos Aires, 2010, p. 49.

19 Isabelle Combès, 'Grigotá y Vitupue. En los albores de la historia chiriguana (1559–1564)', *Bulletin de l'Institut Français d'Études Andines* 41, no. 1 (2012): p. 72.

20 Francisco Pifarré, *Historia de un pueblo*, vol. 2, *Los guaraní-chiriguano* (La Paz: CIPCA, 1989), p. 40; Catherine Julien, 'Colonial Perspectives on the Chiriguana (1528–1574)', in *Resistencia y Adaptación Nativa en las Tierras Bajas Latinoamericanas* (Quito: Abya-Yala, 1997), p. 20.

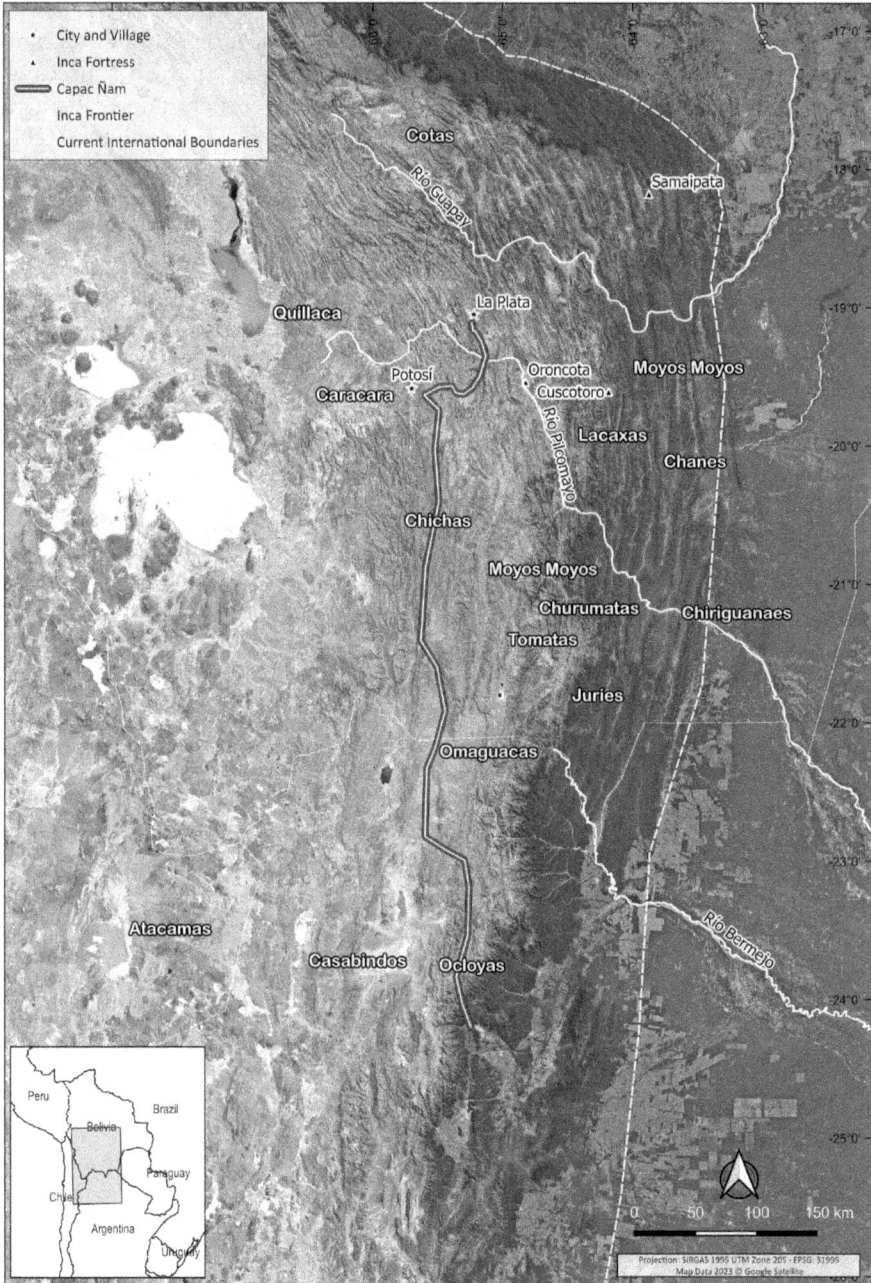

Figure 1.2   Physical map showing the approximate line of the Inca frontier and the Capac Ñam

warriors.[21] They also had captives and servants or *tapii*, who were frequently Chanés or other lowland settlers they regularly captured in battles and raids.[22] The Chiriguana groups are often referred to in Spanish sources as *facciones* (factions), which seem to have had different leaders and disbanded and regrouped over time. This suggests the absence of centralised and stable leadership and a fluid situation. Lacking an organised religion or cult, the Chiriguanaes believed in gods and spirits, and sometimes ancestors.[23] They began their westward expansion by moving into areas not far from the Inca borders during the late fifteenth and early sixteenth centuries.

Three different documents provide some clues to the reasons for this expansion. The first document, by priest Martín González, a 1556 account of abuses by the Spanish of the indigenous peoples of Asunción,[24] refers to the existence of

> infinite gold and silver mines that Indians from Peru who paid tribute to Guayna Caba used to work. These [Chiriguanaes] murdered them and threw them out of the land [...] They are called the old Guayna Caba mines.[25]

A second document, an early seventeenth-century report by priest Diego Felipe de Alcaya, narrates how Inca Huayna Capac sent a relative called Guacane to exert his influence beyond the borders and build a political alliance with Grigota, who was probably a Chané leader. This largely matches Inca politics, which focused on securing alliances and reciprocal ties with other indigenous groups. The outcome of their discussions was the erection

---

21 Fernando Santos-Granero, *Vital Enemies: Slavery, Predation, and the Amerindian Political Economy of Life* (Austin: University of Texas Press, 2009), p. 158.

22 Less is known about the Chanés, who were settled in the Gran Chaco savanna by the early sixteenth century and whose history is mainly connected to that of the Chiriguanaes. They regularly appear in documents as peaceful natives constantly attacked by the Chiriguanaes and driven away from their habitat as a result. Isabelle Combès, *Etno-historias del Isoso: Chané y chiriguanos en el Chaco boliviano (siglos XVI a XX)* (La Paz: Institut Français d'Études Andines, 2005), pp. 41–48.

23 Thierry Saignes and Isabelle Combès, *Historia del pueblo chiriguano* (Lima, La Paz: Institut Français d'Études Andines; Embajada de Francia en Bolivia: Plural Editores, 2007), pp. 34–35.

24 Born in Villarrubia del Campo de Calatrava, Spain, around 1516, González arrived in the Río de la Plata as part of the expedition of Alvar Nuñez Cabeza de Vaca in 1541. Guillaume Candela, *Entre la pluma y la cruz: el clérigo Martín González y la desconocida historia de su defensa de los indios del Paraguay: Documentos inéditos (1543–1575)* (Asunción: Editorial Tiempo de Historia, 2018), p. 13.

25 'Tienen despobladas infinitas minas de oro y plata abiertas y por abrir que los indios del Perú que daban quinto a Guayna Caba labraban. Y estos los mataron y echaron de la tierra [...] A éstas dicen las minas viejas de Guayna Caba', in Archivo Histórico Nacional (from here on AHN), Paraguay, Colección de documentos de Indias, 24, N17, in Candela, *Entre la pluma y la cruz*, p. 120.

of the fortress of Samaipata (close to the present-day city Santa Cruz de la Sierra) (see Figure 0.1) to provide protection to Grigota and his people. In exchange, the Chané leader allowed the exploitation of silver and/or gold mines in Saypurú. News of this wealth spread among the Chiriguanaes who, mustering 8,000 bowmen, clashed with Grigota, Guacane, and their forces at Samaipata. The Spanish priest claimed that these Chiriguanaes managed to carve out a stronghold whose population would be the basis of future Chiriguana settlements in the area.[26]

A third document from 1612, by Spanish captain Ruy García de Guzmán (1559–1629), describes the story of Portuguese captain Alejo or Aleixo García who was stranded off the coast of Brazil with some companions and travelled inland in 1526. García met the Guaraní or Chiriguanaes and raised a force of 2,000 to attack the settlements of Presto and Tarabuco, both under Inca influence (close to what would be the Spanish village of Tomina—see Figure 0.1) where Charca indigenous peoples fought them. After their raid García and his men withdrew to Paraguay, carrying fine clothing and metals they had looted. Shortly after, the captain was murdered by the tribespeople he had led into battle.[27]

The common element in all three narratives is the search for the Inca's fine textiles and metals, something the Chiriguanaes appreciated and wanted. In this light, and although some scholars believe the Chiriguana westward journey to have been part of a wider migration, and others refer to it as occasional raids, the common denominator is the search for items they cherished and saw as luxuries, and which could either be exchanged or seized. Since these attacks became more prominent at the end of the reign of Huayna Capac, they constitute evidence for the delicate situation of the Inca realm, which was engulfed in a civil war. These circumstances probably affected the trade in luxury items between the Chiriguanaes and the Inca. Looking for such precious goods, the Chiriguana were present in the Andean foothills in the 1470s and are recorded as carrying out devastating raids from the 1520s onwards.[28] As had occurred during the Inca period, these valuable

26 AGI, Charcas 21, R1, N2, [1600] Relación cierta de Diego Felipe de Alcaya, fols 18–27v.
27 Ruy Díaz de Guzmán, *Argentina: Historia del descubrimiento y conquista del Río de la Plata* (Buenos Aires: Editorial de la Facultad de Filosofía y Letras, Universidad de Buenos Aires, 2012 [1612]), pp. 93–95. Catherine Julien questions whether García encountered the Inca: Catherine J. Julien, *Desde el oriente: Documentos para la historia del oriente boliviano y Santa Cruz La Vieja, 1542–1597* (Santa Cruz de la Sierra: Fondo Editorial Municipal, 2008), p. XXIII.
28 Catherine Julien, 'Kandire in Real Time and Space: Sixteenth-Century Expeditions from the Pantanal to the Andes', *Ethnohistory* 54, no. 2 (2007): p. 263; Saignes and Combès, *Historia del pueblo chiriguano*, p. 48; Pifarré, *Historia de un pueblo*, Vol. 2, p. 25; Erland Nordenskiold, 'The Guarani Invasion of the Inca Empire in the Sixteenth Century: An Historical Indian Migration', *Geographical Review* 4, no. 2

goods would cement relations between the Spanish and the Chiriguanaes. Exchanging them would engage both parties in the establishment of Spanish villages and towns, and in the provision of captive natives as cheap labour to the Spaniards.[29] Indirectly, these luxury goods would help to establish Spanish jurisdiction in border areas.

González, Alcaya, and Díaz de Guzmán paint a picture of a fragile situation across the borders during the final years of the Inca period, one corroborated by other documentary evidence which refers to clashes around another fortress, Cuscotoro (see Figure 0.1).[30] Scholars rightly point out that such deterioration shows the contradictions of the rapid and merely superficial imposition of Inca rule, under which incessant population relocations did not necessarily mean efficient control. They add that in the south of the empire, where mineral wealth was important but locals were difficult to pacify, as a result control was less direct.[31] Indirect, rapidly imposed, and superficial, the Inca political presence in Charcas and along the borders would quickly vanish as the polity disintegrated in the chaos that succeeded first the death of Huayna Capac and with it a new Inca civil war, and then the assassination of Atahualpa at the hands of the Spanish conquistadors.

4. Transition from the Inca to the Spanish: expeditions and grants

With Huayna Capac's death in 1525, the Inca realm entered a new period of civil war, as had happened at every previous succession. The unrest was almost over when, in 1532, the Spanish encountered Atahualpa (*circa* 1500–1533), one of the two descendants of Huayna Capac having the right to wear the *mascaipacha*, the knitted tassel fringe that only the Inca wore. After Atahualpa's execution by the Spanish and following the distribution of the gold and silver that had been raised as a ransom for his freedom, with help from *quipocamayos*, readers of the knotted cords that stored information

(1917): pp. 103–21; Erick Detlef Langer, *Expecting Pears from an Elm Tree: Franciscan Missions on the Chiriguano Frontier in the Heart of South America, 1830–1949* (Durham, NC: Duke University Press, 2009), p. 12.

29 Lia Guillermina Oliveto, 'Piezas, presos, indios habidos en buena guerra, cimarrones y fugitivos. Notas sobre el cautiverio indígena en la frontera oriental de Tarija en el siglo XVI', in *Vivir en los márgenes. Fronteras en América colonial: Sujetos, prácticas e identidades, siglos XVI–XVIII* (México: Instituto de Investigaciones Históricas, UNAM, 2021), pp. 29–66.

30 Sarmiento de Gamboa, *Historia de los incas*, p. 147; Martín de Murua, *Historia general del Perú. De los orígenes al último inca* (Madrid: Cambio16, 1992 [1606]), pp. 90–91; Joan de Santa Cruz Pachacuti Yamqui Salcamaygua, *Relación de antiguedades deste reyno del Piru: Estudio etnohistórico y lingüístico*, ed. Pierre Duviols and César Itier (Lima: Institut Français d'Études Andines, 1993 [1613]), p. 171.

31 Saignes and Combès, *Historia del pueblo chiriguano*, p. 54; R. Alan Covey, *How the Incas Built their Heartland: State Formation and the Innovation of Imperial Strategies in the Sacred Valley, Peru* (Ann Arbor: University of Michigan Press, 2006), p. 206.

known as *quipos*, the Spaniards started to distribute the indigenous groups under Inca influence via *encomienda*. To be granted *encomienda* was the most precious reward a conquistador could receive from the Crown for military services.[32] They were therefore a key part of the political culture of the Catholic monarchy, as these grants were given as rewards based on service records.[33] Through *encomiendas*, the monarch placed native vassals at the service of an *encomendero*, who received tribute and in return was expected to provide religious instruction and protection. *Encomenderos* had to be based in a Spanish village, town, or city, where they became *vecinos*, with civic duties and rights that were at the core of Catholic monarchy politics. They were expected to exercise some form of tutelage over the indigenous peoples assigned to them, who were perceived as 'perpetual minors' in need of 'paternal' guardianship.[34] This placed these peoples under the supposed supervision of *encomenderos* and their extended families and social networks, who would also benefit from the *encomienda* labour. The system tied *encomenderos* and those assigned to them to urban centres, sometimes remote from the *encomienda*'s sites of settlement. The *encomienda* system placed *encomenderos* in a privileged position as responsible for the implementation, consolidation, and extension of royal jurisdiction among the local populations, in close association with Catholic priests and indigenous leaders. With powers to 'police' their subjects, overseeing their evangelisation and incorporation into the Catholic monarchy as vassals, holders of all three functions were active participants in the extension and installation of jurisdiction in Charcas.[35]

For the indigenous peoples living along the southeast Charcas borders, this shift from the Inca regime, a large-scale polity capable of mobilising armies to fight in remote corners of the realm through its ties with regional elites, to a new political system under the Spanish monarchy that relied on jurisdictions that were frequently vague and overlapped with control by *encomenderos*, was both traumatic and chaotic. It disrupted the provision of gifts that the Inca

---

32 Ana María Presta, *Encomienda, familia y negocios en Charcas colonial: Los encomenderos de La Plata, 1550–1600* (Lima: IEP, Instituto de Estudios Peruanos: Banco Central de Reserva del Perú, 2000), p. 20.

33 Bartolomé Clavero, *Antidora: Antropología catolica de la economía moderna* (Milan: Giuffré, 1991), p. 100.

34 Romina Zamora, *Casa poblada y buen gobierno. Oeconomia católica y servicio personal en San Miguel de Tucumán, siglo XVIII* (Buenos Aires: Prometeo Libros, 2017), p. 52.

35 This was not a unique feature of Charcas and, as Santiago Muñoz Arbeláez shows for the Muisca in sixteenth-century Ubaque, the relations between *encomenderos* and indigenous chiefs cannot be centred exclusively around violence and exploitation; both sides also engaged on personal, political, and economic levels in ways that transformed the other party. Santiago Muñoz Arbeláez, *Costumbres en disputa: Los Muiscas y el Imperio Español en Ubaque, siglo XVI* (Bogotá: Universidad de los Andes, Facultad de Ciencias Sociales, Departamento de Historia, 2015).

had regularly made to the Chiriguanaes, prompting more regular incursions to areas beyond the border, well into Inca territory. It also meant that the protection of these native border settlers moved from Inca armies and fortresses to the small group of men that an *encomendero* could recruit using their own wealth and influence, which might be under compulsion because of their *encomienda* duties. These indigenous peoples were also coerced into participating in Spanish expeditions, sometimes even marched in chains, to new areas and borders. This period coincided with those peoples' fragmentation across different *encomiendas*, and a population decline caused by the arrival of diseases their immune systems could not overcome, combined with generalised violence and a state of war.

After Atahualpa's ransom was distributed, Francisco Pizarro and his companions set their eyes on gaining *encomiendas*. A first round of distribution of such grants took place in Jauja less than a year after Atahualpa's murder; the indigenous peoples of Charcas were placed in *deposito*, this is, held subject to future grants of *encomienda*, as the Spanish had not yet ventured into the region.[36] The conquistadors only knew the region through the references in Inca records at this stage. Two of Pizarro's brothers, Gonzalo (1510–1548) and Hernando (1504–1578), were assigned indigenous peoples in *deposito* in the west and east of Charcas, respectively.[37] Following the arrival of more Spaniards with ambitions to succeed in Peru, including the followers of Diego de Almagro, Pizarro's partner, a period of civil war ensued, and the first distribution was rendered obsolete. This was duly followed by a second round of *encomienda* grants in Cusco.[38] By the end of the 1530s, the Spanish were fully aware of the mineral resources of Charcas and once the first stage of civil wars ended, these grants were finally made effective. *Encomiendas* granted between 1540 and 1549 included indigenous peoples living along the Andean foothills and in the distant region the Spanish had started calling Tucumán. They either fought the Spanish or fled from their settlements, in fear of the Chiriguanaes who were pushing them westwards. As a result the border shifted in the same direction and the Chiriguanaes gained a large measure of control. The Spanish were in no position to defend the fortresses that the Inca had so carefully erected, and their approach, at least for the time being, would be one that combined expeditions (*entradas*), with the actions of individual *encomenderos* trying to protect their subjects from the damaging

---

36 Francisco Pizarro was legally authorised (received royal permission) to grant *encomiendas* in 1534. Gregorio Salinero, *Hombres de mala corte. Desobediencias, procesos políticos y gobierno de Indias en la segunda mitad del siglo XVI* (Madrid: Difusora Larousse – Ediciones Cátedra, 2018), p. 124.

37 Pedro Pizarro, *Descubrimiento y conquista del Perú*, Vol. VI (Lima: Imprenta y Librería San Martí Ca, 1917 [1571]), p. 81; Presta, *Encomienda, familia y negocios en Charcas colonial*, p. 56.

38 Zanolli, *Tierra, encomienda e identidad*, p. 71.

raids. The era of the vast Inca armies parked in garrisons along the borders was certainly over, giving way to an era of downscaled politics.

To take possession of their *encomiendas*, and roll out the process of expanding jurisdiction, the Spanish needed to launch expeditions to explore the land, reach the indigenous populations, and establish villages and towns. *Entradas* and urbanisation were at the core of jurisdiction and the transformation of geographies into territories of the Catholic monarchy. The first large-scale expedition into Charcas was headed by Francisco Pizarro's partner Diego de Almagro (1475–1538). In July 1535, to avoid problems between his men and Pizarro's, and armed with *capitulaciones* (legally binding documents he had secured from the Crown), Almagro set off on an expedition to Chile to take possession of his governorship of the newly created Kingdom of Nueva Toledo, which included Cusco and the land south.[39] Charcas, based on the accounts the Spanish had, promised great wealth. Almagro's *entrada* was in fact part of a major plot by rebel Manco Inca (1515–1544), who had succeeded Inca Tupac Gualpa and was now held prisoner by the Spanish in Cusco, to eliminate Pizarro's main partner and his men, allowing Manco Inca to put Cusco under siege and finally defeat the Spanish.[40] Accompanied by the Inca's half-brother Paullu (1510–1549), the *entrada* gave Almagro and his men, many of whom would settle in Charcas in later years, the opportunity to explore a land with promising potential in terms of populations and resources. Scholars have not managed to agree which conquistador was the first to arrive in the southeastern borders of the Charcas, although this is likely to have happened as part of Almagro's expedition.[41] Almagro survived this expedition and helped to lift the siege of Cusco, imprisoning Hernando and Gonzalo Pizarro, who would later gain *encomiendas* in Charcas. However,

---

39 John Hemming, *The Conquest of the Incas* (London: Macmillan, 1970), p. 170; Josep Barnadas, *Charcas. Orígenes históricos de una sociedad colonial 1535–1565* (La Paz: CIPCA, 1973), p. 32.

40 Ana María Lorandi, *Ni ley, ni rey, ni hombre virtuoso: Guerra y sociedad en el virreinato del Perú, siglos XVI y XVII* (Buenos Aires, Barcelona: Universidad de Buenos Aires, Facultad de Filosofía y Letras; Gedisa Editorial, 2002), p. 54.

41 Barragán Vargas mentions a member of Almagro's expedition, Juan de Saavedra, as the first Spaniard to have ventured into the area. A document published by Catherine Julien suggests Rodrigo de Salcedo was asked by Diego de Almagro to visit Jujuy to punish Chiriguanaes who had murdered six or seven Spaniards. Ana María Presta adds Francisco de Tarifa and gives a date—1536 or 1537—but also stresses that others might have arrived before any of these. Oliveto believes that the identity of the first Spaniard to enter this border region is likely to remain unclear. Mario E. Barragán Vargas, *Historia temprana de Tarija* (Tarija, Bolivia: Grafica Offset Kokito, 2001), p. 24; Julien, *Desde el oriente*, p. 270; Ana María Presta, '"Hermosos fértiles y abundantes." Los valles de Tarija y su población en el siglo XVI', in *Historia, ambiente y sociedad en Tarija, Bolivia* (La Paz: Instituto de Ecología, Universidad Mayor de San Andrés—School of Geography, University of Leeds, 2001), p. 30; Oliveto, 'Ocupación territorial', p. 111.

the captain's position quickly weakened—Gonzalo escaped from prison and Hernando was freed as an ultimate gesture of benevolence to Francisco Pizarro, a move that failed to stave off the predictable end to this episode of the Peruvian Civil Wars (1538–1555) after the sides had faced one another in the battle of Las Salinas on 26 April 1538.[42]

With Almagro's defeat (and subsequent murder), Hernando and Gonzalo Pizarro marched south from Cusco in company of Paullu Inca, who had effectively shifted allegiance to the victorious Pizarro brothers. They faced a first pocket of resistance in Tapacarí, not far from the Cochabamba valley, a fertile area that, as already mentioned, Huayna Capac had turned into a large-scale maize production centre to feed his vast armies, and where Inca general Tiso, summoned by Manco Inca, was waiting for the Spanish. After overcoming Tiso's force, Hernando had to return to Cusco to meet Francisco Pizarro, leaving Gonzalo at the head of the expedition. The next pocket of resistance was in the valley of Cochabamba, where combined armies under the command of Charca and Chicha chiefs Cuysara and Tiori Nasco, paired as 'Warriors of the Incas', faced the Spanish forces and their indigenous auxiliaries in a number of battles and putting them under siege between August and November 1538.[43] The siege was only lifted after Hernando returned with reinforcements and Paullu Inca brought the two sides into negotiations.[44] A resemblance can be noted between this resistance and previous episodes of unrest each time a new Inca had taken over his realm.

Paullu, who became Inca with the support of the Spaniards after the death of his half-brother Manco, had travelled through Charcas before, in Almagro's *entrada* (1535); but then he represented Manco Inca. Now, accompanying the Pizarro brothers' expedition, Paullu entered the region as Inca ruler which guaranteed negotiations between all parties and secured the loyalty of the local peoples. Paullu's mediation was the chief factor that procured the surrender of the armies of Charcas and claimed the region for the Catholic monarchy. It was this Inca, and not his Spanish partners, who extended royal jurisdiction over this new, aggregated territory. Paullu, in effect, conquered Charcas for the Spanish Crown. To seal the arrangements, the *caciques* (local leaders) unveiled to the Spanish the existence of one of their main *huacas*, the silver-rich mine at Porco, which marked the start of a new era in the region.

This move brought together the political cultures of the Catholic monarchy and of the Andean elites, as Porco was at the same time a gift made by those

42 Hemming, *The Conquest of the Incas*, p. 226; Lorandi, *Ni Ley, ni rey, ni hombre virtuoso*, pp. 61–63.

43 Hemming, *The Conquest of the Incas*, p. 236; Platt, Bouysse-Cassagne, and Harris, eds, *Qaraqara–Charka*, pp. 112–15.

44 Platt, Bouysse-Cassagne, and Harris, eds, *Qaraqara–Charka*, p. 111; Thérèse Bouysse-Cassagne, *La identidad aymara. Aproximación histórica (siglo XV, siglo XVI)* (La Paz: Hisbol/IFEA, 1987), p. 29.

elites (like past gifts to the Incas) and a donation that mutually bound them to the Catholic monarch as his loyal vassals. The *caciques* were probably expecting full incorporation as local nobles recognised through the use of the title of 'don', as finally happened.[45] With the presence of precious mineral deposits, there was now the need for a more stable Spanish population in Charcas, one that would give *encomenderos* a place to reside and handle their legal, political, and financial affairs more locally, exercising what they called *vecindad*, a kind of local citizenship, organising themselves politically in an urban settlement. The loyalty of the indigenous elites of Charcas had been sealed and the roll-out of jurisdiction would now commence.

Further expeditions mainly targeted the edges of Charcas and were commanded by men who felt they had not secured a large-enough share of prestige and wealth and/or were simply hoping to find mythical riches. These *entradas* offered the opportunity to assess remote regions and eventually reach indigenous populations the Spanish only knew through the Incas. One such man was the Greek captain Pedro de Candia (1485–1542), someone Hernando Pizarro distrusted. In company of Pedro Anzúrez de Campo Redondo, he set off south from Cusco, following the line of Inca *tambos* in an expedition that they funded themselves in 1538.[46] Candia marched into Tarija on his own, after Pedro Anzúrez went north to Cusco on orders from Francisco Pizarro, leaving his men in charge of Captain Diego de Rojas (1500–1544). Rojas and Candia eventually met in Tarija and began preparations for the first documented expedition into the Chiriguanaes. However, without a precise knowledge of the area, the expedition ended up following the wrong path, one that led away from Chiriguana settlements.[47]

Upon his return to Charcas, Pedro Anzúrez founded the first Spanish settlement in the district—Villa Plata, called La Plata later, present-day Sucre—between 1539 and 1540, finally giving *encomenderos* a legal, political, and juridical site of residence. In Villa Plata, a new, urban, political community was established, beginning the long process of settling and extending royal jurisdiction in Charcas, through installing a *cabildo* with authority over a vast area that included the region's southeast borders. This process of settling jurisdiction would reach momentum with the establishment of the Audiencia de Charcas in the same city in 1561.

Key to Villa Plata's foundation was the fact that the natives in the area were granted in *encomiendas* to the citizens of this new urban centre. Spanish villages and towns required regular labour and were not able to function

---

45 Tristan Platt and Pablo Quisbert, 'Tras las huellas del silencio: Potosí, los incas y Toledo', *Runa* XXXI, no. 2 (2010): p. 116.

46 José Antonio del Busto, *La hueste perulera* (Lima: Pontificia Universidad Católica del Perú, Fondo Editorial, 1981), pp. 160–63; Hemming, *The Conquest of the Incas*, p. 234.

47 Rafael Sanchez Concha Barrios, 'Las expediciones descubridoras: La entrada desde Larecaja hasta Tarija (1539–1540)', *Boletín del Instituto Riva Agüero* 16 (1989); Oliveto, 'Ocupación territorial', p. 116.

without such grants. Although their home settlement was far from the new village, the Chichas, a group this book follows because of their proximity to the border with the Chiriguanaes, were given in *encomienda* to Hernando Pizarro on 27 April 1539.[48] Others also present in the border region, such as the Moyos-Moyos, Apatamas, Juríes, and Churumatas, were assigned to Francisco de Retamoso and Alonso de Camargo in 1540.[49] These groups lived in areas difficult to access that by then were regularly exposed to raids by Chiriguanaes.[50]

Further south, in the region the Spanish called Tucumán, Juan de Villanueva was assigned the Omaguaca, and Martín Monje the indigenous peoples in Casabindo and the Chichas.[51] In documents years later Monje would acknowledge that it had been impossible for him to exact any tribute from his indigenous subjects because they were too distant and were at war.[52] These type of *encomienda*, known as *de guerra* ('war' *encomiendas*) clearly show the limitations of a model that did not work with peoples who resisted Spanish rule.[53] This was also the situation with the Chiriguanaes, the Chanés, and other lowland peoples who were politically fragmented and whose organisation made them 'unsuitable' for *encomienda* arrangements. The expansion of jurisdiction and implementation of *encomiendas* relied on indigenous cooperation, coercion, and the existence of societies that were politically organised in a hierarchy, without which these Spanish models were destined to fail. Furthermore, post-Inca alliances, such as those the Spanish were able to secure with Andean chiefs, were simply impossible among border groups who had not been integrated into the Inca realm. For such groups, the only alternative was a fragile coexistence that combined peace and war, and that transformed the borders into 'lands of warrying indigenous peoples' (*tierras de Indios de guerra*), a status some of these areas would not lose for many centuries.[54]

For those *encomenderos* whose grants were in areas where Inca control had never been deep and the indigenous populations were now hostile, and

---

48 Platt, Bouysse-Cassagne, and Harris, eds, *Qaraqara–Charka*, pp. 311–16; Zanolli, *Tierra, encomienda e identidad*, p. 71.

49 Oliveto, 'Ocupación territorial', p. 127.

50 AGI, Justicia, 1125, N5, R1, [1551] El capitán Cristóbal Barba, con el adelantado Juan Ortiz de Zárate, ambos vecinos de la ciudad de La Plata, sobre el derecho a los indios moyos.

51 José Toribio Medina, *Colección de documentos inéditos para la historia de Chile*, Vol. VI (Santiago de Chile: Imprenta Elzeviriana, 1896), pp. 168–70.

52 Marcos Jiménez de la Espada, *Relaciones geográficas de Indias: Perú*, Vol. II (Ministerio de Fomento, Madrid: Impreso en la Casa Real, 1885), p. XLIII; Presta, 'Los valles mesotérmicos de Chuquisaca', p. 52; Zanolli, *Tierra, encomienda e identidad*, pp. 72–81.

53 Thomas Calvo and Aristarco Regalado Pinedo, *Historia del reino de la Nueva Galicia* (Jalisco: Universidad de Guadalajara, 2016), pp. 217–18.

54 Langer, *Expecting Pears from an Elm Tree*, Introduction.

had regained a large degree of freedom, the task of reaching their native tributaries and taking possession of their *encomiendas* became challenging and required new expeditions. The assassination of Francisco Pizarro in July 1541 opened another chapter in the Spanish civil wars, as the thirst for expansion seemed not to stop. Captain Diego de Rojas, a veteran of the Conquest who had previously been with Hernando and Gonzalo Pizarro in Charcas, secured permission for his own expedition to Tucumán in 1543. Rojas lost his life in this *entrada* and was replaced by Francisco de Mendoza (1515–1547).[55] Mendoza's main achievement was the discovery of a route between Charcas and the Río de la Plata, after reaching the confluence of the Paraná and Carcarañá rivers. The new route, which would offer a new connection with Spain that avoided the viceregal capital Lima, was strategic for Charcas, reorienting the region geopolitically to the Atlantic Ocean. This gave the Spanish elite in Charcas a new objective and the ambition to eventually detach the district from the influence of Lima. However, for the time being, such a journey was perilous owing to the hostility of indigenous populations and a largely unknown geography. This discovery of the Río de la Plata route and the recent foundation of Villa Plata, nonetheless, made stabilisation of the southeastern borders of Charcas an urgent matter.

Peru would not see peace for another decade. The first blow to the power of the *encomenderos* would come from Blasco Nuñez Vela (1543–1546), who reached Peru as its first viceroy with orders to see the implementation of the New Laws of 1542. Their aim was to limit *encomendero* authority by failing to extend grants of *encomienda* beyond the life of the first holder, compromising future generations of *encomendero* families and descendants. The Laws also banned obligations on indigenous peoples to provide personal services to *encomenderos*, something the latter relied upon.[56] This was perceived by the *encomendero* group as an attack on its core values and ambitions. They felt betrayed by the Crown and partly dispossessed of their well-earned grants, in contravention of the rules of war.[57] Because Nuñez Vela proved inflexible in implementing these new regulations, Peru's *encomenderos* relied on Gonzalo Pizarro, the last relative of the Marquis of the Conquest in the area and so able to impose seigneurial authority as his heir, to lead them and potentially overturn the New Laws. Pizarro began a large-scale rebellion that resulted in Nuñez Vela's death (January 1546), prompting the arrival in 1548 of a new Crown envoy, Licenciado Pedro de La Gasca (1485–1567). Contrary to the Crown's intentions, this period of anarchy saw the revival of *encomendero* factions, a situation invigorated by a new development. Around this time, news of Potosí, a silver mine that would become Peru's main source of wealth, had reached all corners of the viceroyalty and beyond. The new riches would

---

55 Oliveto, 'Ocupación territorial', pp. 117–18.
56 Lorandi, *Ni ley, ni rey, ni hombre virtuoso*, pp. 72–73.
57 David García Hernán, *La cultura de la guerra y el teatro del Siglo de Oro* (Madrid: Sílex, 2006), pp. 158–59.

finance, first Gonzalo Pizarro's war efforts against Nuñez Vela and then his fresh campaign against the Crown's new envoy. Mining at Porco and Potosí, located close to the natives Gonzalo managed through his *encomienda*, made the *encomiendas* in Charcas more valuable and the availability of native labour an asset.

However, with the arrival of La Gasca, Gonzalo Pizarro's days were numbered. After his defeat and execution, there was a new redistribution of *encomienda* grants to reward those who had sided with the victors. With so many candidates and so few *encomiendas*, La Gasca asked for assessments of the actual value and size of these grants and these data were used for the redistribution pursued in Guaynarima in August 1548.[58] Because of the need for indigenous labour, Potosí had inflated the value of *encomiendas* in Charcas significantly. The mining settlement, or *asiento* as it was initially called, created new mercantile opportunities for those with labour and money to invest. The valleys not far from the Chiriguana borders, which could be used for agriculture to feed the crowds of miners and Potosí's *vecinos*, merchants, and mining entrepreneurs, acquired new significance, but the threat of the Chiriguanaes was difficult to overcome. As Catholic priest Reginaldo de Lizárraga said, remembering this period half a century later, 'Potosí was crowding' these valleys.[59] By then, prominent *encomenderos* of Charcas and their clients had farms along the southeast borders.[60] In time, the farms would be starting points for many of the settlements, villages, and towns that were planned and built around them. At this point, the Chiriguanaes had become a nuisance to the authorities in La Plata, who were seeking ways to penetrate their lands, and establish law, order, and monarchy in an environment they perceived as chaotic, or in their terms, that lacked *policía* (civic and religious order).[61]

To wrap up this section of this chapter, with the disintegration of the

---

58 Rafael Loredo, 'Relaciones de repartimientos que existían en el Perú al finalizar la rebelión de Gonzalo Pizarro', *Revista de la Universidad Católica del Perú* VIII, no. 1 (1940): pp. 51–62; Rafael Loredo, *Los repartos; Bocetos para la nueva historia del Perú* (Lima: no identified publisher, 1958).

59 Reginaldo de Lizárraga, *Descripción colonial*, Libro uno (Buenos Aires: Librería de la Facultad, 1916 [1605]), p. 274.

60 Roberto Levillier, *Audiencia de Lima. Correspondencia de presidentes y oidores (1549–1564)*, Vol. I (Madrid: Juan Pueyo, 1922), pp. 95–96; Nathan Weaver Olson, 'A Republic of Lost Peoples: Race, Status, and Community in the Eastern Andes of Charcas at the Turn of the Seventeenth Century', PhD dissertation, University of Minnesota, 2017, pp. 62–63; Catherine Julien, Kristina Angelis, and Zulema Bass Werner de Ruiz, *Historia de Tarija. Corpus documental*, Vol. VI (Tarija: Editora Guadalquivir, 1997), p. xiii.

61 On *policía* see Jesús Vallejo, 'Concepción de la policía', in *La jurisdicción contencioso-administrativa en España. Una historia de sus orígenes*, ed. Marta Lorente (Madrid: Consejo General del Poder Judicial, 2010), pp. 117–44; and Zamora, *Casa poblada y buen gobierno*, pp. 201–09.

Inca empire, the southeastern border, built over the years through imperial policies that included the construction of fortresses and the relocation of native colonists, simply collapsed. The border enabled both confrontation and trade. As part of their efforts to implement and expand jurisdiction, through expeditions, the Spanish learned more about the border, yet they also realised that the *encomienda* system that was installed elsewhere in Peru would not work among indigenous populations of the lowlands. Under pressure from Chiriguana raids, some of those natives given in *encomienda* to different Spaniards moved westwards, and with them so did the border. The Chiriguanaes posed a challenge and set a limit to Spanish jurisdiction. This situation, however, was not unique to Charcas. As this book is about to explore, elsewhere across Spanish America conquistadors faced similar situations that prompted heated discussions about the nature of the Spanish conquest, the role of the monarchy, and the nature of its newest vassals: the indigenous populations.

4.1 The Spanish and the unconquered and unconquerable natives

As the conquistadors moved from north to south, from the Caribbean and Mexico to Peru, they encountered peoples who had not been conquered and wanted to remain that way.[62] This triggered ethical and religious discussions that, in 1512, prompted the Laws of Burgos, cementing the idea that the Crown was obliged to protect the natives of the New World. This only applied, however, if these peoples had first accepted royal jurisdiction. The use of violence as part of the process of extending jurisdiction over new possessions was questioned and remained a controversial subject, as it placed the monarchy in a difficult position both at home and abroad.[63]

---

62 Juan David Montoya Guzmán, 'La fabricación del enemigo: Los indios pijaos en el Nuevo Reino de Granada, 1562–1611', *TRASHUMANTE. Revista Americana de Historia Social* 19 (2022): pp. 96–117; Linda Newson, *Supervivencia indígena en la Nicaragua colonial* (London: University of London Press, 2021); Linda Newson, *Life and Death in Early Colonial Ecuador* (Norman: University of Oklahoma Press, 1995); Alvaro Jara, *Guerra y sociedad en Chile. La transformación de la guerra de Arauco y la esclavitud de los indios* (Santiago de Chile: Editorial Universitaria, 1971); Salvador Alvarez, 'La guerra chichimeca', in Calvo and Pinedo, eds, *Historia del reino de Nueva Galicia*, pp. 211–62. For a more general review of all these borders: Thierry Saignes, 'Las zonas conflictivas: Fronteras iniciales de guerra', in *El primer contacto y la formación de nuevas sociedades*, Vol. II (Madrid: Ediciones UNESCO, Ediciones Trotta, 2007), pp. 269–99.

63 Spain's medieval code, the Siete Partidas de Alfonso X, had identified the waging of religious war against infidels, as part of the Reconquista struggle against the Moors, as a just cause based on three considerations: first, to expand religion and destroy those who oppose it; second, as part of vassal–lord ties; and third, to protect and honour one's dwelling place. *Las Siete Partidas del Sabio Rey don Alonso El Nono, Nuevamente Glosadas por el Licenciado Gregorio López del Consejo Real de Indias de Su*

A document best known as Requerimiento seemed the best way forward.[64]
It was supposed to convey the rights the natives possessed and the
corresponding duties on them, and was first read out loud in the Spanish
American jungles in 1514. Adjusted in 1526 to make room for interpreters to
ensure that the message was understood by its recipients, the Requerimiento
was subject to further changes: written consent from priests was added as
an extra requirement before any war could be declared.[65] Despite all the
legalities, such adjustments did not change the fact that indigenous peoples
who were faced with the 'illocutionary force' of this document either had to
surrender or be cast as hostile and suffer outright violence in the process.[66]
This document did not certainly solve the polemics about the way the
jurisdiction of the Crown over the New World was being extended, often (to
quote contemporaries) '*a sangre y fuego*', 'with blood and fire'.

These debates, or 'polemics of possession',[67] eventually resulted in the New
Laws of 1542, designed to curb *encomendero* abuses. Further changes were
introduced making it clear that natives could not be enslaved by war or for
any other reason, but the discussions continued. Between 1550 and 1551, Juan

Magestad, Vol. 1 (Salamanca: Andrea de Portonari, 1555), Segunda Partida, Título
XXIII, Ley II, p. 79.

64 This document descends from medieval legal traditions circulating across Christian
Europe in relation to just war and the rights of non-Christians, and from traditions
from the Reconquista and Moorish genres, specifically the Islamic *jihad*. Like many
other legal documents of the period, the Requerimiento was staged. Paja Faudree,
'Reading the "Requerimiento" Performatively: Speech Acts and the Conquest of the
New World', *Colonial Latin American Review* 24, no. 4 (2015): pp. 456–78. Widely
mocked, it was controversial from its beginnings, yet Cañizares-Esguerra suggests
a contextual reading from the Bible: he states that, for those jurists who drafted the
Requerimiento, the conquest was the fulfilment of 'Joshua 3:7 and 6:16–21: Israelites/
Spaniards gave the Canaanites/Indians an ultimatum to clear the Promised Land or
face destruction'. Jorge Cañizares-Esguerra, 'Typology in the Atlantic World: Early
Modern Readings of Colonization', in *Soundings in Atlantic History: Latent Structures
and Intellectual Currents, 1500–1830* (London: Harvard University Press, 2009),
p. 251. Cervantes proposes to understand it as a sign that the Crown was becoming
all too aware of its obligations to indigenous peoples and in response was attempting
to cover itself legally. Fernando Cervantes, *Conquistadores: A New History* (London:
Penguin Books, 2021), p. 82.
65 Lewis Hanke, *The Spanish Struggle for Justice in the Conquest of America* (Philadelphia:
University of Pennsylvania Press, 1949), p. 112.
66 José Rabasa, *Writing Violence on the Northern Frontier: The Historiography of Sixteenth
Century New Mexico and Florida and the Legacy of Conquest* (Durham, NC: Duke
University Press, 2000), pp. 10–11; Tamar Herzog, *Frontiers of Possession: Spain and
Portugal in Europe and the Americas* (Cambridge, MA: Harvard University Press,
2015), p. 106.
67 Understood as debates over the right to possess and govern the Indies and its peoples.
Rolena Adorno, *The Polemics of Possession in Spanish American Narrative* (New Haven,
CT: Yale University Press, 2007).

Ginés de Sepúlveda (1494–1573) and Bartolomé de Las Casas (1486–1566) hosted two sessions in Salamanca to debate the nature of Spanish conquests and whether they were lawful and just.[68] The question was never actually settled, but by the 1550s there were regulations on the rights of natives and how to extend and settle jurisdiction over them, even if this had to be done with violence.[69] Stressing the 'minority condition' of indigenous peoples, who were perceived as lacking civic order because they were not living in fixed settlements and leading what the Spanish saw as a 'civic life', and because they did not know the Catholic faith, such regulations dictated how to wage war against unconquered natives, and when such actions would be just or unjust.[70] With religion as a key argument for intervention and expansion, the Crown could arrange with individuals the extension of its own jurisdiction on grounds that this was an instrument of conversion to Christianity, thus justifying war, a practice that would continue well beyond the New Laws of 1542.[71] Cannibalism, among other 'sins' attributed to some indigenous groups, provided moral ground for just war and their subsequent enslavement.[72] This argument was conveyed as part of strategic narratives and would resonate in letters and official documents every time the Spanish needed to justify expeditions to lands occupied by 'indigenous peoples at war', from the Chichimecas in Mexico, the Pijaos in Nueva Granada, to the Araucanos in Chile, and the Chiriguanaes in Charcas. It was an argument that fed into a wider stereotype of native peoples who were hostile to Spanish jurisdiction. It was also part of a narrative that would end up being manipulated by those

68 What was at a stake was the application of infidel rights to the natives, which, as David Lantigua suggests, became a legal precedent for international relations between non-Europeans and Europeans. This was a debate that originated from experiences along the Catholic monarchy's borders. David Lantigua, *Infidels and Empires in a New World Order: Early Modern Spanish Contributions to International Legal Thought* (Cambridge, New York: Cambridge University Press, 2020), pp. 2–3.

69 Richard Konetzke, *Colección de documentos para la historia social de la formación de Hispanoamérica 1493–1810*, Vol. 1 (1493–1592) (Madrid: Consejo Superior de Investigaciones Científicas, Instituto Francisco de Vitoria, 1953), pp. 335–39.

70 Although the enslavement of indigenous peoples was banned by Royal Decrees of 1526, 1530, 1532, 1540, 1542, and 1543, as Patricia Seed rightly points out 'both Spanish and Portuguese monarchs consistently made exceptions for their general decrees of freedom [of Indians] if the natives were accused of eating human flesh'. *Recopilación de leyes de los reynos de las Indias*, Vol. 2 (Madrid: Julian Paredes, 1681), p. 194; Patricia Seed, *American Pentimento: The Invention of Indians and the Pursuit of Riches* (Minneapolis: University of Minnesota Press, 2001), p. 103.

71 Nancy Van Deusen, 'Why Indigenous Slavery Continued in Spanish America after the New Laws of 1542', *The Americas* 80, no. 3 (2023): pp. 395–432; José Javier Ibáñez and Gaetano Sabatini, 'Monarchy as Conquest: Violence, Social Opportunity, and Political Stability in the Establishment of the Hispanic Monarchy', *The Journal of Modern History* 81, no. 3 (2009): p. 515.

72 Seed, *American Pentimento*, p. 104.

same indigenous peoples to extract goods from the Spanish, in exchange for members of other indigenous groups they had taken prisoner in their own battles. This narrative worked both ways, in practice, and underpinned the exchange of goods and peoples between the Spanish and the unconquered and unconquerable natives.

Native captivity was extremely common despite bans and regulations.[73] Captives were generally by-products of war, acquired largely in expeditions organised by the Spanish and their indigenous allies, or taken as prisoners by other indigenous peoples. The organisers could petition the authorities to be allowed to keep such prisoners in captivity. This offered an extra incentive for expedition members who were entitled to the 'spoils of war', which included captives. It created a market for captive indigenous peoples in border areas and away from them. Moreover, it also made some indigenous populations dependent on securing prisoners to obtain from the Spanish commodities they treasured. Their raids probably became more regular, while they also took more precautions to seize and retain as many enemies as possible, just for the purpose of trading them with the Spanish afterwards.[74] Native captivity, hostages, and prisoners played an important role in the settlement, extension, and consolidation of jurisdiction in(to) the border areas. Dressed as the moral and religious duty to rescue indigenous peoples who were already captive, or were the spoils of just war, captivity was integrated into the system of merits and rewards for services provided to the Crown and went hand in hand with stereotypes of border indigenous peoples.[75]

4.2 'Cannibals, savages, and sinners'

Stereotypical views of indigenous peoples were largely based on 'hegemonic knowledges', which constituted a philosophical and religious matrix through which the Spanish perceived their new vassals as mentally and morally inferior and therefore lacking capacity and in need of guardianship.[76] Scholars disagree on the issue of early perceptions of the Chiriguanaes. One view indicates that they had different names in Asunción (Paraguay) and Charcas, being called Guaraní in the former and Chiriguanaes in the

---

73 Jaime Valenzuela Márquez, 'Los indios cautivos en la frontera de guerra chilena: entre la abolición de la esclavitud y la recomposición de la servidumbre esclavista', in *Espaços Coloniais: Domínios, Poderes e Representações* (São Paulo: Alameda Casa Editorial, 2019), pp. 229–61; and Andrés Reséndez, *The Other Slavery: The Uncovered Story of Indian Enslavement in America* (Boston, MA, New York: Mariner Books, Houghton Mifflin Harcourt, 2017).

74 Santos-Granero, *Vital Enemies*, p. 25.

75 Paola Revilla Orías, *Entangled Coercion: African and Indigenous Labour in Charcas (16th–17th Century)* (Boston, MA: De Gruyter Oldenbourg, 2020).

76 Germán Morong Reyes, *Saberes hegemónicos y dominio colonial. Los indios en el Gobierno del Perú de Juan de Matienzo (1567)* (Rosario, Argentina: Prohistoria Ediciones, 2016), Capítulo III.

latter. This argument adds that the Spanish in Asunción were fewer and had sufficient land and because the Guaraní/Chiriguanaes met their needs for food supplies and labour, they were seen as allies and friends. In contrast, in Charcas, where Chiriguanaes resisted meeting such needs and were seen as an obstacle to the local elite's plans to control the southeast borders and exploit their fertile lands, these local peoples were seen as outsiders, invaders, and enemies.[77] A second view stresses that, in both areas, Spanish perception of the Chiriguanaes changed over time, hardening as more of these indigenous peoples moved to the borders.[78] Both views point however to the same argument: they stress the changing perception of the Chiriguanaes based on how far they adapted, or did not, to the extension of jurisdiction by the Spanish into the region. Chiriguana identity was thus structured around their political agency, which was limited by jurisdiction since this defined them in relation to ability to establish law and deliver justice and in line with Spanish concepts of status, race, and religion. This is consistent with the political culture of the Spanish monarchy in which identities were relational: individuals largely defined themselves in relation to others.[79]

As with other unconquerable natives in Spanish America, one main feature of the stereotypical views of the Chiriguanaes was attributing cannibalism to them. It has been argued that there was a different approach to them in Asunción and Charcas. If the Guaraní of Asunción practised cannibalism of any kind, it was certainly frowned upon by their Spanish allies, but it was never construed as an obstacle to alliance.[80] In Charcas, the allegation was regularly made by the Spanish, to depict the Chiriguanaes as savages. This shows that when the Chiriguana were seen as 'cooperative' by the Spanish, they were classed as 'peaceful' and 'friendly', where otherwise they were 'warring indigenous peoples'. The demonisation of the Chiriguanaes in Charcas was a narrative reworked and built by local authorities and *vecinos* that fed into the views the Crown had of those peoples through letters, reports, and assessments that came from the district. It was also a narrative that was deployed politically and one that ideologically underpinned the expeditions, the merits and rewards that could be obtained through these, including captives and other spoils of war, and the extension of jurisdiction over the border areas.

Tracing this stereotype back to its roots can be challenging, yet correspondence shows its widespread and systematic use. As early as 1549, Licenciado La Gasca wrote to the Consejo de Indias, the royal council responsible for

---

77 Julien, 'Colonial Perspectives on the Chiriguana (1528–1574)', p. 18.
78 Isabelle Combès, 'De luciferinos a canonizables: Representaciones del canibalismo chiriguano', *Boletín Americanista*, 2, LXIII, no. 67 (2013): pp. 134–35; Combès, 'Grigotá y Vitupue', p. 74.
79 António Manuel Hespanha, *A ordem do mundo e o saber dos juristas: Imaginários do antigo direito europeu* (Lisbon: independently published, 2017), pp. 101–02.
80 Julien, 'Colonial Perspectives on the Chiriguana (1528–1574)', p. 36.

the Indies, of the need to establish border towns to solve the problem of cannibalism:

> And [if] a town [were] established in Tucumán not only would the Indians of Charcas be defended from the Chiriguanaes, but the Chiriguanaes would also be settled and overcome their bestial habit and custom [i.e. cannibalism].[81]

It is interesting to note the extension of political jurisdiction through urban spaces based on such stereotypes. Jurisdictional politics relied on expansion of towns, and this required indigenous peoples to be classified either as hostile or friendly to the Spanish presence. The letter conveys the idea that Spanish towns, and the civic and religious life that they could bring, extending the monarch's presence along the border, would transform 'barbaric' natives into the Catholic king's vassals.[82]

Despite La Gasca's ambitions, for the monarchy the border remained a lawless area. By the early 1550s there were even fears of a large-scale attack by Chiriguanaes, headed by Spaniards who were living in the area and engaged in trade with them. This prompted calls for the establishment of an Audiencia in Charcas.[83] Without the presence of such an institution, and therefore the 'monarch's presence', it was argued that it was impossible either to settle and expand jurisdiction or to keep the land 'in order'.

Yet the stereotype persisted unabated. After the establishment of the Audiencia in 1561, in a letter one of its judges, Juan de Matienzo, stressed that:

> [i]n this land, near this city, are some Indians who have recently arrived called Chiriguanaes, cruel and warring people, savages who eat human flesh and fight those Indians who live in the lowlands and, when they want to catch them, they do so and capture 600 or 1,000 Indians, and then eat them, just after they seize them, or keep them to fatten them up, whereas they sell others, or keep others as slaves.[84]

---

81 '[Y] hecho el pueblo en Tucumán no solo se defenderá a los indios de los Charcas destos Chiriguanaes, pero aún los subjetarán y quitarán desta bestial costumbre e uso'. Letter by Pedro de La Gasca to the Consejo de Indias, 17 july 1549, in Marqués Miraflores and Miguel Salva, *Colección de documentos inéditos para la historia de España*, Vol. L (Madrid: Imprenta de la Viuda de Calero, 1867), p. 79.

82 Jorge Díaz Ceballos, *Poder compartido: Repúblicas urbanas, monarquía y conversación en Castilla de Oro, 1508–1573* (Madrid: Marcial Pons Historia, 2020), Ch. 4.

83 Levillier, *Audiencia de Lima*, pp. 95–96.

84 'En esta tierra bien cerca desta cibdad ay vnos yndios aduenedizos que se dicen chiriguanaes gente cruel y de guerra yndomitos que comen carne humana y pelean con los yndios comarcanos que habitan en los llanos y quando quieren hazen tal presa en ellos, que toman y captiuan seiscientos y mill yndios y dellos comen luego en tomandolos, y otros tienen a engordar para este efecto otros venden y de otros se siruen como esclauos.' Letter by Juan de Matienzo to the King, 20 October 1561,

Further evidence of Matienzo's role in the construction and propagation of this narrative comes from his political treatise *Gobierno del Perú* from 1567:

> In this land and province of Charcas, near this city and its area, are some Indians who have only just arrived called Chiriguanaes, warring people, very cruel, who eat human flesh, and live in the hills, and whose only occupation is to fight, kill, and eat Indians and use them as slaves.[85]

Matienzo's views summarise very well the reworking by local elites of the cannibal stereotype already employed against other unconquerable indigenous peoples in Spanish America.[86] The Crown relied on letters and other documents from officials and settlers to build an image of the situation. Through such communication channels this stereotype travelled to the Consejo de Indias and the monarch. In contrast, where no local connection prompted them, travellers and distant chroniclers presented a different image from which such stereotypes are absent.[87]

While they probably practised ritual cannibalism, this was not the only label attached to the Chiriguanaes. They were also seen as newcomers, invaders who occupied land that belonged to others, perhaps providing a reminder that they had only moved into the Andean slopes early in the sixteenth century. They were also seen as inclined to engage in acts of a 'sinful' nature.[88] Finally, they were also labelled apostates, as some had been baptised, yet rejected the

Roberto Levillier, *La Audiencia de Charcas. Correspondencia de Presidentes y Oidores. 1561–1579*, Vol. 1 (Madrid: Colección de Publicaciones Históricas de la Biblioteca del Congreso Argentino, 1918), p. 54.

85 'En esta tierra e provincia de los Charcas, e junto a esta ciudad y sus términos, hay unos indios advenedizos que se dicen chiriguanaes, gente de guerra, muy cruel, indómitos, que comen carne humana, habitan en las cordilleras, y no tienen otro oficio sino pelear y matar y comer indios y servirse de ellos como de esclavos.' Juan de Matienzo, *Gobierno del Perú* (Paris, Lima: IFEA, 1967 [1567]), p. 256.

86 Luis Miguel Córdoba Ochoa, 'Guerra, imperio, y violencia en la Audiencia de Santa Fe, Nuevo Reino de Granada 1580-1620', PhD dissertation, Universidad Pablo de Olavide, 2013, p. 13.

87 A revision of the description of the Chiriguanaes among chroniclers shows a completely different picture. Betanzos [1551] mentioned the Chiriguanaes but does not describe them at all. Murúa [1600] called them 'raiders'. Guaman Poma [1615] referred to them as 'warring and strong'. Juan de Betanzos et al., eds, *Suma y narración de los incas* (Madrid: Atlas, 1987 [1551]), pp. 25, 32; Murua, *Historia general del Perú*, p. 71; Felipe Guamán Poma de Ayala, *El primer nueva corónica y buen gobierno* (México: Siglo Veintiuno, 2006 [1615]), p. 913. The only chronicler to call them cannibals was Pedro Sarmiento de Gamboa, who was very close to Viceroy Toledo who also shared this view of the Chiriguanaes. Sarmiento de Gamboa, *Historia de los incas*, pp. 146–47.

88 Such as the sin of *nefando*, which was understood at the time as what were seen as unnatural sexual practices, some of which are today associated with homosexuality. Combès, 'De luciferinos a canonizables', p. 132.

Catholic faith. All these elements built a stereotype that, first the Cabildo in La Plata and then, after 1561, the judges of the Audiencia de Charcas, would regularly invoke every time they needed justification for expeditions and ultimately the captivity of Chiriguanaes to secure labour and extend the border. The Chiriguanaes were also aware of this stereotype which at times they would use to secure concessions from the authorities. They would stress they were ready to accept evangelisation, only to go back on their promises when their goals were not achieved. Cannibalism also provided grounds for engagement with the Spanish, who made the practice an excuse for acquiring indigenous captives, to 'rescue' them. In exchange the Chiriguanaes would receive iron tools, fine clothing, and even the seashells that the Inca had provided. Cannibalism, or the threat of it, brought the Chiriguanaes and the Spanish together, ensuring the circulation of these goods.

For as long as the Chiriguana were seen as cannibals, there was going to be a trade in captive natives and both the Spanish and the Chiriguanaes knew it. Also, for as long as this stereotype was alive, the *entradas* could be easily justified by Spanish conquistadors, captains, and other soldiers who, as members of the expeditions, were able to accumulate merits for future rewards and secure extra labour for a range of businesses and duties in Charcas. The stereotype also helped the monarchy justify its support for the expeditions, as a moral duty to rescue from the Chiriguanaes captives who would otherwise be eaten.

5. Invented borders, invented peoples

This opening chapter has discussed the Inca southeastern border and its transformation during the early years of Spanish presence in Charcas. The southeast border occupied a transitional area from a geographical point of view. In ecological terms, it lay between the high plateau and the mesothermal valleys, and the more tropical rainforest and savanna areas of the *yungas* and lowlands. Under the Inca, a sophisticated system of roads and fortresses created a border that could be used for both defence and trade. In typical Inca fashion, the indigenous polity both negotiated the defence of its vast border-land with, and outsourced this defence to, its allies, who gained privileged status as a result. Under this approach, Chicha and other peoples deployed at the heart of Charcas to watch the borders were reinvented by the Incas as 'Warriors of the Inca'. All this was put to the test under Inca Huayna Capac (1493–1525) as the first Chiriguana incursions took place. The border established under the Inca was one that mirrored the type of reciprocal ties that the regime fostered with all those cultures it encompassed. However, it was also a border that acknowledged that the Inca realm and the Andean groups were radically different from those that inhabited the lowlands.

With the disintegration of this polity and the advance of the Spanish conquistadors, the border was engulfed in chaos. Populations were decimated by disease and regular Chiriguana raids. Some moved westwards as a result. Through launching expeditions, the Spanish built their knowledge about the Chiriguanaes, who were increasingly hostile to Spanish presence. As happened in other areas across Spanish America, stereotypes of the unconquerable natives were deployed, to justify recurrent *entradas* that were needed to keep them at bay, safeguarding populations near the border, and more importantly in the case of Charcas, making safe the crucial route between Charcas and the Rio de la Plata. Furthermore, the stereotypes were known by the Chiriguanaes themselves, and used by them to extract gifts and concessions from the Spanish. The stereotypes also fuelled trade in local people enslaved by the Chiriguana under the pretext that otherwise the captives would be eaten by their 'cannibal' captors. From Charcas, the labels travelled to Spain and the monarchy used them to give ultimate meaning to the successive expeditions, promising those who went rewards, so long as the *entradas* were narrated in an epic way and reports of merit were presented in the legal format, *probanzas*. A new border was created, one that mirrored the Spanish monarchy's jurisdictional politics, just as the previous one had mirrored Inca imperial politics. This new border, and its invented inhabitants, drove a further reinvention of conquistadors, priests, and idle armed men as heroes or *beneméritos*. Taking from this theme, Chapter Two focuses on the *encomendero* group, through the expeditions of one of the most prominent *vecinos* of La Plata, Captain Martín de Almendras, in 1564–1565.

Jurisdictional Entanglements
The Expeditions of Martín de Almendras

'¿Qué príncipes ocupan los catálogos de la fama, sino los
guerreros? A ellos se les debe en propiedad el renombre de
magnos. Llenan el mundo de aplauso, los siglos de fama, los
libros de proezas, porque lo belicoso tiene más de plausible que
lo pacífico.'[1]

'What princes occupy the catalogues of fame, but warriors? Only
they deserve the renown of Great Ones. They elicit the applause
of the world, centuries of fame, books of exploits, for war
exploits elicit greater admiration than peaceful enterprises.'[2]

Baltasar Gracián

'Porque bien save vuestra señoría que todo el Perú sin Potosí y
Porco no vale más que Tucumán.'[3]

'You are well aware, our lord, that the entire of Peru without
Potosí and Porco is not worth more than Tucumán.'

Audiencia de Charcas judges

1 Biblioteca Nacional de España (from here on BNE), Ms. 6,643. Baltasar Gracián,
   El héroe, fol. 21, http://bdh-rd.bne.es/viewer.vm?id=0000128386&page=1, accessed
   24 April 2024.
2 Translation by David Castillo, 'Gracián and the Art of Public Representation',
   in *Rhetoric and Politics: Baltasar Gracián and the New World Order* (Minneapolis:
   University of Minnesota Press, 1997), p. 206.
3 Letter from the Audiencia de Charcas to the King, 1566, in Blas Garay, *Colección de
   documentos relativos a la historia de América y particularmente a la historia de Paraguay*,
   Vol. 2 (Asunción: Talleres Nacionales de Martín Kraus, 1901), p. 449.

1. Introduction

Through an analysis of the final expeditions of *encomendero* Martín de Almendras between 1564 and 1565, first to the Chichas and subsequently to the region of Tucumán—in present-day Argentina—the present chapter navigates a crucial time in the early history of Charcas. The founding in the district of an Audiencia, the highest court of justice and government, in 1561, initially removed all territories within a radius of one hundred leagues around La Plata, including the city of La Paz, from the jurisdiction of the Audiencia de Lima, which created friction and tensions between the two Audiencias. Tucumán, where many indigenous groups had been given in *encomienda* to *vecinos* of La Plata, thus remained outside the new Audiencia's jurisdiction and under control of the governorship of Chile, which was under the jurisdiction of the Audiencia de Lima.[4] The presence of those indigenous peoples and the district's strategic position along the route to the Atlantic made Tucumán a natural target for the young Audiencia's expansion plans.

With this new body eager to confirm, exercise, and extend its jurisdiction, La Plata's political sway over the southern portion of Peru would increase dramatically, boosting the aspirations of the new Audiencia's *encomendero* group. Beginning with a description of *encomenderos* and men who, unable to secure a grant of *encomienda*, were regarded as a potential source of political unrest, the chapter then focuses on how the ambitions of the first group and the needs of the second, generally known as soldiers, brought them close to the young Audiencia and its own political plans. It continues with an analysis of the *encomendero* network in the region built by Francisco de Almendras and his nephews Diego and Martín over several decades. Martín de Almendras would play an important role in the Audiencia's consolidation and expansion plans.

Through two expeditions, designed to restore peace in an area under attack by indigenous groups, Almendras was expected to help the Audiencia de Charcas effectively bring Tucumán—whose governor, Francisco de Aguirre (1507–1581), was allegedly dead—within its sphere of political influence. To justify these expeditions, the Audiencia overplayed fears of a large native revolt, resorting to stereotypes of indigenous peoples.[5] It also

---

4 Tucumán was at the time a district much larger than the present Argentine province, involving a vast area from the north of Cordoba to Jujuy, and included Santiago del Estero which was a centre of important gravitation for some time. The northern border was the Bermejo River, which was under the influence of the Chiriguanaes. Roberto Levillier, *Gobernación de Tucumán. Correspondencia de los cabildos en el siglo XVI* (Madrid: Sucesores de Rivadeneyra, 1918), pp. XIII–XXIII.

5 Aguirre had been born in Talavera de la Reina, and moved to Peru in 1536 after participating in the wars in Italy: Luis Silva Lezaeta, *El conquistador Francisco de Aguirre* (Santiago de Chile: Imprenta de la Revista Católica, 1904), pp. 5–35. Overplaying fears of a native revolt seems to have been something not uncommon

secured the title of governor of Tucumán for Almendras, on condition that Aguirre's death could be confirmed. Despite the rumours, Aguirre was found safe, but he was taken prisoner to La Plata, never to recover the governorship of Tucumán. This chapter illustrates how, in the mid-1560s, through its *encomendero* group, the Audiencia de Charcas began the journey to settle its jurisdiction and that of the monarchy along the southeastern borders, turning them into regions run by its political allies. This process of confirmation and settlement of the monarchy's political presence also involved a large degree of localisation, as borders increasingly adopted a local character and the Crown had to negotiate, through its agents and regional elites, the terms of its presence there.[6] This transformation involved indigenous groups who argued and fought over the terms of either their inclusion or their exclusion from the political project of the Audiencia de Charcas.

2. A wealthy elite

The journey from conquistador to *encomendero* was one that many Spaniards hoped to make, yet only a few succeeded in accomplishing it. There were never more than 500 *encomenderos* in the whole of Peru, including Charcas, a figure reached by 1540 that was stable after that date.[7] Each of the 168 men who were present when Francisco Pizarro distributed the treasure of Cajamarca in 1533 were effectively entitled to an *encomienda* and, with that, the possibility of holding a public office in a *cabildo* as city council members. *Encomiendas* were part of a wider 'economy of privileges and rewards' through which the Crown recompensed with *mercedes* the merits and services of its loyal vassals in line with their honour, status, and background.[8]

Although *encomiendas* were many conquistadors' dream, they were also, in effect, grants created and held at the discretion of viceroys, governors, *adelantados*, or captains and were therefore a better basis for the accumulation of wealth and perpetuation of family status than rents and properties

among *encomenderos* at the time. Aguirre and his family employed similar tactics to remain in control of the Copiapó valley in Chile: Francisco Garrido and Erick Figueroa, 'Establishing Colonial Rule in a Frontier *Encomienda*: Chile's Copiapó Valley under Francisco de Aguirre and His Kin, 1549–1580', *Latin American Research Review*, August 2023, pp. 1–17.

6 Carlos Garriga, 'Patrias criollas, plazas militares. Sobre la América de Carlos IV', in *La América de Carlos IV*, Vol. 1 (Buenos Aires: Instituto de Investigaciones de Historia del Derecho, 2006), p. 18; Oscar Mazín Gómez, 'Architect of the New World. Juan Solórzano Pereyra and the Status of the Americas', in *Polycentric Monarchies: How Did Early Modern Spain and Portugal Achieve and Maintain a Global Hegemony?* (Eastbourne: Sussex Academic Press, 2012), pp. 27–42.

7 James Lockhart, *Spanish Peru, 1532–1560: A Colonial Society* (Madison: University of Wisconsin Press, 1974), p. 12.

8 Clavero, 'Justicia y gobierno. Economía y gracia', pp. 121–48.

held in Spain, a situation that drove *encomenderos* into a constant search for business diversification and political recompense. Those with good connections were therefore in a much better position than others to secure and retain good *encomiendas* and escape, as unscathed as they could, the turbulent years of Peru's civil wars (1538–1555).[9] Also, *encomiendas* could not be held *in absentia*, since *encomenderos* had to defend the jurisdiction to which their grants belonged with their arms, horses, and men. They could however justify a short absence from their place of residence.[10] Such restrictions and the characteristics of *encomienda* tenure anchored *encomenderos* and their political clients to a specific region, a situation that turned them into the first local elites in Spanish America. They were therefore key agents in the implementation and expansion of royal jurisdiction in areas where such authority was absent.

By the 1560s, those *encomenderos* in Peru who had survived the civil wars shared one or more traits in common, such as a respectable social background in Spain, military experience from the conquest period, strong political ties, and/or seniority in the conquest of Peru. They were a tiny group, and even when there were significant differences between them, they often treated one another as equal. To ensure the continued existence of their grants, they were only permitted to leave their *encomiendas* to rightful heirs or wives; however, if a widow received the *encomienda*, a subsequent marriage was anticipated, to ensure the grants remained in the family. In effect, like other privileges at the time, *encomiendas* were granted to an individual but were supposed to realise the expectations of an extended family, including clients and countrymen, who also made their living from the enterprise.[11] *Encomenderos* built social networks around their grants that influenced not only *cabildo* politics but also institutions such as the Audiencias. With the wealth acquired from the labour of the people assigned to them, *encomenderos* were able to enjoy a lifestyle that imitated or even exceeded that of Spanish noblemen, with the ideal of setting up a family home (*casa poblada*), a large unit populated with relatives, friends, and servants, to show the social status they held.[12]

As already stressed, the *encomenderos* were a minority in Peru as in Charcas. With an estimated 8,000 Spaniards in Peru, the 500 or so holders of *encomienda* were clearly a small percentage.[13] For between 2,000 and

---

9 Ida Altman, *Emigrants and Society: Extremadura and America in the Sixteenth Century* (Berkeley: University of California Press, 1989), p. 222.

10 This was a particular issue among highland *encomenderos*, who tended to spend part of the year in Lima and away from the towns where they exercised their *vecindad*. Lockhart, *Spanish Peru, 1532–1560*, p. 21.

11 Lockhart, *Spanish Peru, 1532–1560*, p. 17.

12 Presta, *Encomienda, familia y negocios en Charcas colonial*, pp. 31–32; Zamora, *Casa poblada y buen gobierno*, Ch. 2.

13 Based on two documents, Lohmann Villena states that by the early 1560s there were thirty-two *encomenderos* in La Plata. Checking both documents, I find that only one,

Figure 2.1   Drawing of a wealthy *encomendero* taken from don Felipe Guamán
Poma de Ayala's *Nueva Coronica y Buen Gobierno* of 1615
Source: Royal Danish Library, GKS 223: Guaman Poma, *Nueva corónica y
buen gobierno* (c. 1615). Page [548 [562]].

López de Velasco, provides an accurate, much lower, figure—14—and the other does
not give any clear indication on numbers. Another 200 Spaniards lived in La Plata,
and a further 800 within its area of influence. Guillermo Lohmann Villena, *Juan de
Matienzo, Autor del 'Gobierno del Perú' (su personalidad, su obra)* (Sevilla: Escuela de
Estudios Hispanoamericanos, 1966), p. 48; Marcos Jiménez de la Espada, *Relaciones
geográficas de Indias: Perú*, Vol. II (Ministerio de Fomento, Madrid: Impreso en la
Casa Real, 1885); Juan López de Velasco, *Geografía y descripción universal de las Indias*
(Madrid: Establecimiento Tipográfico de Fortanet, 1894 [1571–1574]), p. 497.

4,000 Spaniards, who were not ecclesiastics, *mayordomos*, notaries, miners, doctors, artisans, merchants, or sailors, an *encomienda* was simply out of reach. These men without a craft or religious function were rootless and unemployed, and frequently perceived as a potential threat; they were normally referred to as soldiers, even though in Peru at the time there was no regular army.[14] Such unoccupied and transient men were 'neither paid, nor forced' to join expeditions and battles, and were certainly not part of a Spanish war machine.[15] Many had arrived too late to benefit from the 'booty' of Cajamarca in 1533 and were struggling to find a place in a society that was becoming more settled.[16] Governors regularly called for the 'land to be drained' of these men, and expeditions were a good excuse to dispatch them out of cities and towns, giving them hope to find a better future. They were expected to fight, and their participation could be an opportunity for social redemption. The authorities sometimes offered individuals clemency in exchange for their service in these events.[17] Their presence in the numerous *entradas* organised by the Spanish to border areas is difficult to estimate, but it was certainly pronounced.[18] Apart from the experience and skills they could gain, which could form the basis for claims for rewards from the monarchy, these *soldados* may have been entitled to a share of the booty from expeditions. If the expedition involved the establishment of a village or town, they could secure land and potentially an *encomienda*, finally fulfilling their dream of being able to settle down with an extended family home, thus starting their path to the accumulation of wealth and eventually their return to Spain.

2.1 A family business

Martín de Almendras' social position in Charcas was attributable to the strong connection between his uncle Francisco de Almendras (1510–1545) and the Pizarros: they shared the same origin—Extremadura—and were

---

14 Matienzo, *Gobierno del Perú*, pp. 270–71; Lockhart, *Spanish Peru, 1532–1560*, pp. 136–37.

15 Matthew Restall, *Seven Myths of the Spanish Conquest* (New York: Oxford University Press, 2003), Ch. 2.

16 Barnadas, *Charcas*, pp. 242–43.

17 Alejandro Agüero, *Castigar y perdonar cuando conviene a la república. La justicia penal de Córdoba del Tucumán, siglos XVII y XVIII* (Madrid: Centro de Estudios Políticos y Constitucionales, 2008), pp. 149–50.

18 The lists of all men involved in expeditions existed yet in most cases are now missing. While researching this book, I found three such lists in seventeenth-century *probanzas* relating to expeditions carried out in the sixteenth century. They show that men of this background did not originate only from Charcas; many were from Paraguay, Rio de la Plata, Mexico, or even Spain. AGI, Lima, 241, N9, [1648] Informaciones de oficio y parte: Alonso Troncoso Lira y Sotomayor, capitán de infantería española, vecino de las fronteras de Tomina; AGI, Charcas, 81, N11, [1610] Informaciones de oficio y parte: Julio Ferrufiño, contador y juez oficial de La Paz; AGI, Charcas, 58, [1656] Información de servicios de Diego Moreno Contreras.

countrymen or *paisanos* as a result. This loyalty was rewarded with gold and silver when the Cajamarca booty was shared between Pizarro and his men in 1533 and when *encomiendas* were distributed.[19] In a culture in which family ties and origin played such an important role, coming from the same region of Spain made these men feel close to one another.[20] Francisco de Almendras lived and died in the shadow of the Pizarros. These ties brought him *encomiendas*, and *vecindad* in Cusco in 1537. In the first distribution of grants in 1534, Francisco de Almendras was given the *encomienda* of Caracollo in Paria, in Charcas, along with someone else close to the Pizarros: Lucas Martínez de Vegazo (1511/1512–1566).[21] After the foundation of Villa Plata in Charcas both men lost their *encomienda* on grounds that by then they had too many, but Almendras received another that would be passed down through his family for many decades, in Tarabuco, on the eastern border of Charcas, which made him a *vecino* of Villa Plata. An active participant in the rebellion by Gonzalo Pizarro, to whom he was loyal until the end, Francisco de Almendras suffered the same fate as many of those who were present in Cajamarca. He was executed in 1545 by someone he had loved as a son, Diego de Centeno, after Centeno decided to switch sides.[22] His nephews Diego and Martín survived him and became the beneficiaries of their uncle's Tarabuco *encomienda*. Cleverly, and at the last minute, just before Gonzalo Pizarro's defeat, both changed sides and Licenciado La Gasca granted each brother half of the *encomienda* previously enjoyed by their uncle.[23]

With their uncle Francisco murdered, after Diego de Almendras died in 1554 his brother Martín became the head of the *encomendero* family and network. An anonymous document written by a Dominican priest in the aftermath of Gonzalo Pizarro's rebellion calls Martín '*bullicioso*', which could be translated as 'bellicose'.[24] Arrogant and ambitious, Martín de Almendras had characteristics held in high esteem in his time, such

19 James Lockhart, *The Men of Cajamarca: A Social and Biographical Study of the First Conqueror of Peru* (Austin: University of Texas Press, 1972), pp. 312–13.

20 Ties of that type, as Hespanha stresses, were not just emotional and frequently involved a political connection: Hespanha, *A ordem do mundo*, Ch. V.

21 Martínez de Vegazo was also from Trujillo in Extremadura. Efraín Trelles Arestegui, *Lucas Martínez de Vegazo: Funcionamiento de una encomienda temprana inicial* (Lima: Pontificia Universidad Católica del Perú, Fondo Editorial, 1991).

22 Pedro Gutiérrez de Santa Clara, *Historia de las guerras civiles del Perú (1544–1548)*, Vol. 2 (Madrid: Librería General de Victoriano Suárez, 1904), pp. 270–76; Pizarro, *Descubrimiento y conquista del Perú*, p. 167.

23 Presta, *Encomienda, familia y negocios en Charcas colonial*, Ch. 3.

24 José Toribio Medina, *Colección de documentos inéditos para la historia de Chile*, Vol. VII (Santiago de Chile: Imprenta Elzeviriana, 1896), p. 164; Real Academia Española, *Diccionario de la lengua castellana en que se explica el verdadero sentido de las voces su naturaleza y calidad con las phrases o modo de hablar, los proverbios y refranes y otras cosas convenientes al uso de la lengua*, Vol. I (Madrid: Imprenta de la Real Academia Española, 1726).

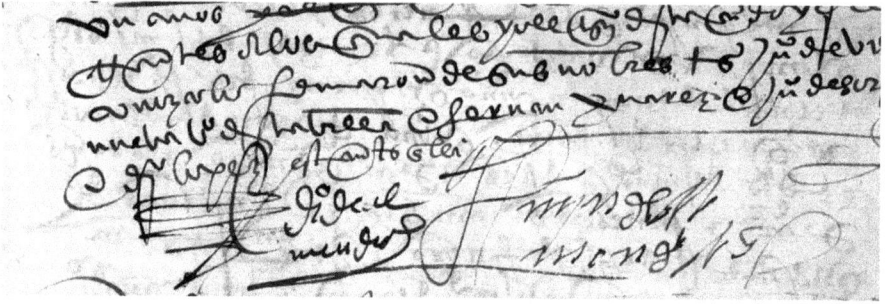

Figure 2.2   Handwritten signatures of Diego de Almendras and his brother
Martín de Almendras
Source: Used with permission of Archivo y Biblioteca Nacionales
de Bolivia EP 1.

as liberality and magnificence, virtues that embellished his lifestyle and emboldened his persona. In the footsteps of his uncle, by the 1550s Almendras had secured a place in La Plata's *cabildo* and marriage to a *mestiza*, doña Constanza Holguín de Orellana, that brought together two networks of prestige and wealth.[25] Doña Constanza was an illegitimate daughter of Pedro Alvarez Holguín (1490–1542), an Extremadura-born *hidalgo* who died in the battle of Chupas on 16 September 1542 fighting Almagro's son Diego de Almagro 'the younger'. Her father's position and assets, and his relatives and business partners from Cáceres, made possible the marriage by offering a substantial dowry and the necessary status. All this added to Martín de Almendras' public persona, carefully built over decades to show, through paperwork and in ceremonies and festivities, his virtues and values, those any true vassal of his Catholic majesty was supposed to display or should aspire to.[26]

3. Prelude to the 1564 expedition

With the triumphal arrival in La Plata of the Sello Real (Royal Seal) on 7 September 1561, a symbolic step and one of paramount importance, the creation of an Audiencia and Chancilleria came to fruition, yet the

25 By 1558 Almendras was Alcalde Mayor de Justicia, helping Polo de Ondegardo (who was Corregidor) with the running of Charcas. Bartolomé Arsans de Orzúa y Vela, *Historia de la villa imperial de Potosí*, Vol. 1 (Providence, RI: Brown University Press, 1965 [1705]), p. 110.

26 Hespanha, *A ordem do mundo*, pp. 20, 32, 56, and 102; Amedeo Quondam and Eduardo Torres Corominas, *El discurso cortesano*, trans. Cattedra di Spagnolo del Dipartimento di Scienze Documentarie, Linguistico-filologiche e Geografiche dell'Univ. Roma 'La Sapienza' (Madrid: Ed. Polifemo, 2013), pp. 82, 98, and 319.

settlement, confirmation, and consolidation of its jurisdiction across the vast land it oversaw had only started.[27] It still had to be negotiated in a process that was sometimes long and challenging. The seal was carried by judge Juan de Matienzo all the way from Lima, via Arequipa. In a spectacle that recreated the royal entry to his domains, it was welcomed in La Plata by crowds who marked the momentous occasion of the creation of a new court of law and government in Charcas—one that combined the Audiencia and its *oidores* (judges and president)—and a Chancilleria (the body that hosted the seal, symbol of the royal presence).[28] The new court left the Audiencia de Lima without jurisdiction over a large portion of its territories in the south. In the political patchwork to which the Spanish monarchy actually amounted, where jurisdictional boundaries were unclear, overlapping, and variable, a new Audiencia only created additional tensions, mainly between existing governors—such as those of Santa Cruz de la Sierra, Tucumán, and Chile—and the Audiencia de Lima and its president.[29] Through a *cédula real*, the Audiencia de Charcas was given jurisdiction over a radius of more than one hundred leagues which, although it included the city of La Paz, left Tucumán, Santa Cruz de la Sierra, Arequipa, Chile, and other important districts outside its ambit. As a result, disputes with the Audiencia de Lima erupted very soon.[30] The Audiencia de Charcas tried to confirm and extend its jurisdiction through a paperwork exercise that involved letters from *cabildo* and Audiencia officials in La Plata to Philip II asking for a wider geographical scope that would include Tucumán, Chile, the Rio de la Plata, and Santa Cruz de la Sierra, all to be put under the new Audiencia's influence.[31]

The death in 1564 of Peru's viceroy, Diego López de Zúñiga, Conde de Nieva, and the lack of an immediate successor, presented further problems, yet the Audiencia de Charcas would see in this an opportunity to assert its political authority and move forward with the process of confirming and consolidating its jurisdiction. Peru was left without a viceroy for five years and Licenciado Lope García de Castro, in his position of president of the Audiencia de Lima, automatically became governor of the entire district. This aggravated the clashes between the new Audiencia and the Audiencia de Lima, which was now presided over by someone with influence over the whole of Peru, meaning that both Audiencias' jurisdictions now in effect overlapped. On one hand, García de Castro's position was equivalent to that of the president of the Audiencia de Charcas yet, as governor of Peru, his jurisdiction extended further than that of the Audiencia de Lima and covered

---

27 Letter from the King to the Audiencia de Charcas, 22 October 1561, in Levillier, *La Audiencia de Charcas*, p. 23.
28 Clavero, 'Justicia y gobierno. Economía y gracia', p. 2.
29 Hespanha, 'The Legal Patchwork of Empires'.
30 Royal Decree, 22 May 1561, in Levillier, *La Audiencia de Charcas*, pp. 526–29.
31 Barnadas, *Charcas*, p. 526.

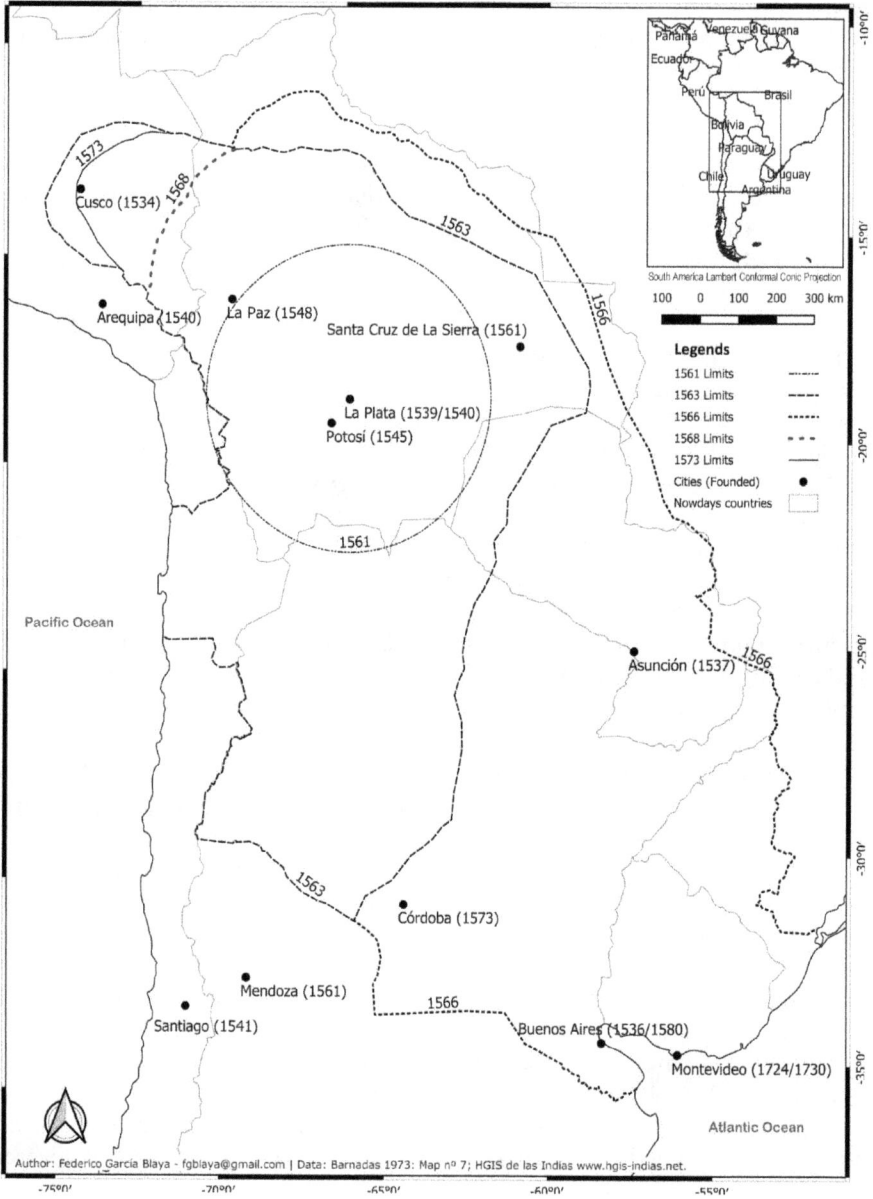

Figure 2.3   Changes to the limits of the jurisdiction of the Réal Audiencia de
Charcas in the sixteenth century
Source: Revilla Orías, *Entangled Coercion*, p. 18. Reproduced with permission
of Paola Revilla Orías.

the Audiencia de Charcas.[32] In a political culture that meticulously followed ceremonies and enforced protocol, and observed hierarchies, this was a situation that fuelled conflict. Scholars rightly highlight that Audiencias were more active in periods without viceroys, as they shared the administration of royal privileges and rewards with the viceroy and in the latter's absence were able to dramatically increase the scope of their government.[33] In the 1560s, this situation put the Audiencia de Lima and its president, Castro, on one side, and the Audiencia de Charcas on the other, at odds with each other, and in these power games the well-established Charcas *encomendero* Martin de Almendras was situated to help de Almendras play his part.

As I discussed in Chapter One, the founding of the Audiencia de Charcas was a geopolitical response to developments in silver mining in Potosí and the need for a route to the Atlantic Ocean via Tucumán. The Audiencia's leading judge, the 'strategist of Charcas', Juan de Matienzo, was convinced that the region's future lay not in the Pacific but in the Atlantic Ocean. In 1567 Matienzo would write one of the Catholic monarchy's most important political treatises, the *Gobierno del Perú*, and his opinion and suggestions mattered.[34] The *oidor* saw the Chiriguanaes as a menace to the Audiencia de Charcas' plans to keep open communications between Charcas and the Río de la Plata, via Tucumán. They were a challenge to such geopolitical schemes.[35]

By the early 1560s, the situation with the Chiriguanaes had deteriorated further and there were permanent raids in the region the Spanish called Chichas, after the indigenous groups of that name. The Spanish decided to contain the pressure the Chiriguanaes were putting on other populations along the borders.[36] Peru's third viceroy, Andrés Hurtado de Mendoza (1556–1561), Marqués de Cañete, made an agreement with Captain Andrés Manso that the captain should found a village in land occupied by the Chiriguanaes. Manso had planned an expedition to the area in 1541, being convinced of the existence of mineral deposits in Saypurú, a site of symbolic importance noted in Chapter One. This was a boost to ambitions held by the elite of Charcas, to expand eastwards, establishing an urban presence in land not far from Santa Cruz de la Sierra. Manso was made governor with the task of carving a new governorship in the area and in the first half of 1559 he established Santo Domingo de la Nueva Rioja along the Parapetí River (see Figure 0.1), named to honour La Rioja, his birthplace. The village

32 Royal Decree, 12 June 1559 in Víctor Maurtua, *Juicio de límites entre el Perú y Bolivia. Prueba peruana presentada al gobierno de la República Argentina*, Vol. 2 (Barcelona: Imprenta de Henrich y Cia, 1906), pp. 3–4.
33 Eugenia Bridikhina, *Theatrum mundi. Entramados del poder en Charcas colonial* (Lima: Institut Français d'Études Andines, 2015), p. 29.
34 Matienzo, *Gobierno del Perú*.
35 Barnadas, *Charcas*, pp. 459–60; Matienzo, *Gobierno del Perú*, pp. 216–18.
36 Barnadas, *Charcas*, p. 47.

was also known as Condorillo, carrying the name of the local Chiriguana leader, who is likely to have provided the new settlement with the labour and materials needed.

From the opposite direction, the east, the governor of Santa Cruz de la Sierra, Captain Ñuflo de Chaves (1518–1568), was also advancing; he established the settlement of La Barranca, with the idea of setting the boundaries of his own future governorship (see Figure 0.1).[37] The proximity of the two villages created a conflict over political jurisdiction between Chaves and Manso. Chaves travelled to the Audiencia de Lima to legally challenge Manso's presence in the area and returned to arrest Manso who, after some time defending his case in Potosí, went back to Condorillo/Santo Domingo de la Nueva Rioja. Despite the legal quarrel between the two conquistadors, which shows the conflictive character of jurisdictions, neither of these villages would last. Santo Domingo de la Nueva Rioja and La Barranca were both destroyed by a group of Chiriguanaes headed by their leader Vitapué in 1564.[38] Manso is likely to have perished, being caught up in internal disputes among different groups of Chiriguanaes.[39] He was accused of participating with the Chiriguanaes in raids aimed at securing captives, and of using Condorillo, which did not even resemble a Spanish town, as a base for these raids.[40] It is clear that both Manso and Chaves only managed to hold on to their settlements for as long as the Chiriguanaes allowed them to do so. The tribespeople were probably aware of the conflict between the two Spaniards and played one side against the other. Once in land where Spanish presence was more tenuous, both captains became entangled in a web of Chiriguana factions that made their presence there precarious and totally reliant on indigenous allies. Apart from containing the Chiriguanaes, La Barranca and Condorillo also had another ultimate objective: to establish

---

37 Ñuflo de Chaves had been born in Santa Cruz de la Sierra, not far from Trujillo in Spain, to Alvaro de Escóbar and María de Sotomayor. His surname was taken from his mother's side. He joined the expedition of Río de la Plata *adelantado* Alvar Nuñez Cabeza de Vaca in 1540 and married doña María Elvira de Mendoza in the early 1550s. Hernando Sanabria, *Cronica sumaria de los gobernadores de Santa Cruz (1560–1810)* (Santa Cruz de la Sierra: Publicaciones de la Universidad Boliviana Gabriel René Moreno, 1975), pp. 9–10.

38 José María García Recio, *Análisis de una sociedad de frontera: Santa Cruz de La Sierra en los siglos XVI y XVII* (Sevilla: Excma. Diputación Provincial de Sevilla, 1988), p. 94; Barnadas, *Charcas*, pp. 61–62.

39 Julien, 'Colonial Perspectives on the Chiriguana (1528–1574)', p. 48.

40 In Manso's case, a letter by Audiencia de Charcas judge Juan de Matienzo suggests that the captain was murdered after taking part in a Chiriguana raid on lowland peoples. Manso and his Chiriguana allies captured more than 2,000 local people in this raid, and shared these captives equally. When the Spaniard's allies felt that his presence there was no longer needed, they simply murdered him and his men. Letter from Matienzo to the King, 1566, in Garay, *Colección de documentos, historia de Paraguay*, p. 432.

new routes for communication with the Atlantic Ocean. This was never met.[41] Expansion of Spanish jurisdiction in the Charcas border region had to accommodate the needs of the Chiriguanaes who challenged, shaped, and altered the process, although they failed to stop it altogether.

There were also obstacles for the Audiencia de Charcas in Tucumán, where some La Plata *encomenderos* had been granted indigenous people who were either hostile to Spanish presence or inhabited land seen as still not conquered. Tucumán had a native population that largely refused to be put under the *encomienda* system. In the years before the establishment of the Audiencia, and with the less important title of lieutenant rather than governor, Juan Pérez de Zurita (1516–1595) headed to the region in 1557 with endorsement from Viceroy de Mendoza, and with the purpose of establishing new Spanish towns.[42] Paying homage to King Philip II's new wife, Queen Mary I (Mary Tudor), Zurita and his men, mostly from Charcas, founded Londres in 1558, then Córdoba del Calchaquí in 1559, and Cañete in 1560—see Figure 0.1. Pérez de Zurita was extending royal jurisdiction on behalf of the viceroy and with support from La Plata's *cabildo*.

However, when news broke of the founding of the Audiencia de Charcas, the new governor of Chile, Francisco de Villagra (1511–1563), quickly moved to appoint someone to replace Zurita—who was perceived as too close to the Audiencia—and to exercise and display his district's jurisdiction over Tucumán, naming Gregorio de Castañeda to the post. Castañeda arrived in Tucumán in 1562 and his first job was to undertake a *residencia* on Zurita, a legal review of the lieutenant's period in office, which resulted in Zurita's arrest and transfer to Chile.[43] Determined to erase his predecessor's legacy in Tucumán, Castañeda decided to change the names of the towns Zurita had founded, establishing a new town called Nieva, in honour of Peru's new viceroy, Diego López de Zúñiga (1561–1564), Conde de Nieva. This was an affront to the *vecinos* who had actively participated in founding the more southerly towns and deprived them from the status as founders and privileged members of these political spaces. Furthermore, it was a move to remove, at least in name, the basis for the jurisdiction that Zurita had tried to establish in the area on behalf of the new Audiencia in Charcas; a jurisdiction that was being built from the ground up, through the foundation of towns by members of successive expeditions with limited support, and sometimes against fierce resistance, from indigenous populations.

---

41 García Recio, *Análisis*, p. 347.
42 Born in Córdoba, Spain, from a very young age Juan Pérez de Zurita served under Charles V in campaigns against the Ottomans in the Mediterranean. He arrived in Perú in the 1550s. Sanabria, *Cronica sumaria Santa Cruz*, p. 15.
43 Roberto Levillier, *Francisco de Aguirre y los orígenes del Tucumán, 1550–1570* (Madrid: Imprenta de Juan Pueyo, 1920), p. 25.

Castañeda's new town of Nieva did not survive, because of the hostility of the natives around it.[44] Tucumán's new governor had prompted radical changes that also altered the arrangements that Spanish *vecinos* had with local indigenous groups, who were key participants in the establishment of towns in the new territory. Eventually this triggered a rebellion among these groups, headed by Juan Calchaquí. Córdoba del Calchaquí was destroyed in the fighting, and Londres and Cañete had to be evacuated.[45] This incident shows the complexity of jurisdictional politics and how they involved the Spanish and the indigenous groups around them. Without the cooperation of such groups, the distances involved made the transformation of such geographies into territories of the Catholic monarchy a challenging and risky task.

By 1562, and benefiting from local circumstances, Juan Calchaquí managed to position himself as an indigenous leader of the peoples of Tucumán and this raised fears in the Audiencia de Charcas that he was trying to spread his influence even over the Chiriguanaes.[46] As much as Castañeda tried to please Peru's new viceroy, the events in Tucumán prompted a new governor for the unruly district to be named, and the post went to the Chile *encomendero* Francisco de Aguirre.[47] Aguirre's main task was to bring the local rebellion to an end, but his appointment was not welcomed in Charcas where the young Audiencia had pinned its hopes on Zurita's return to Tucumán to finish what he had started. Although in 1563 the Crown finally placed Tucumán under the Audiencia de Charcas, Aguirre remained as governor and his presence was seen as an obstacle to the consolidation of the Audiencia's jurisdiction over its territory, and its strategy to fully integrate Tucumán into its sphere of influence.[48]

In brief, the Audiencia de Charcas was facing challenging conditions at the crucial time right after its establishment. There were jurisdictional conflicts with the Audiencia de Lima, and with the government in Chile over Tucumán. Attempts by Manso and Chaves to establish a presence in areas occupied by the Chiriguanaes failed with considerable losses. Chichas, located at the west of Chiriguana territory, was under pressure from regular raids. In Tucumán, actions taken by the government of Castañeda triggered

44 Silva Lezaeta, *El conquistador Francisco de Aguirre*, p. 184.
45 Pedro Mariño de Lovera, *Crónica del reino de Chile*, Vol. VI (Santiago de Chile: Imprenta del Ferrocarril, 1865 [1594]), p. 263; Levillier, *Francisco de Aguirre*, p. 26.
46 Ana María Lorandi, 'La resistencia y rebeliones de los diaguito-calchaquí en los siglos XVI–XVII', *Cuadernos de Historia* 8 (1988): pp. 103–04; Ana María Lorandi and Roxana Boixados, 'Etnohistoria de los valles calchaquíes en los siglos XVI y XVII', *Runa* XVII–XVIIII (1987, 1988): pp. 263–419; Lorandi, *Ni ley, ni rey, ni hombre virtuoso*, pp. 134–35.
47 Barnadas, *Charcas*, p. 52.
48 On 29 August 1563 Phillip II placed Tucumán under the jurisdiction of the Audiencia de Charcas. Levillier, *La Audiencia de Charcas*, pp. 588–90; BNE, Ms. 2,927, http://bdh-rd.bne.es/viewer.vm?id=0000134117&page=1, accessed 24 April 2024.

a rebellion among indigenous peoples, headed by Juan Calchaquí, and this began to unsettle other indigenous groups such as Casabindos, Omaguacas, and Chichas. The Audiencia feared this could result in an alliance between those peoples and the Chiriguanaes. The arrival of Francisco de Aguirre as new governor in Tucumán was expected to bring this rebellion to an end, yet a victorious Aguirre would also bring Tucumán closer to Chile, and away from the Audiencia de Charcas, which was determined to confirm and exercise its jurisdiction over the district. All this was happening against the backdrop of the Taqui Onkoy indigenous movement in the central Andes and a general feeling of crisis in the whole viceroyalty caused by difficulties with the articulation of the different layers of government, problems with the implementation of adequate fiscal policies, exhaustion of mineral resources because of the use of obsolete technology, and a worrying demographic collapse among the indigenous populations of Peru.[49] At a local level, the Audiencia de Charcas needed to remove what it saw as the 'indigenous threat' in the region between La Plata and Tucumán, and politically reattach the district to Charcas. It would recruit someone with the experience, background, and status to do these things. Their choice fell on the renowned *encomendero* of Tarabuco, Martín de Almendras; he would head two expeditions, first to Chichas and then, his final journey, to Tucumán.

4. Marching to the borders: Staging jurisdiction in remote lands

The scholarship on Martín de Almendras' expedition to the Chichas has framed the event as part of a process, as the relations between indigenous peoples and the Spanish deteriorated. That process includes the raids by Chiriguana groups along the southeastern border and the Taqui Onkoy

---

49 Taqui Onkoy is seen by scholars either as a nativist movement, or as an attempt by priests to boost their own careers by accusing indigenous peoples of idolatry, or a mixture of the two. It peaked in the mid-1560s and might well have been a symptom of a critical time in Peru. There is a vast bibliography on the subject: Pierre Duviols, *La lutte contre les religions autochtones dans le Perou colonial. 'L'extirpation de l'idolatrie' entre 1532 et 1660* (Lima: IFEA, 1971); Luis Millones, *El retorno de las huacas. Estudios y documentos del siglo XVI* (Lima: IEP, 1990); Gabriela Ramos, 'Política eclesiástica y extirpación de idolatrías: Discursos y silencios en torno al Taqui Onkoy', in *Catolicismo y extirpación de idolatrías. Siglos XVI–XVIII. Charcas. Chile. México. Perú*, Vol. 5 (Cusco: Centro de Estudios Andinos 'Fray Bartolomé de las Casas', 1993), pp. 137–68; Nathan Wachtel, *Los vencidos. Los indios del Perú frente a la conquista española (1530–1570)*, trans. Antonio Escohotado (Madrid: Alianza Editorial, 1976), p. 289; Nicholas Griffiths, *The Cross and the Serpent: Religious Repression and Resurgence in Colonial Peru* (Norman: University of Oklahoma Press, 1996), p. 13; Steve J. Stern, *Peru's Indian Peoples and the Challenge of Spanish Conquest: Huamanga to 1640* (Madison: University of Wisconsin Press, 1986), pp. 51–76; Sabine MacCormack, *Religion in the Andes: Vision and Imagination in Early Colonial Peru* (Princeton, NJ: Princeton University Press, 1991), pp. 181–204.

movement.[50] This book suggests a different reading, one that integrates the Almendras expedition, with the subsequent *entrada* to Tucumán, framing both in the wider context of the jurisdictional conflicts between the Audiencias of Charcas, Lima, and Chile over the remote district.[51] With Aguirre feared dead at the hands of indigenous peoples in Tucumán, and the Viceroyalty of Peru in charge of the Audiencia de Lima's president, a window of opportunity opened up for the Audiencia de Charcas to mount a number of expeditions with help from La Plata's *encomenderos*. These jurisdictional battlefields would be a collective work that would bring together *encomenderos*, indigenous populations in the disputed area, idle men without an occupation in La Plata and Potosí, and Andean chiefs and their peoples with knowledge of the terrain. The result would be the installation of a new governor in Tucumán bringing that district under the jurisdictional scope of the new Audiencia. To achieve this, in letters and reports the Audiencia de Charcas would overplay fears of a major indigenous revolt, conveying them in a strategic narrative underpinned by stereotypical views of the peoples supposedly involved, to effectively confirm and settle its jurisdiction over the Chichas first, and then Tucumán.[52] The first stage of this process would involve an expedition to the Chichas.

The origin and identity of this group or tribe are issues that still puzzle scholars today. Chicha was a generic denomination that may well conflate many indigenous peoples that were only loosely related. However, the Chichas appear in historical records in association with other groups sharing a similar area, which may indicate that this identity was largely built around the agency of one group in relation to these others.[53] In Chapter One I stressed that the Chichas were paired with other Andean groups as 'Warriors of the

50 Barnadas, *Charcas*, p. 179; Presta, *Encomienda, familia y negocios en Charcas colonial*, p. 76; Zanolli, *Tierra, encomienda e identidad*, pp. 110–12; Presta, 'Hermosos, fértiles y abundantes', p. 33; Palomeque, 'Casabindos, cochinocas y chichas', p. 245; Oliveto, 'Ocupación territorial', p. 153.

51 This idea is present to an extent in Levillier, in his suggestion of different ideologies that underpinned the actions of Francisco de Aguirre; and Barnadas, who refers to the conflict between Charcas and Chile over Tucumán in 'geopolitical' terms. A viewpoint based on the political culture of the Catholic monarchy brings a new and different dimension that also encompasses these approaches. See Roberto Levillier, *Nueva crónica de la conquista del Tucumán. 1563–1573*, Vol. II (Buenos Aires: Editorial 'Nosotros', 1931); Barnadas, *Charcas*, p. 52.

52 Thierry Saignes, 'La reencontré', quoted by Nathan Wachtel, 'The Indian and the Spanish Conquest', in *The Cambridge History of Latin America*, Vol. I (Cambridge: Cambridge University Press, 1984), p. 242.

53 Palomeque, 'Casabindos, cochinocas y chichas', p. 243; Silvia Palomeque, 'Los chicha y las visitas toledanas. Las tierras de los chicha de Talina (1573–1595)', in *Aportes multidisciplinarios al estudio de los colectivos étnicos surandinos reflexiones sobre Qaraqara-Charka tres años después* (La Paz: Plural-IFEA, 2013), p. 119; Raffino, Vitty, and Gobbo, 'Inkas y chichas', p. 260; Scholl, 'At the Limits of Empire', p. 110.

Incas' and this status might give clues to that relationship. The 'warring' Chichas were effectively established in the area crossed by the Camblaya and San Juan Mayo or del Oro rivers, scattered over the region between Talina and Culpina—see Figure 0.1.[54] Early in the sixteenth century they were established along the Capac Ñam.[55] This exposed them to regular raids by the Chiriguanaes, as well as to periodic expeditions by Spanish conquistadors on their way to Tucumán. Their territory was strategically situated along the route between Charcas and the Atlantic Ocean which made settlement and pacification of the Chichas of paramount importance.

As Chapter One mentioned, the Chichas were granted to Hernando Pizarro, who became an absent *encomendero* after he was imprisoned in Spain. They had to pay tribute—a total of 3,500 pesos and 200 bushels of maize every year, both substantial amounts for a region that was constantly at war. Unsurprisingly, by the Almendras expedition their tribute payments to the Spanish were long overdue.[56] Instead, they had begun paying tribute to the Chiriguanaes, in goods those peoples appreciated, such as silver objects, axes, and fine clothing.[57] It was probably more economic for the Chichas to pay for Chiriguana protection, knowing that the Spanish would be kept away from the area, than to support the Spanish expeditions that regularly travelled through Chicha lands, pay the rate of tribute established by the Spanish, and probably become labour for mining in Potosí. Regardless of the reasons, this provides clues to how the area had drifted away from the core of Charcas, where Spanish authority was more consolidated.[58] It is also an example of the type of ties that the Chiriguanaes constructed with border populations, whatever their origin; the Spanish would also regularly hand similar gifts to their Chiriguana partners.

Concerned about the situation, and as part of its wider plans to confirm and settle its jurisdiction, in March 1564 the Audiencia de Charcas entrusted Hernando Pizarro's *mayordomo* Martín Alonso de los Ríos with the task of collecting the overdue tribute from the Chichas.[59] Prepared for what was supposed to be the ceremonial welcoming of the Chichas back into the sphere

54 Presta, 'Hermosos, fértiles y abundantes', p. 28.
55 Palomeque, 'Los chicha y las visitas toledanas', p. 120.
56 Rafael Varón Gabai, *La ilusión del poder: Apogeo y decadencia de los Pizarro en la conquista del Perú* (Lima: Instituto de Estudios Peruanos, Instituto Francés de Estudios Andinos, 1996), p. 343.
57 AGI, Patronato, 137, N1, R2, [1598] Información de los méritos y servicios del capitán Luis de Fuentes y Vargas, corregidor y poblador de la villa de San Bernardo de la Frontera de Tarija y conquistador de otros pueblos de Perú, fol. 36v.
58 Varón Gabai, *La ilusión del poder*, p. 345.
59 José Miguel López Villalva (dir.), *Acuerdos de la Real Audiencia de La Plata de los Charcas (1561–1568)*, Vol. 1 (Sucre: Corte Suprema de Justicia de Bolivia, Archivo y Biblioteca Nacionales de Bolivia, Embajada de España en Bolivia, Agencia Española de Cooperación Internacional para el Desarrollo, 2007), 5 October 1564, p. 117.

of the monarchy, as the payment of tribute by indigenous peoples was seen as indicating acceptance of status as the monarch's vassals, de los Ríos promptly travelled to the area in company of two priests and three other Spaniards. The region, however, was already in flames. Early in August 1564 two letters from the Mercedarian friar Gonzalo Ballesteros brought news to La Plata that the Chicha settlement of Suipacha, where Ballesteros and other Spaniards had taken shelter after fleeing Tucumán, had been besieged by Casabindo and Omaguaca natives. Seven churches had been burned down in the area.[60] Assessing the situation, and fully aware that, in the absence of a viceroy, military duties fell within its jurisdiction, the Audiencia de Charcas began planning an expedition to the region. La Plata *encomendero* Martín de Almendras, someone with *encomienda* peoples within reach of the Chiriguanaes, was seen as the most suitable leader for the task. The expedition was going to be financed either with funds that the Chichas owed or with a loan from assets collected from vacant *encomiendas*. A group of fifty Spaniards would accompany Almendras, including *encomenderos* whose indigenous populations lived in the region at war. In addition, 20 or 25 men were to come from Potosí, mainly Spaniards who owned mines that relied on the labour of Chicha natives, 200 Chichas— 'because they should defend their own land'—and a further 200 indigenous people from the rest of Charcas.[61]

It was also decided to combine this expedition with a second journey, as Almendras was expected to be hosted at the Chichas' expense until he and his men could move forward and travel to Tucumán where Aguirre, the incumbent governor, was reported to be under siege by local people. By August 1564 no news of Aguirre's fate had been received for eight months and speculation was mounting whether he was still alive or not. As a reward for Almendras' efforts, the Audiencia de Charcas promised him the title 'governor of Tucumán', providing Aguirre's death was confirmed. Since this type of expedition was a collective effort, Almendras, who probably had secret instructions from the Audiencia de Charcas about his mission to Tucumán, may have shared these with his men, as a way to strengthen their support and discourage defections.[62] If Almendras should succeed, the Audiencia de Charcas would bring the Chichas back within the monarchy's realm, clear the path to Tucumán, and more importantly, confirm and settle royal jurisdiction over Tucumán by placing one of its *encomenderos* at the helm of the district. For Almendras and the *encomenderos* and men who would go along with him this was a great opportunity to add official recognition to their already long list of merits, gain status, and amass extra wealth. They would

60 López Villalva (dir.), *Acuerdos de la Real Audiencia de La Plata de los Charcas*, Vol. 1, 14 August 1564; AGI, Patronato, 137, N1, R2, [1598] Luis de Fuentes y Vargas, fols 37r, 68v.

61 López Villalva (dir.), *Acuerdos de la Real Audiencia de La Plata de los Charcas*, Vol. 1, 14 August 1564, pp. 104–05.

62 Levillier, *Francisco de Aguirre*, p. 33.

be able to enjoy the *encomiendas* already granted to them, maybe gain others, and build prestige by participating in an *entrada* on behalf of the Audiencia and therefore His Majesty.

Negotiations between Audiencia judges and those who would head an expedition were tough and complex and involved several meetings and copious amounts of paperwork. Unfortunately, only a small fraction of the *capitulaciones* agreed for the expeditions examined in this book have been found, but summaries of agreements reached with the Audiencia de Charcas have survived as part of the Audiencia's *Acuerdos*.[63] Expedition documents were legally binding and gave the Audiencia the authority to check the task had been accomplished, and impose punishments and fines if things went wrong. Once an agreement had been made, a summary of what had been agreed was written down in the *acuerdos* and, in a ceremony typical of such a highly ritualised society, those responsible for undertaking the task were asked to enter the exclusive *Acuerdos* room at the Audiencia, remove their hats, and swear allegiance to the arrangements by placing the documents above their bare heads. All the documents were filed in the coffers of the *Acuerdos*, along with any correspondence between the Audiencia and the expedition's leaders.[64] News of the expedition were made public through a crier and further documents were issued, giving the titles of those involved. All aspects close to the expedition had to be monitored by the Audiencia, at least in theory. If at any point a problem should arise, the Audiencia would step in. As a royal body, it had to make sure that the running of the expedition, a task arranged in this case with Almendras, would be smooth and conform to the arrangements made.

Returning to the specific set of events surrounding this expedition, the Omaguacas and Casabindos were not the only groups active at the time. The Chiriguanaes took advantage of the fragile situation in Tarija and in September 1564 dramatic news from the farms of Juan Ortiz de Zárate arrived in La Plata. These had been raided by Chiriguanaes who caused considerable damage.[65] Ortiz de Zárate, a wealthy *encomendero* with homes in Potosí and La Plata, rural property elsewhere in Charcas that included

---

63 Of the three expeditions in this book, only a fraction of the *capitulaciones* that must have been agreed have survived, transcribed as part of the report on the merits and services of Pedro de Cuellar Torremocha in 1606. They include some sections of the *capitulaciones* signed by Potosí factor Juan Lozano Machuca for his 1584 expedition. Since many such legal processes were standard, it has been possible to reconstruct the process of the negotiations based on this account. AGI, Patronato, 126, R17, [1606] Información de los méritos y servicios de Pedro de Cuéllar Torremocha, maese de campo, en la conquista de Perú, con el presidente Gasca, sirviendo contra Gonzalo Pizarro, fols 73v–76r.

64 López Villalva (dir.), *Acuerdos de la Real Audiencia de La Plata de los Charcas*, Vol. 1, 14 August 1564, p. 105.

65 Matienzo, *Gobierno del Perú*, p. 283.

mills, and Carangas *encomienda* peoples settled in both Tarija and Chichas, asked the Audiencia de Charcas for permission to travel to his farms.[66] When *vecinos* in Potosí learned about Aguirre and the raid on those farms, panic ensued and they began to build a fortress in anticipation of the remote chance of a (fairly improbable) indigenous attack.[67] A month later, and with the situation deteriorating fast, the Audiencia de Charcas discussed the possibility of sending to the borders La Plata *vecinos* Juan de Cianca and Martín Monje; the former, married to an *encomendera* with indigenous peoples in the hostile area; the latter Martín de Almendras' brother-in-law and an *encomendero* with native people in the same area.[68] Having already come to an agreement with Almendras, the Audiencia de Charcas sent him with twenty-four men to assess the situation and 'clear the land all the way to the Chiriguanaes'.[69] The Audiencia had at this point asked García de Castro for Almendras' appointment as governor of Tucumán, but the president of the Audiencia de Lima put off deciding, perhaps hoping that Aguirre was still alive. Given that García de Castro was in charge of Peru, this raised concerns that the Audiencia de Charcas' bold and fearless decision to name Almendras governor and arrange such expeditions might have political consequences.

Despite such concerns, using its military and governmental functions, the Audiencia de Charcas moved ahead with the standard process of consulting its *vecinos* on its plans.[70] On 9 October 1564, an advisory committee was set up with Martín de Almendras, Diego Pantoja, Polo de Ondegardo, and Antonio Alvarez, all well-established *encomenderos*, assisting the Audiencia in any matters of urgency.[71] Polo de Ondegardo was also a well-known jurist with a deep knowledge of the Andes and its peoples.[72] Without exception, all had been conquistadors and had recently participated in the civil wars (1538–1555). However, there was still frustration since support for an expedition was lacking, as an Audiencia letter to the monarch from late October 1564 indicates. Arrangements for the expedition had been made, but

66 Presta, *Encomienda, familia y negocios en Charcas colonial*, Ch. 5.
67 López Villalva (dir.), *Acuerdos de la Real Audiencia de La Plata de los Charcas*, Vol. 1, 2 October 1564, p. 115.
68 Presta, *Encomienda, familia y negocios en Charcas colonial*, p. 74.
69 Letter from the Audiencia de Charcas to the King, 1566, in Garay, *Colección de documentos, historia de Paraguay*, p. 449.
70 AGI, Charcas, 418, L1, [1563] Registro de oficio y partes: reales cédulas y provisiones, etc., conteniendo disposiciones de gobierno y gracia para las autoridades y particulares del distrito de la Audiencia de Charcas, image 29.
71 López Villalva (dir.), *Acuerdos de la Real Audiencia de La Plata de los Charcas*, Vol. 1, 9 October 1564, p. 119.
72 Gonzalo Lamana, *Pensamiento colonial crítico: textos y actos de Polo Ondegardo* (Lima, Cusco: IFEA; CBC [Centro Bartolomé de las Casas], 2012); Laura González Pujana, *Polo de Ondegardo: un cronista vallisoletano en el Perú* (Valladolid: Universidad de Valladolid, Instituto de Estudios de Iberoamérica y Portugal, 1999).

[i]t could not proceed because, before things could move on, we thought it better to explain our plan to the *regidores* [aldermen] and old *vecinos* in this land so they, as experts in such matters, could give us an opinion. Instead, they did their best to derail the plan, saying that providing weapons to *vecinos* should be enough and even when two of us supported our plan, because one of us agreed with the old *vecinos*, we decided to put everything on hold.[73]

Without a royal army, and based on the old medieval tradition of *auxilium*, the defence of the realm fell on *vecinos* who had the capacity to command their men, clients, dependants, and indigenous peoples, and it was organised by viceroys or, in their absence, by the Audiencias. *Entradas* required a collective effort and as such they needed to be negotiated. Consensus was not something that could be easily attained and in line with the 'economy of privileges and rewards', it required appointments, concessions, and grants to engage these men. Faced with decisions that could jeopardise the credibility of the tribunal, Audiencia judges would frequently seek advice and garner support from aldermen and *vecinos*. This provides further evidence of the decentralisation and localisation of authority in the Catholic monarchy at the time. Faced with immense territories and communication hurdles, the political system was therefore structured around consensus and negotiation and the implementation of jurisdiction was indeed a negotiated matter.

After months in the making and weeks of public displays of propaganda, with announcements by town criers and banners, Martín de Almendras and his men left La Plata for the Chichas in November 1564. The *encomendero* was in company of only fifty other Spaniards and large numbers of native auxiliaries with their *caciques*, priests, and probably slaves and notaries. The sight reflected previous Spanish *entradas* that, like other public rituals such as festivals and celebrations in general, had endured little change from medieval times.[74] Similar to past missions, Almendras travelled in splendour, being carried by an army of indigenous peoples in a sedan chair or litter, fed and assisted each time the expedition stopped along the route.[75] War was a luxurious matter and those involved made sure that they wore the

73 '[m]as no se efectuo porque antes que se hiziese no parecio que hera bien dar quenta dello a la justicia y rregidores y vezinos mas antiguos desta tierra para que ellos como persona mas esperta en semejantes negocios nos diesen su parescer los quales lo estorvaron y dixeron que bastaba se apercibiese la tierra de armas y avnque dos fuimos de parescer que se pusiese en efecto lo que primero se avía acordada por ser vno de nosotros de contrario parescer siguiendo el que los vezinos havian dado se suspendio.' Letter from the Audiencia de Charcas to the King, 30 October 1564, in Levillier, *La Audiencia de Charcas*, pp. 137–38.
74 Teofilo Ruiz, *A King Travels: Festive Traditions in Late Medieval and Early Modern Spain* (Princeton, NJ: Princeton University Press, 2012), p. 22.
75 Pedro Cieza de León, *Crónica del Perú*, Cuarta Parte. Vol. 2 (Lima: Pontificia Universidad Católica del Perú, 1994 [1551]), p. 141.

best garments and carried the most impressive equipment they could afford. Quillaca, Charca, and Colla chiefs don Juan Colque Guarache, don Fernando Ayavire Cuysara, and don Juan Calpa, alongside other indigenous chiefs such as don Diego Soto and don Martín Alata, who were respected and collaborative regional lords, accompanied Almendras, probably also carried in their Tahuantinsuyu-era litters and surrounded by their relatives and their people.[76] Their participation was essential as they knew the area; they (or their predecessors) had accompanied several expeditions—the 1535 *entrada* by Diego de Almagro received assistance from don Juan Colque Guarache's father Guarache.[77]

Also in Almendras' company was friar Ballesteros, who had already been in Tucumán and knew the area relatively well. The Mercedarians were an order close to conquistadors and *encomenderos* and their presence in Tucumán had been disrupted by jurisdictional disputes. Francisco de Aguirre was not fond of the presence of religious orders in the area and Ballesteros was hoping to secure stronger support from Almendras, and through him the Audiencia, to establish the Mercedarians in Tucumán under their protection, and help extend royal jurisdiction in the area.[78]

Almendras and his expedition made their first stop at Ortiz de Zárate's farms, to expel the Chiriguanaes who were besieging Zárate and his men, and from there continued their journey to Chichas.[79] Upon arrival, Almendras and his entourage encountered the Chichas in the valley of Suipacha (see Figure 0.1).[80] They probably camped in an old fortress, later renamed Almendras' *Pucará*.[81] According to don Juan Colque Guarache's *probanza*, after seizing those responsible for the rebellion, negotiations ensued. Witnesses to his

---

76 The Audiencia in La Plata appointed don Juan Colque Guarache captain of the indigenous peoples that went on the expedition. AGI, Charcas, 53, [1574–1576] Información de méritos y servicios de don Juan Colque Guarache, fol. 48r; Platt, Bouysse-Cassagne, and Harris, eds, *Qaraqara–Charka*, pp. 825, 871.

77 AGI, Charcas, 53, [1574–1576] Juan Colque Guarache, fol. 3r.

78 Fray Pedro Nolasco Pérez, *Religiosos de la merced que pasaron a la América española* (Sevilla: Tipografía Zarzuela, 1924), pp. 293–95; Francesco Leonardo Lisi, *El tercer concilio limense y la aculturación de los indígenas sudamericanos: estudio crítico con edición, traducción y comentario de las actas del concilio provincial celebrado en Lima entre 1582 y 1583* (Salamanca: Universidad de Salamanca, 1990), p. 41.

79 Letter from the Audiencia de Charcas to the King, 1566, in Garay, *Colección de documentos, historia de Paraguay*, p. 450.

80 AGI, Patronato, 124, R9, [1580] Información de los méritos y servicios de los generales Pedro Álvarez Holguín y Martín de Almendras, desde el año de 1536 en la conquista y pacificación de Perú, habiéndose hallado en el cerco de la ciudad de Cuzco perseguidos por Mango Inca, cuyos servicios hicieron en compañía de los capitanes Hernando y Juan Pizarro. Constan asimismo los servicios hechos por Diego de Almendras, hermano del general Martín de Almendras, image 529. There are two reports of merits and services by Almendras' descendants.

81 Quechua for fortress. Archivo y Biblioteca Nacionales de Bolivia (from here on

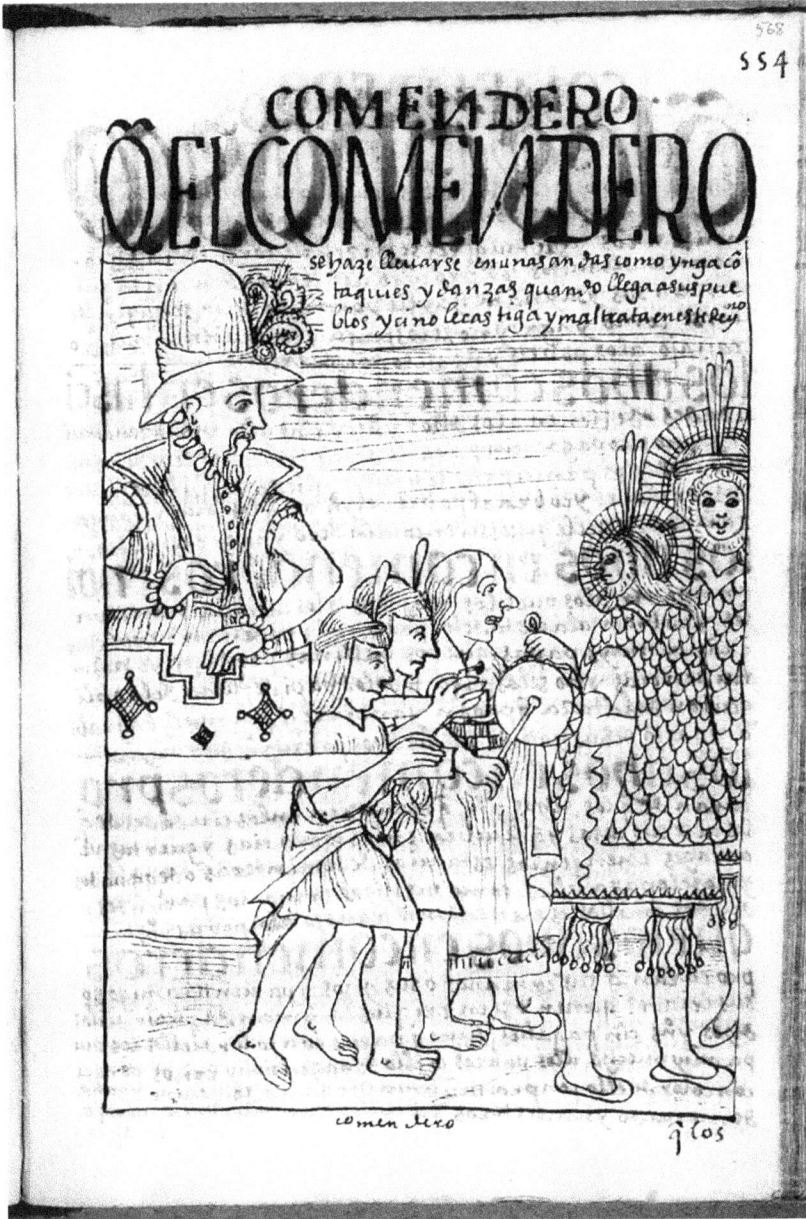

Figure 2.4 Drawing of a wealthy *encomendero* being carried by his Indians, taken from don Felipe Guamán Poma de Ayala's *Nueva Coronica y Buen Gobierno* of 1615

Source: Royal Danish Library, GKS 223: Guaman Poma, *Nueva corónica y buen gobierno* (c. 1615). Page [554 [568]].

report suggest that such discussions did not follow the Spanish but the Andean 'etiquette'. This probably involved gifts from both parties, and food and drinks provided by a hostess, while Almendras would keep to the background, overseeing the process, as the following statement suggests:

> And this witness heard from *caciques* of Chichas Indians how the said don Juan Colque played a big part in these Indians' pacification because he praised them and treated them in a manner that brought them to peace.[82]

The notary and translators used the word '*halagar*', 'to praise' in Spanish, reflecting the reciprocal bonds between native chiefs. It was don Juan Colque Guarache and the chiefs of the other 'naciones de Charcas' that brought the Chichas back to the ambit of the Catholic monarchy. As Paullu Inca had done before, helping Gonzalo and Hernando Pizarro, these *naciones* supported Almendras in his royal commission to make the King symbolically and theatrically present in a remote border region. From this point of view, the expeditions and the rituals that accompanied them played essential roles in the confirmation and consolidation of jurisdiction, and through it, royal presence. Soon after all this, the main Chicha chiefs travelled back to La Plata where they paid tribute and received baptism, confirming their identity as Catholic and loyal vassals of His Majesty.[83]

5. A final journey

With the Audiencia's jurisdiction over the Chichas confirmed, Almendras was able to move on with the second step of their plans, the *entrada* to Tucumán. The *encomendero* returned to La Plata to raise funds and put together the expedition. Learning that there was still no news of Aguirre, Almendras stressed that it was impossible for him to go on a new expedition without financial support and accordingly entered a new arrangement with the Audiencia. The *encomendero* would borrow 10,000 gold pesos from the tribute paid by the Chichas that had been deposited in the royal coffers in Potosí. Ambitiously thinking of the rewards that would be obtained from his journey to Tucumán, Almendras pledged to repay the loan over three

ABNB), 1674, EC25, Visita de Agustín de Ahumada a los Chichas, 24 July 1573, in Palomeque, 'Los chicha y las visitas toledanas', p. 177.

82   '[O]yo este testigo dezir a caciques e yndios chichas que el dicho don juan colque fue mucha parte para que se pacificasen los yndios chichas porque los halago mucho y tuvo con ellos tales tratos que los hizo benir de paz.' AGI, Charcas, 53, [1574–1576] Juan Colque Guarache, fol. 59v.

83   This process would be consolidated, and the Chichas' identities as the Catholic monarchy's vassals reconfirmed, during their resettlement, which was arranged by Viceroy Toledo early in the 1570s. See Palomeque, 'Los chicha y las visitas toledanas', p. 136; AGI, Charcas, 53, [1574–1576] Juan Colque Guarache, fol. 64r.

years, putting up the revenues from his *encomienda* as collateral.[84] This loan was insufficient, and the *encomendero* borrowed a further 30,000 pesos to buy supplies in Potosí. Almendras and his men would travel to Tucumán in a glorious display. They planned to instal the *encomendero* as the district's new governor, and this would be achieved through an aggressive, loud, and colourful stance that (it was hoped) would prompt negotiations with Aguirre, if he still lived, or simply trigger the process of Almendras' installation as governor. Once in Tucumán, *encomiendas* and rewards would be distributed and the Audiencia would be able to confirm and settle on the ground the jurisdiction that had been secured on paper.

In March 1565, Peru governor Lope García de Castro finally appointed Captain Martín de Almendras governor of Tucumán, but this appointment was entirely conditional on confirmation that Aguirre was deceased (or effectively so).[85] Pushed by Castro's decision, Almendras had to rush to assemble his expedition to Tucumán. Even so, a month later he had not still left, having assembled only 70 of the 120 Spaniards he was supposed to take south. An expedition to the distant district was difficult to sell, even among the 'idle' soldiers in La Plata and Potosí, who were always seeking opportunities for wealth and rewards, on top of the honour they could obtain from joining in. The *encomendero* also struggled to secure native auxiliaries, as many never returned from such events. Concerned that he might not be able to recruit the necessary men, and therefore fail to accomplish his side of the bargain, the Audiencia made it clear to Almendras that there would be inspections along the path to Tucumán, four days' journey from Potosí.[86] The young Audiencia's own prestige was at risk if anything went wrong.

Almendras finally left for this final *entrada* between May and June 1565. Unexpectedly, before his departure, news arrived in Charcas via Aguirre's son-in-law that the governor was in fact alive. Once the news reached García de Castro at the Audiencia de Lima, he reconfirmed Aguirre in the post of governor, expecting the Audiencia de Charcas to withdraw the nomination of Almendras and bring him and his men back to La Plata.[87] The Audiencia de Charcas did not acknowledge García de Castro, but did recommend Almendras to shorten his journey and stop in Salta (present-day northwest Argentina), to avoid confronting Aguirre and have two governors

---

84 López Villalva (dir.), *Acuerdos de la Real Audiencia de La Plata de los Charcas*, Vol. 1, 21 February 1565, p. 136; Presta, *Encomienda, familia y negocios en Charcas colonial*, p. 76.

85 Letter from Licenciado Castro to the King, 6 March 1565, in Roberto Levillier, *Gobernantes del Perú. Cartas y papeles. Siglo XVI*, Vol. 3 (Madrid: Sucesores de Rivadeneyra, 1921), pp. 55–56.

86 López Villalva (dir.), *Acuerdos de la Real Audiencia de La Plata de los Charcas*, Vol. 1, 12 April 1565, p. 149.

87 Letter from Licenciado Castro to the King, 23 September 1565, in Levillier, *Gobernantes del Perú*, p. 97.

of Tucumán in the district at the same time. Almendras was to wait, 'at least until the governor [Aguirre] or the Audiencia command otherwise'.[88]

Following the well-known route through the Chichas, Almendras moved into Tucumán with 120 Spaniards, including his lieutenant and partner Jerónimo González de Alanís; encomenderos having subjects in the area, such as his brother-in-law Martín Monje; a large number of local auxiliaries with supplies; and 300 horses.[89] They travelled as wealthy gentlemen, wearing the best armour and garments they could afford, surrounded by crowds of indigenous servants, and in company of friends, acquaintances, and relatives. With plans for the establishment of a village in Salta, there was also a sense among the party that, as a group, they would eventually form a political community as vecinos, members of the cabildo of a new town. The journey was arduous and after months of marching the group had its first skirmishes with indigenous people at Jujuy.[90] Almendras died at the hands of the Ocloyas in a clash in the province of Omaguaca (present-day northwest Argentina), probably early in September 1565.[91]

Leaderless, his men continued with Alanís at their head, searching for Francisco de Aguirre. They auctioned off Almendras' belongings, including horses, clothing, and weapons worth up to 8,000 pesos.[92] This sum represents nearly a quarter of the second loan that Almendras negotiated to buy supplies, which demonstrates that an encomendero, emulating feudal Castilian lords, would travel only if surrounded with the comforts and perquisites required by someone of his social status. After facing starvation and hostile natives, who murdered several members of the party including Juan de Cianca, Almendras' men eventually found Aguirre, who by then had received support from Chile.[93] The governor had orders to march towards the Río de la Plata and consolidate the Atlantic Ocean route for Charcas. Instead, he decided to

88 López Villalva (dir.), *Acuerdos de la Real Audiencia de La Plata de los Charcas*, Vol. 1, 14 August 1564, p. 105.

89 The route was the Capac Ñam. See Figure 1.2. AGI, Patronato, 124, R9, [1580] Pedro Álvarez Holguín and Martín de Almendras, image 14; Presta, *Encomienda, familia y negocios en Charcas colonial*, p. 76.

90 AGI, Patronato, 132, N2, R8, [1590] Información de Juan Mejía Miraval, fol. 15v.

91 In his statement as witness to the *probanza* of Juan Mejía Miraval, Lope de Quevedo recalled that Almendras was killed by natives from Ocloyo. Ocloyas is today an area in the Argentine province of Jujuy. AGI, Patronato, 132, N2, R8, [1590] Juan Mejía Miraval, fol. 15v; AGI, Justicia, N1, R2, [1565–1571] Jerónimo de Alanís, mercader, vecino de la ciudad de La Plata contra los herederos del Capitán Martín de Almendras, sobre el pago de 8.000 pesos, fols 75, 88, 93, and 106v (with thanks to Dr Ana María Presta who gave me access to this document).

92 The inventory of the goods Almendras took with him was reportedly left in Santiago del Estero. It has not been located yet. AGI, Patronato, 124, R9, [1580] Pedro Alvarez Holguín and Martín de Almendras, images 165 and 602.

93 Letter from Lope García de Castro to the King, 12 January 1566, in Levillier, *Gobernantes del Perú*, p. 149.

Figure 2.5   Drawing of a Réal Audiencia meeting taken from don Felipe
Guamán Poma de Ayala's *Nueva Coronica y Buen Gobierno of 1615*
Source: Royal Danish Library, GKS 223: Guaman Poma, *Nueva corónica y
buen gobierno* (c. 1615). Page [484 [488]].

shift route and head to Cuyo—in present-day Argentina—planning to add this new area to his own jurisdiction in Tucumán.[94] Cuyo was dangerously close to Chile in the eyes of the Audiencia de Charcas, which probably saw Aguirre's move as another attempt to detach Tucumán from Charcas. At this point it became clear to Almendras' men that securing the rewards they had been promised when they left La Plata offered very slim chances. Supported by the bishop of Tucumán, Licenciado Martínez, and under Gerónimo de Holguin—a countryman of Almendras; they both were from Extremadura— the men mutinied and took Aguirre prisoner under charges of heresy. The governor was taken to La Plata where he spent three years in prison.[95] Without significant, substantiated evidence for what would otherwise have been classed as minor offences, on 15 October 1568 Aguirre was sentenced to pay a fine of 1,500 pesos.[96] Many of the men on Almendras' expedition eventually settled in the recently founded villages of Esteco, Nuestra Señora de la Talavera, and San Miguel de Tucumán.[97]

Aguirre had the misfortune (or fortune, depending on how it is looked at) to have been found alive. The Audiencia de Charcas had placed its hopes on Almendras, who had reattached the Chichas to the Catholic monarchy, confirming the Audiencia's jurisdiction over the district; and who was expected to reaffirm the Audiencia's presence in Tucumán, clearing the path to the Atlantic Ocean, a geopolitical project of Audiencia de Charcas judge Licenciado Juan de Matienzo. Almendras was an *encomendero* in La Plata and his political clients and loyalties were there. He represented the Audiencia de Charcas and its elite groups with their aspirations to an Atlantic connection that, in their eyes, would make Charcas as important as Lima. To make a strong argument for the expedition, the Audiencia overplayed the threats posed to Potosí and Porco by Taqui Onkoy, the Chiriguanaes, the Chichas, and the leader Juan Calchaquí and his people. Looking at how far most of these groups' territories were from the mines, it would have been impossible for any of the Omaguaca, Casabindo, Chichas, or Chiriguanaes

---

94 Letter from Licenciado Pedro Ramirez to the King, 1566, in Garay, *Colección de documentos, historia de Paraguay*, p. 463. In a letter by Hernando de Retamoso to the monarch dated 25 January 1582, the correspondent clearly explains that Aguirre never had any intention to open the path between the Atlantic and Perú. Roberto Levillier, *Gobernación de Tucumán. Probanzas de méritos y servicios de los conquistadores. Documentos del Archivo de Indias (1583–1600)*, Vol. 1 (Madrid: Sucesores de Rivadeneyra, 1920), p. 521.

95 Levillier, *Francisco de Aguirre*, pp. 40–41.

96 José Toribio Medina, *Diccionario biográfico colonial de Chile* (Santiago de Chile: Imprenta Elzeviriana, 1906), pp. 25–26; José Toribio Medina, *Historia del Santo Oficio de la Inquisición de Lima (1569–1820)*, Vol. I (Santiago de Chile: Imprenta Gutenberg, 1887), p. 42.

97 AGI, Patronato, 124, R9, [1580] Pedro Álvarez Holguín and Martín de Almendras, image 14; Matienzo, *Gobierno del Perú*, p. 321.

to ever mount a full-scale invasion of those mines. Many of these indigenous peoples were politically fragmented and while Juan Calchaquí had provided leadership, it was not strong enough for a pan-indigenous movement. The original Audiencia plan did not quite work as intended because of Almendras' death. However, with Aguirre in prison, the Audiencia de Charcas was able to consolidate its presence in Tucumán and pursue its plans for the region through new channels to continue with its plans.[98]

Almendras' final journey shows the risks for those who, following ambitions founded on uncertain or false information, decided to borrow to assemble resources and men and embark upon what they saw as the next step up a ladder of social progress. He travelled as a royal agent on a commission agreed with the Audiencia de Charcas and held a royal post, governor of Tucumán. Such expeditions, if successful, offered advantages to all sides involved. For the Audiencia de Charcas and the *vecinos* in La Plata they were the perfect opportunity to 'drain the land' of men—a frequent expression in documents at the time—who would otherwise cause trouble. Those in charge of such expeditions would also gain political recognition and formalise their ties with royal officers of high rank, and would thereby expand their network of political clients into new districts. These expeditions enabled the Crown to expand at the expense of ambitious individuals, who were expected to provide the financial backing. The monarchy could also be ritually and theatrically staged and made present in remote parts of its realm, confirming its presence through ceremonies of possession. The expeditions were also supposed to provide unemployed and potentially problematic men with the chance to become *vecinos* of newly founded towns and rebel natives the opportunity to negotiate concessions and their status within the Catholic monarchy, if only provisionally.

With the Audiencia de Charcas at odds with García de Castro (president of the Audiencia de Lima and governor of Peru), two sides emerged. Wary of the Audiencia de Charcas' growing authority and strength, García de Castro backed Francisco de Aguirre, to keep in check the plans of the Audiencia de Charcas in Tucumán and the consolidation of its Atlantic route, even though the Audiencia de Charcas effectively had jurisdiction over the unruly province.[99] Viceroys in Peru, as well as those in similar roles such as García de Castro, often tried to exercise their own authority through playing one Audiencia against another.[100] The Audiencia de Charcas found in Martín de Almendras the possibility, first of pacifying the Chichas and then conquering

---

98 Presta, *Encomienda, familia y negocios en Charcas colonial*, p. 79.

99 Letter from Lope García de Castro to the King, 15 June 1565, in Levillier, *Gobernantes del Perú*, p. 92.

100 This was a political system in which conflict was not the exception but the norm. Ultimately, this placed the monarch as the only legitimate and valid mediator. Domingo Centenero de Arce, '¿Una monarquía de lazos débiles? Circulación y experiencia como formas de construcción de la Monarquía Católica', in *Oficiales*

the unruly Tucumán, to confirm and settle its jurisdiction. With Almendras dead, the Audiencia had to arrest and imprison Aguirre.

The expeditions show the difficulties of a political system of juxtaposed and often overlapping jurisdictions, which emerged in conflicts over the appointment of governors and other authorities. García de Castro, via his two posts, and the Audiencia de Charcas both had such authority, yet the final decision would be made in Spain, sometimes months or even years after the appointment. Such distances helped or undermined different causes and agents and created jurisdictional problems and clashes between those who intended to expand their rights to exercise authority. This also kept the monarch as the overseer and only person with a final say on all matters. Finally, as far as the southeastern border of Charcas was concerned, the expeditions did very little to either expand jurisdiction or restore peace—the area remained under the influence of the Chiriguanaes and their various factions.

6. A localised empire

The first years of the Audiencia de Charcas were decisive as it struggled to confirm and settle its presence over its own political space, having recurrent disputes with the Audiencia de Lima and its president, the governor of Peru, Lope García de Castro. This translated into copious correspondence between Audiencia de Charcas members and the monarch, aimed at securing jurisdiction over a geographical area larger than the initial one hundred leagues. This also had to be negotiated and confirmed on the ground. With royal confirmation in 1563 of the Audiencia de Charcas' jurisdiction over Tucumán, a space disputed with the governorship of Chile, it was a matter of time before the Audiencia de Charcas tried to move into the remote area with help from its *encomenderos*. Aguirre's appointment as governor of Tucumán was an obstacle to such plans, but rumours over his death at the hands of indigenous peoples prompted the organisation of two expeditions by the ambitious *encomendero* Martín de Almendras and his men. One *entrada* would confirm Almendras' credentials as a warrior and peacemaker by pacifying the Chichas and rescuing Juan Ortiz de Zárate and his men, who were under attack by the Chiriguanaes in Tarija. The other would have placed Almendras as the new governor of Tucumán, if it had found Aguirre to be dead.

Jurisdiction, the authority to establish law and deliver justice, was at the centre of these political conflicts. Because jurisdiction was shared by the Crown with a myriad of agents, competition over who could exercise authority and who could make the monarchy present in Charcas was intense. Along the Catholic monarchy's borders, which were perceived as void of 'law and order', this 'absence' of jurisdiction was filled with stereotypes that made

reales. Los ministros de la Monarquía Católica (siglos XVI–XVIII) (Valencia: Universitat de Valencia, 2012), p. 142.

the border regions meaningful to both the Spanish and the peoples that inhabited them. The indigenous populations along the southeastern borders of Charcas had begun to adapt, or not, to a new political reality that, based on the polycentric character of the Catholic monarchy, shared authority and with it, its jurisdiction. Stereotyped and labelled in a strategic narrative hyped by the imaginary threat of the destruction of Potosí and Porco, these indigenous peoples unwillingly helped the Audiencia de Charcas and the local elite to advance their ambitious plans.

The clash of the Spanish monarchy on one hand, with its ideology of sharing authority and political agency, and the worlds of indigenous groups such as the Chiriguanaes on the other, fostered further political fragmentation on both sides as well as stimulating debate about the unconquerable natives and the alternatives the monarchy faced in order to incorporate them into the realm. A state of permanent captivity, albeit an ultimate option, was always on the table, but also required local adaptation of royal provisions that, although seen as guidance, clearly opposed that option. Such debates encouraged a pragmatic approach that privileged local experience and knowledge. This was a view shared in Charcas by its elites and its Audiencia judges and president. Beneath a thick layer of political rituals and ceremonies lay a down-to-earth approach that recognised the vast distance between Charcas and the court in Madrid and the need for decisive action, compromise, and adaptation. For all this, jurisdiction also had to be staged and ritualised. The physical absence of a monarch who ruled his vast possessions from Spain meant that jurisdiction on the ground was more than simply authority over a district. It had to be negotiated and agreed upon. This meant decisions over how to make the monarchy present in its territories and what type of symbolic and political tools were needed for the task. A political geography was always a geography of presence. Such presence was always negotiated at a local level and based on the circumstances and situation at the time. Political battles arose over presence, which made political posturing necessary, and this required the display of imagery through visual and public rituals that ornamented every political stage, among them the *entradas*.

In Chapter Three, this book will move to the land of the Chiriguanaes and the 1574 expedition by Peru viceroy don Francisco de Toledo, who took theatricality and visual display to a level not seen before and never seen in the Charcas borders after. While Almendras exploited the juxtaposition of jurisdictions by travelling to the Chichas and Tucumán with the aim of expanding the jurisdiction of the Audiencia de Charcas, Toledo only went to the Chiriguanaes after all other attempts to organise expeditions to punish the rebel natives had failed and with the aim of restoring law and order and expanding the authority of the Crown. In 1574, with an *encomendero* group largely reluctant to participate, Toledo had to rely on his own political clients. Without support from local elites and consensus, the monarch or his alter ego were faced with a daunting task.

CHAPTER THREE

La Flor del Perú
Viceroy Toledo's Journey to the Borders

'La biografía de Don Francisco de Toledo podría llevar de subtítulo: "Doce años de vida del virreinato del Perú, en su período de mayor organización legislativa y administrativa, y en su brillo máximo de creación de ciudades".'

'Don Francisco de Toledo's biography should bear the subtitle "Twelve years of viceroyalty of Peru's life, during the period of its highest legislative and administrative organisation, and its brightest in terms of the establishment of cities".'

Roberto Levillier, 1935[1]

'Yo salí de la cordillera harto flaco y malparado por averme dado en ella una enfermedad muy rrezia, bendito sea nuestro Señor que me ha dado salud después que llegué a esta ciudad.'

'I left the cordillera [of the Chiriguanaes] very thin and unwell due to a harsh illness. God bless Our Lord that gave me health afterwards when I reached this city [La Plata].'

Don Francisco de Toledo, November 1574[2]

---

1 Roberto Levillier, *Don Francisco de Toledo. Supremo organizador del Perú. Su vida, su obra (1515–1582)* (Buenos Aires: Colección de Publicaciones Históricas de la Biblioteca del Congreso Argentino, 1935), p. 13.
2 Letter from don Francisco de Toledo to Mercedarian friar Diego de Porres, November 1574, in Fray Víctor Barriga, *Los mercedarios en el Perú en el siglo XVI. Documentos del Archivo General de Indias 1518–1600*, Vol. 3 (Arequipa: Establecimientos Gráficos La Colmena SA, 1942), p. 314.

1. Introduction

This chapter is at the centre of this book and shows, through the expedition to the Chiriguanaes in 1574 by Peru viceroy don Francisco de Toledo (1569–1581), how the administration and government of the Catholic monarchy's most troublesome and wealthy possession, Peru and more particularly Charcas, was a negotiated ground that exposed the tensions and conflicts between the Crown and the local elites. Toledo has been admired and vilified, described by scholars as 'the supreme organiser of Peru',[3] 'the most outstanding figure in the history of the viceroyalty of Peru';[4] and the opposite, 'the great tyrant of Peru';[5] and more recently, 'the first applied anthropologist of the modern period'.[6] An analysis of this expedition to the southeastern borders of Charcas through the political culture of the time conveys a completely different image of Toledo, one of a viceroy forced to seek consensus, accommodate and concede, while still at centre-stage as the King's alter ego. It also shows the difficulties that the ambitious viceroy encountered in consolidating royal jurisdiction and implementing a programme to establish the monarchy in an area with a weak tradition of regal authority and largely run by regional elites. This book departs from the early twentieth-century historiography of Toledo's rule that, in a search for the origins of the nation-state, scrutinised his long period at the helm of Peru for clues to the foundations of a stable and long-lasting 'colonial state'. It also marks a radical shift from recent scholarship that, in line with those same concerns, explored the consolidation of a 'modern state' and the strengthening of royal sovereignty during the Toledan years.[7] Also, this may well explain why the expedition to the Chiriguanaes, an event that quickly moved from epic to tragedy, only fills limited space in many accounts of Toledo's government and has not been given the scholarly attention that it deserves.

Based on an approach that explores the political culture of the time and its theatrical representations, challenging the traditional view of a 'colonial

3 Levillier, *Don Francisco de Toledo*.
4 Arthur Franklin Zimmerman, *Francisco de Toledo: Fifth Viceroy of Peru, 1569–1581* (New York: Greenwood Press, 1938), p. 7.
5 Luis E. Valcárcel, *El virrey Toledo, gran tirano del Perú: una revisión histórica* (Lima: Universidad Garcilaso de la Vega, 2015).
6 Antonino Colajanni, 'El virrey Toledo como "primer antropólogo aplicado" de la Edad Moderna. Conocimiento social y planes de transformación del mundo indígena peruano en la segunda mitad del siglo XVI', in *El silencio protagonista. El primer siglo jesuita en el virreynato del Perú 1567–1667* (Quito: Abya-Yala, 2004), pp. 51–95.
7 Javier Tantaleán Arbulú, *El virrey Francisco de Toledo y su tiempo: Proyecto de gobernabilidad, el imperio hispano, la plata peruana en la economía-mundo y el mercado colonial*, 2 vols (Lima: Universidad de San Martín de Porres, Fondo Editorial, 2011); Manfredi Merluzzi, *Politica e governo nel Nuovo Mondo: Francisco de Toledo viceré del Perù (1569–1581)* (Rome: Carocci, 2003).

state' organised top-to-bottom, this chapter describes the painstaking process involved in organising an expedition, with a focus on the Catholic monarchy's polycentrism. It shows a viceroy with strong views on the implementation of a number of reforms largely focused on Potosí and on how the Crown should be present in Peru, who was only able to travel to the Andean slopes, after many setbacks, with his close entourage (and a few *encomenderos*, at the King's expense), as local elites were reluctant to join and/or finance the dangerous journey and only took part after royal funding had been secured and certain conditions met. Nonetheless, as Jesuit priest José de Acosta (c. 1539–1600) commented, Toledo took with him 'la flor del Perú' (the flower of Peru)[8] and positioned himself at the centre of the theatrical stage mounted to travel to the eastern slopes. As 'the King's living image' in Peru, Toledo summoned a 'mystic body' made of all the different parts of the Catholic monarchy's local society, who under his command would help him to exercise the most important duty of political government at the time: the delivery of justice. In this context this meant the punishment, settlement, and evangelisation of indigenous groups either by persuasion, by force, or a combination of the two. Toledo's expedition was not only a 'costly stage'; it was also the weakest point in the viceroy's career. The final image portrayed in sources written after the event includes one propagated by *mestizo* chronicler and writer Inca Garcilaso de la Vega, of an ill and delirious man carried out of the mosquito-infested lowlands in a basket/litter chased by laughing indigenous people referring to Toledo as 'that old woman' and demanding that the Spanish release the viceroy and let them eat 'her'.[9] In the expedition's aftermath, Toledo handed *mercedes* to a loyal few just before sailing back to Spain, while leaving many others craving rewards, rushing to draft *probanzas* in the hope that what the viceroy had not delivered, the King might. The expedition also left behind a stronger Audiencia de Charcas and an empowered local elite now aware that any further expeditions had to involve captains and soldiers with knowledge of the border area. This would eventually clear the way to more formal arrangements to extend Spanish Crown influence over the most conflictive areas of the southeastern Charcas borders between the Audiencia de Charcas and groups headed by Spanish captains which included poor Spaniards, *mestizos*, and even Chiriguanaes. Bows and arrows and a hostile environment seem to have been enough to bring down the strategist and law maker.

---

8 José de Acosta, *Historia natural y moral de las Indias* (Sevilla: Casa de Juan León, 1590), p. 590.
9 El Inca Garcilaso de la Vega, *Primera parte de los commentarios reales* (Lisbon: Oficina de Pedro Crasbeeck, 1609), p. 184.

2. The initial plan

In its search to find the origins of nation- and state-building in nineteenth-century Latin America, early twentieth-century historiography of the government of don Francisco de Toledo as Peru's fifth viceroy focused mainly on his personal qualities as a political strategist and law maker, seeing his character and position in the context of a more centralised administration with a well organised and structured bureaucracy, characteristic of a nation-state. This focus prioritises those aspects of Toledo's government that highlight organisation and control, such as the arrangement of drafts of native labour to extract mercury in Huancavelica and silver in Potosí; the resettlement of indigenous peoples across the Andes; and the dense *corpus* of legislation produced during his twelve years at the helm of the viceroyalty.[10] The historiography of the second half of the twentieth century does not change this focus but explores the same issues in depth, concerning itself with the impact of Toledo's 'reforms' on 'subalterns'—more specifically, indigenous peoples.[11] More recent research revisits Toledo's time in Peru from the perspective of governability and institutionalisation and the expansion of royal sovereignty. It also explores his multiple roles as a juridical reformist, as a traveller in search for vital information to understand Peru's indigenous peoples, and behind the 'Great Resettlement of Indigenous Populations'—the *reducciones toledanas*—through which the viceroy supposedly reimagined himself as an heir to the Incas.[12]

Toledo's expedition to the Chiriguanaes in 1574 occupies only a small part of scholarly output on the viceroy and his government, if it is mentioned at all.[13] The event, for instance, is only superficially described in a few pages of Arthur Zimmerman's biography of Toledo, in the chapter dedicated to the viceroy's work in Charcas.[14] A more recent monograph by Italian historian Manfredi Merluzzi also addresses the topic only briefly, within the wider

---

10 Levillier, *Don Francisco de Toledo*; Zimmerman, *Francisco de Toledo*.

11 Peter Bakewell, *Miners of the Red Mountain: Indian Labor in Potosí, 1545–1650* (Albuquerque: University of New Mexico Press, 1984); Jeffrey A. Cole, *The Potosí Mita, 1573–1700: Compulsory Indian Labor in the Andes* (Stanford, CA: Stanford University Press, 1985); Jeremy Ravi Mumford, *Vertical Empire: The General Resettlement of Indians in the Colonial Andes* (Durham, NC: Duke University Press, 2012).

12 Tantaleán Arbulú, *El virrey Francisco de Toledo y su tiempo*; Merluzzi, *Política e governo nel nuovo mondo*; Antonino Colajanni, *El virrey y los indios del Perú: Francisco de Toledo (1569–1581), La política indígena y las reformas sociales* (Quito: Abya Yala, 2018); Mumford, *Vertical Empire*, p. 7.

13 Surprisingly, in Tantaleán Arbulú's *magnum opus* on the viceroy, which covers over 800 pages in 2 volumes, there is not one mention of the expedition. The subject is not discussed in Colajanni's work either, even though the monograph is centred on Toledo and Peru's indigenous peoples.

14 Zimmerman, *Francisco de Toledo*, pp. 196–200.

context of the efforts made to reaffirm the Crown's sovereignty over Peru.[15] One of the reasons for this silence might be the expedition's outcome. When he left the mountains inhabited by the Chiriguanaes, Toledo was ill and defeated. This is an image that fits neither with the strategist and law maker, nor the heir to the Incas; nor it is particularly well suited to a 'royal bureau- crat' or a 'colonial reformer'.

An interpretation of this *entrada* in the context of the political culture and representations of the period evokes a different picture: one of a viceroy forced to negotiate, regularly review his plans, and adapt to the challenging conditions in Charcas, where the elites, although loyal to the monarch, had become accustomed to run the land largely on their own terms, with tacit or explicit support from royal officials. Toledo's determination to *govern* Peru, overseeing every aspect of reality with zeal and obsession, emulated Philip II's approach to government. It would clash with *cabildos* and *vecinos* having their own agendas and reluctant to accept orders for which no consensus had been built. Inevitably, the pragmatism of the region's elites would succeed, and the viceroy's *entrada* would also be the grave for his ambitions.

Toledo, a member of the Oropesa noble house of Spain, arrived in Peru at the end of his career and in the autumn of his life. The 53-year-old royal officer had served Emperor Charles V in Italy for many years.[16] His time in Peru was expected to be the culmination of a long period in the Crown's service and he hoped it would be brief. As viceroy, Toledo was, in effect, the King's alter ego, supposed to mirror the monarch's image and be accorded the same ceremonial treatment. However, he was also the monarch's servant and minister, someone who served someone else, and society in general was aware of this ambiguity.[17] As recent historiography shows, the administration and delivery of justice was at the core of government in the early modern period, and in an area like Peru this could be summarised as keeping the land 'trouble-free' (*quieta*, using the vocabulary of the time).[18] Toledo had clear royal instructions that offered him advice on how to run the challenging viceroyalty. The instructions should not be interpreted as orders and were largely for guidance. They reflected both the spirit of the Junta Magna of 1568—a meeting of Crown advisers to discuss future global royal policy—and

---

15 Merluzzi, *Politica e governo nel nuovo mondo*, pp. 170–73.
16 Ambassador to the Council of Trent from 1546 and prior to that involved with different duties of the Alcantara knightly order in Rome. León Gómez Rivas, *El virrey del Perú don Francisco de Toledo* (Toledo: Instituto Provincial de Investigaciones y Estudios Toledanos, Diputación Provincial, 1994).
17 Alejandro Cañeque, *The King's Living Image: The Culture and Politics of Viceregal Power in Colonial Mexico*, New World in the Atlantic World (New York: Routledge, 2004), p. 28.
18 António Manuel Hespanha, *La gracia del derecho. Economía de la cultura en la Edad Moderna* (Madrid: Centro de Estudios Constitucionales, 1993), p. 62; Clavero, 'Justicia y gobierno. Economía y gracia', p. 2.

Figure 3.1   Drawing of don Francisco de Toledo, viceroy of Peru between 1569 and 1581, taken from don Felipe Guamán Poma de Ayala's *Nueva Coronica y Buen Gobierno* of 1615
Source: Royal Danish Library, GKS 223: Guaman Poma, *Nueva corónica y buen gobierno* (c. 1615). Page [444 [446]].

key advice from those already in Peru.[19] Such advice came from characters like Audiencia de Charcas judge Juan de Matienzo, the author of *Gobierno del Perú,* a political treatise intended to bring the knowledge of Peru and its peoples to the Spanish court and the Consejo de Indias, published only a year before the Junta Magna.[20]

Because of the importance of silver mining in Potosí, Charcas and the routes to carry that silver to Spain occupied a central place in the Crown's global policy. However, the Chiriguanaes, who refused evangelisation and permanent settlement—the Spanish *policía*—and who by the late 1560s were occupying a crescent-shaped area between the Guapay or Grande and Pilcomayo rivers, stood in the way of a new route to funnel Potosí's riches to Seville via the Atlantic. Furthermore, by the early 1570s the Chiriguana had reached their westernmost point, pushing other populations westwards, making farming in areas near the southeastern Charcas border a hazardous task.[21] The royal advice given to Toledo in 1568 recommended the creation of a network of *presidios* or fortified villages, towns, and settlements along the border with the purpose of trading and contacting the indigenous population hostile to Spanish presence as an alternative to punitive expeditions.[22] The *cédula real* that the viceroy received stressed that

> having exhausted all the human means to bring these Indians to the service of our Lord, if they are unwilling to cooperate, you may wage war against them until they are brought to one place and settled (*reducidos*), and we grant you licence to do this with all the consequences that such action might entail.[23]

19 Demetrio Ramos Pérez, 'La crisis indiana y la Junta Magna de 1568', *Jahrbuch für Geschichte Lateinamerikas,* no. 23 (1986): pp. 1–61; Max Deardorff, *A Tale of Two Granadas: Custom, Community, and Citizenship in the Spanish Empire, 1568–1668* (Cambridge: Cambridge University Press, 2023), p. 66.

20 Gómez Rivas, *El virrey del Perú,* Ch. VI; Merluzzi, *Politica e governo nel nuovo mondo,* pp. 46–67; Matienzo, *Gobierno del Perú;* Morong Reyes, *Saberes hegemónicos y dominio colonial.*

21 France Marie Renard-Casevitz et al., *Al este de los Andes: relaciones entre las sociedades amazónicas y andinas entre los siglos XV y XVII* (Quito: Abya-Yala, 1988), pp. 168, 176.

22 'Cédula dirigida al Virrey del Perú, cerca de la orden que ha de tener y guardar en los nuevos descubrimientos y poblaciones que diere, assi por mar como por tierra', 1568, in Alfonso García-Gallo and Diego de Encinas, *Cedulario indiano o cedulario de Encinas,* Vol. IV (Madrid: Boletín Oficial del Estado, 2018 [1596]), pp. 229–32.

23 'Y aviendo vos usado de todos los medios humanos para reducir estos yndios al servicio de Dios y nuestro y no lo queriendo ellos hacer, les podays hacer guerra, hasta reducirlos, que para ello os damos poder cumplido con todas sus incidencias y dependencias'. BNE, Ms. 3,044, Papeles varios tocantes al gobierno de Indias, Real Cédula, Madrid, 19 December 1568, fols 309–10.

The instructions could not be clearer in indicating that war against the Chiriguanaes should be the last resort.

Academics are divided about the viceroy's intentions. On one hand, some argue that Toledo's initial plan for the southeastern Charcas border suggests that the viceroy was determined to gather sufficient evidence to justify war against the populations there. Such views emphasise how, based on preconceptions and the demonisation of these peoples, using the trope of cannibalism among other labels, Toledo organised the evidence in a manner that eventually gave him reasons to attack the Chiriguanaes.[24] Other scholars put forward a different argument, one explored in this chapter, that stresses that the viceroy was open to finding a peaceful solution, only coming to the conclusion that an expedition was needed after negotiations failed.[25] Toledo, a minister with hopes to receive recognition for his long career and therefore with his eyes on the court in Madrid, planned to follow royal advice as much as possible. He therefore arranged to found new towns as a way to establish a stronger presence along the Charcas border, and pushed for small-scale punitive expeditions headed by his political allies. Such *entradas* would be funded by *encomenderos* to whom had been assigned peoples exposed to attacks from the Chiriguanaes, as part of their duty to protect those they had received in *encomiendas*.

In a political culture that brought together patrons and their clients through a system of rewards and mutual and quasi-legal obligations, Toledo could add to his own clients—who would join expeditions expecting to receive rewards for their services and merits—any *encomenderos* whom he could enlist.[26] The military obligation would fall upon the few *encomenderos* whose subject peoples farmed along the border area. This move was also the least expensive option for a financially exhausted Crown, only a few years away from defaulting on its debts, that was reluctant to finance expeditions unless this was extremely necessary.[27] Only the fear of losing Potosí could prompt such drastic intervention and, even though news from Charcas was concerning, the information was far from alarming, as Toledo was about to find out.

---

24 Oliveto, 'Ocupación territorial', p. 161; Julien, 'Colonial Perspectives on the Chiriguana (1528–1574)', pp. 20–22; Lia Guillermina Oliveto, 'Chiriguanos: la construcción de un estereotipo en la política colonizadora del sur andino', *Memoria Americana* 18, no. 1 (2010): p. 61.

25 Scholl, 'At the Limits of Empire', p. 270; García Recio, *Análisis*, p. 95; Manfredi Merluzzi, *Gobernando los Andes: Francisco de Toledo virrey del Perú (1569–1581)*, trans. Patricia Unzain (Lima: Fondo Editorial, Pontificia Universidad Católica del Perú, 2014), p. 229.

26 Clavero, *Antidora*.

27 A first default took place in 1575: John Elliott, *Imperial Spain, 1469–1716* (Harmondsworth: Penguin, 1970), p. 269.

3. A viceroy on tour: Toledo inspects the land and encounters Charcas

In 1570, months after his arrival in Peru, don Francisco de Toledo did something no other viceroy had done before, and no other viceroy would do after him: he embarked on a Visita General, a general inspection of Peru, that would last a total of five years. As recent historiography shows, *visitas* were more than simply bureaucratic tasks—they were also an effective way to make the monarch present in remote and sometimes inaccessible parts of his realm. They were means of staging jurisdiction. Beyond the 'propaganda' effect, *visitas* were a form of bringing the 'mystic body' of society together, through either coercive or peaceful means, sometimes combined, in a political ritual that demonstrated the government in action through the gathering of information at meetings with notables and locals, through the publication and enactment of decrees and laws, and most importantly, through the delivery of justice, righting wrongs.[28] As the King's 'living image', Toledo was hoping to bring the monarch and his vassals close together, narrowing the vast distance between Madrid and Peru in what, for many of the King's vassals, would be one, if not the only, opportunity to come into the presence of his 'physical representation'. Because of their symbolic importance, the theatrical stage of *visitas* was conducted with great pomp and ceremony, and the viceroy was accompanied by many officials, including notaries and translators. The long 'procession' also involved priests, physicians, relatives, *criados*, and political clients who accompanied the viceroy along the lengthy path that separates Lima and Charcas, to keep him constantly informed, amused, and provide advice on different urgent matters. Replicating the regular journeys of his old and by then deceased patron, Emperor Charles V, the 'court in motion' that Toledo arranged for his Visita General would stop at key locations along the route to meet *cabildo* representatives, local elites, and indigenous leaders. The inspection had as its main objectives the resettlement of indigenous populations and the reorganisation of labour drafts to boost mineral production in Potosí and mercury extraction in Huancavelica. It would also give the viceroy first-hand knowledge of a large section of Peru and its peoples and the opportunity to 'act like the monarch', overseeing the implementation of rules and execution of orders.

With Charcas, and more importantly Potosí, at the core of Toledo's *visita*, the monarchy was not only preoccupied with silver and mercury production, but also with the logistics involved in carrying silver to Spain. Traditionally, silver left Charcas via Lima and Panama, but the Atlantic route was a desirable alternative and one that had been under threat from

28 Armando Guevara-Gil and Frank Salomon, 'A "Personal Visit": Colonial Political Ritual and the Making of the Indians in the Andes', *CLAHR* 3, nos 1–2 (1994): pp. 3–36; Tamar Herzog, *Ritos de control, prácticas de negociación: Pesquisas, visitas y residencias y las relaciones entre Quito y Madrid (1650–1750)* (Madrid: Fundación Ignacio Larramendi, 2000).

the Chiriguanaes for some time. With the information on these indigenous peoples at his disposal, Toledo, aware of the reluctance to volunteer to fight, was still pondering different options just before leaving Lima, and in a letter in June 1570 he stated that he 'did not want to burden those who already had to go to fight in Chile [against the Araucanos] so unwillingly' by forcing an expedition to another border in conflict.[29]

Toledo knew that in 1564 the Chiriguanaes had destroyed two Spanish border towns situated not far from Santa Cruz de la Sierra, causing great consternation: Santo Domingo de la Nueva Rioja, also known as Condorillo, and La Barranca, as described in Chapter Two. At the time, the duty to respond to these attacks fell upon Pedro de Castro, husband of doña Inés de Aguiar, a wealthy *mestiza* who had inherited half an *encomienda* over indigenous peoples exposed to the Chiriguanaes.[30] Disguised as part of his *encomendero* military duties, Castro's *entrada* had an ulterior and more lucrative motive: the capture of lowland natives, largely Chanés, whom the Chiriguana normally captured themselves, to exchange for goods with farmers along the border.[31] The growing need for local labour in Charcas was a driving force behind such expeditions, one that the authorities eventually had to accommodate, and one that was met either through expeditions or the direct trade in captives with the Chiriguanaes themselves. This trade was also disguised as an act of mercy, the rescue of indigenous people who otherwise were supposedly at risk of being eaten by the cannibal Chiriguana. However, and unfortunately for Castro and his men, the Chiriguanaes saw the task of taking Chané and other neighbouring native captives as their monopoly and, as true lords of their lands, they were not prepared to accept competition over the Chané or other lowland tribes from any other groups, not even the Spaniards. Castro and most of his men did not survive their *entrada* into Chiriguana territory.

Castro's request for authority to mount an expedition was processed and approved by the Audiencia de Charcas, as at the time Peru did not have a viceroy at its helm and the Audiencia took on the responsibility, not without controversy. With Toledo in Peru, military matters fell under the viceroy's jurisdiction and the Audiencia de Charcas only provided advice. Throughout the whole of Toledo's time in Peru, the Audiencia de Charcas would act largely as witness to such matters, acceding to decisions taken by Toledo and offering suggestions, which gave its judges the right to criticise the viceroy's role, after an expedition. Aware of this sidelined role and in

29 Letter from Toledo to the King, Lima, 10 June 1570, in Levillier, *Gobernantes del Perú*, Vol. 3, p. 436.
30 Ana María Presta, 'Portraits of Four Women: Traditional Female Roles and Transgressions in Colonial Elite Families in Charcas, 1550–1600', *Colonial Latin American Review* 9, no. 2 (2000): pp. 237–62.
31 Letter from Matienzo to the King, 1 December 1567, in Levillier, *La Audiencia de Charcas*, p. 241.

accordance with the viceroy's initial plan for small punitive expeditions, one of Toledo's *criados*, Hernando Díaz, secured his permission for an *entrada* to the Chiriguanaes to avenge their attacks and the death of Castro. With the viceroy's authorisation, the Audiencia de Charcas approved powder and lead, for ammunition for Díaz's weapons, while also insisting that he was not supposed to wage war against this people.[32] Díaz did not follow their advice and, travelling with fifty men, set two Chiriguana settlements on fire, returning to La Plata with numerous captives.[33] This brief episode illustrates Toledo's refusal to support large-scale expeditions, at least at this stage, and his preference for low-profile *entradas* involving his *criados* and *encomenderos*, which would not cost the Crown very much.[34] Toledo would reward Díaz with a permanent post, in the Compañía de Lanzas, later.[35]

This *entrada* gave the Audiencia de Charcas a taste of what was to come. It was clear that the viceroy wanted a more direct approach to the district's border policy, one that would try to avoid consultation with local authorities and tight scrutiny, and one that was widely supported by his own household, which saw it as an opportunity to fight indigenous peoples, secure cheap captive labour, and accrue merits for future rewards. It would also save the Crown's coffers the expense. While this worked well for Díaz, it was a different matter for larger expeditions that required ground support, ammunition, and materials, as well as plenty of men, and hence needed the involvement and cooperation of local authorities. If this was going to be the policy for settling the southeastern border, then sooner or later Toledo would be forced to negotiate and agree compromises with local elites.

With the Chiriguanaes punished for the murder of Castro and his men,

---

32 López Villalva (dir.), *Acuerdos de la Real Audiencia de La Plata de los Charcas*, Vol. 2, 19 June and 6 July 1570, 96, p. 101.

33 'Información de los daños causados por los chiriguanos mandada practicar por el Virrey Francisco de Toledo, los testigos declaran que dieron muerte a un religioso de la merced', Yucay, October 1571, in Victor Barriga, *Mercedarios ilustres en el Perú. El padre fray Diego de Porres, misionero insigne en el Perú y en Santa Cruz de La Sierra*, Vol. II (Arequipa: Establecimientos Graficos La Colmena SA, 1949), p. 40; Ricardo Mujía, *Bolivia–Paraguay. Exposición de los títulos que consagran el derecho territorial de Bolivia, sobre la zona comprendida entre los rios Pilcomayo y Paraguay, presentada por el doctor Ricardo Mujía, enviado extraordinario y ministro plenipotenciario de Bolivia en el Paraguay. Anexos*, Vol. II (La Paz: Empresa Editora 'El Tiempo', 1914), p. 503.

34 Letter from Toledo to the King, Cusco, 1 March 1572, in Levillier, *Gobernantes del Perú*, Vol. 4, pp. 292–98.

35 This was an elite group of soldiers that followed the viceroy and were frequently based in Lima. Guillermo Lohmann Villena, 'Las compañías de gentilhombres de lanzas y arcabuces de la guarda del virreinato del Perú', *Anuario de Estudios Americanos* no. 13 (1956): pp. 141–215; AGI, Patronato, 190, R23, [1577] Representación de Diego de Porras sobre el origen y estado de las compañías de lanzas y arcabuceros en Perú. Acompaña una relación de lo que han supuesto los tributos en Perú, destinados al pago de dichas lanzas y arcabuces, image 12.

Toledo began listening to different members of the body politic, to collect and process the information available about the Chiriguanaes and the southeastern Charcas border area, in search of a more permanent solution that would involve the settlement and evangelisation of these peoples. In March 1571 the viceroy met the attorney—*procurador*—of Santa Cruz de la Sierra, Cristóbal de Saavedra, in Cusco, one of the stops in his Visita General, to discuss the issue.[36] As *procurador*, Saavedra represented the *cabildo* of Santa Cruz de la Sierra and, through it, its *vecinos*. Cities had a prominent place in the political edifice of the Catholic monarchy and Saavedra was asked to give an assessment of the situation, on behalf of the town he represented.[37] At this time, Toledo still thought the situation to be under control as silver mining in Potosí was deemed safe.[38] As noted in Chapter Two, unless the Crown perceived a serious risk, it would try to avoid outright confrontation. Following this initial meeting, in September 1571 Saavedra travelled back to Cusco to see Toledo again, but this time, in company with Francisco de Mendoza, brother of don Diego de Mendoza, the governor of Santa Cruz de la Sierra—who was probably trying to meet the viceroy officially and gather information about his intentions in relation to the Chiriguanaes and Santa Cruz de la Sierra.

Because of its proximity to Chiriguana settlements, Santa Cruz de la Sierra was always going to occupy a key role in any move against these peoples. Securing support from the district's *vecinos* was of paramount importance. This was not an easy task, however. Santa Cruz de la Sierra had grown largely as an autonomous outpost between Asunción and Charcas and its *vecinos* had a strong tradition of self-reliance. Even the Chiriguanaes were perceived in a different manner in Santa Cruz de la Sierra, where they were considered more similar to the Guaraní in Asunción, than they were elsewhere in Charcas. Any expedition would have to rely on the district's singular elite who by then were focused on other unconquered indigenous peoples, those of Mojos, and the minerals that might be found in nearby Itatín.

Toledo met these men in the ancient resting place of the Incas, Yucay valley, surrounded by his courtiers. He asked for a wider enquiry into the situation along the southeastern Charcas border.[39] *Vecinos* from La Plata and Santa Cruz de la Sierra travelled to Cusco and carried out a series of

---

36 Julien, *Desde el Oriente*, pp. 212–17.

37 Alejandro Agüero, 'Ciudad y poder político en el Antiguo Régimen. La tradición castellana', in *El derecho local en la periferia de la Monarquía Hispana. Río de La Plata, Tucumán y Cuyo. Siglos XVI–XVIII* (Buenos Aires: Editorial Dunken, 2013).

38 Letter from Toledo to the King, Cusco, 25 March 1571, in Levillier, *Gobernantes del Perú*, Vol. 3, p. 452.

39 Julien, *Desde el Oriente*, pp. 218–21. AGI, Patronato, 235, R1, [24 October 1571] Chiriguanaes. Ynformacion que se hizo por mandado del excelentisimo señor visorrey del Peru sobre la cordillera de los chiriguanaes por su persona que su excelencia ymbio y lo que piden los dichos yndios que se haga con ellos para salir de paz.

interviews, kickstarting the enquiry, between 24 and 29 October 1571. The interview findings confirmed Toledo's suspicions that there was growing disquiet about the administration of don Diego de Mendoza in Santa Cruz de la Sierra. With this information, the viceroy began considering replacing don Diego with one of his own allies, Juan Pérez de Zurita, a veteran of the Jornada de Argel, a 1541 expedition against the Ottoman stronghold Algiers that had ended in disaster for the Spanish, in which a much younger Toledo had participated.⁴⁰ As mentioned in Chapter Two, Zurita had also been governor of Tucumán, and was therefore familiar with the hardships and with the rebellious indigenous peoples. At this point, Toledo had a much better idea of the situation along the southeastern Charcas border, but decided to wait before entering Charcas, to move forward with the enquiry and have a more accurate assessment of the district.⁴¹

With what Toledo saw as the 'success' of Díaz's expedition in mind, the viceroy decided that small *entradas* were the best way to tackle the Chiriguana threat. He therefore hoped to ask the governors of Tucumán, an area that also bordered with these peoples, and Santa Cruz de la Sierra, to organise separate expeditions, which would be financed by *vecinos* in those jurisdictions, with some royal support in terms of supplies and ammunition.⁴² Opting for smaller *entradas* meant that Toledo was planning to rely on the duties these *vecinos* held as loyal royal vassals to enlist in and join such expeditions.⁴³ It would have potentially given them access to land and resources, mainly native labour for farming activities and domestic service. However, because those local elites were supposed to bear the cost of such expeditions, they wanted clear benefits from such hazardous enterprises and without such clarity it was hard for governors and viceroys to organise *entradas*. Despite being aware of all this, Toledo was not prepared to allow expedition members who seized Chiriguanaes as prisoners to trade them, and limited such prisoners' term of captivity to the life of their captor, which made it impossible for the captor to pass these captives down to successors, as *encomiendas* could be. The viceroy had sought clarification from the King on such matters in March 1573:

40 AGI, Patronato, 127, N1, R12, [1584] Información de los méritos y servicios de Juan Pérez de Zorita en la conquista y pacificación de Perú y persecución de Francisco Hernández Girón, habiendo servido también en las guerras de Italia, Argel, y Tremecén, fol. 1r; Gómez Rivas, *El virrey del Perú*, pp. 53–54.
41 Letter from Toledo to the King, 1572, in Levillier, *Gobernantes del Perú*, Vol. 4, p. 401; Comisión a don Gerónimo de Cabrera, gobernador de Tucumán, para poblar en dichas provincias los pueblos de españoles que le pareciere, 1571, in Roberto Levillier, *Gobernación del Tucumán. Papeles de gobernardores en el siglo XVI* (Madrid: Sucesores de Rivadeneyra, 1920), pp. 401–03.
42 Letter from Toledo to the King, Cusco, 1 March 1572, in Levillier, *Gobernantes del Perú*, Vol. 4, pp. 98, 312.
43 This choice by Toledo is mentioned in García Recio, *Análisis*, p. 97, but not in Scholl, 'At the Limits of Empire'.

Until now, as I have written to Your Majesty, I have not allowed the governors of Tucumán and Santa Cruz (as part of their war against the Chiriguanaes) to make use of prisoners for any longer than the duration of their own lives, and banned trade in these prisoners [...] I beg Your Majesty to send me a clear indication of policy because of the confusion that this seems to be causing.[44]

4. A drastic change: Toledo revisits his plan

As the Visita General moved on, and having decided that a large expedition was not an option for the time being because of the expense involved, Toledo reached his next destination, La Plata, in 1573.[45] Following the obligatory festivities that accompanied his arrival, he met the Audiencia de Charcas judges, and discussed the situation along the southeastern border.[46] Unlike the viceroy, the monarch's living image, an Audiencia was the actual monarch in presence, in any jurisdiction subject to that court. *Vecinos* would write to the Audiencia in the same style they would use to write to their King.[47] The coexistence of the two authorities, and the two 'presences', in the same jurisdiction was always cause for problems and tensions given the similarities of their functions and representations in a theatre in which royal officers and tasks overlapped on a complicated and elaborated stage. This was more pronounced given Toledo's personality, his approach to the viceregal role, and his interpretation of the Crown's government of Peru. In May 1573 and following the established protocol, Toledo consulted the

---

44 'Hasta agora, como escreví a V.M. yo no e permitido a los Governadores de Tucumán y Sancta Cruz que en la guerra de los Chiriguanaes puedan hazer mas que servirse de estos prisiones [*sic*] por sus dias que le tomare, sin que los puedan bender y trocar [...] Ymporta mandar V.M. embiar con dicicion y claridad estas dudas, porque cada día se padece en la confusion y contradición que causa no estar rresueltos'. Letter from Toledo to the King, 20 March 1573, in Maurtua, *Juicio de límites entre el Perú y Bolivia*, Vol. 1, pp. 88–89.

45 The viceroy stopped first in Potosí where he stayed for three to four months: letter from Toledo to the King, 1572, in Levillier, *Gobernantes del Perú*, Vol. 4, p. 401; Lizárraga, *Descripción colonial*, Vol. 2, pp. 111–12.

46 Toledo had not even entered the village before disagreements broke out with the Audiencia judges. The issue was over the seats that would be used during the viceroy's entrance ceremony. Toledo wanted simpler seats for the judges, and they wanted more luxurious ones. To further assert his authority, Toledo walked into La Plata under a canopy [*palio*], whereas he had entered Lima without one: Lizárraga, *Descripción colonial*, Vol. 2, p. 112. On entrances of viceroys and their ceremonies: Juan Chiva Beltrán, *El triunfo del virrey* (Madrid: Universitat Jaume I. Servei de Comunicació i Publicacions, 2012).

47 Carlos Garriga, 'Concepción y aparatos de justicia: Las reales audiencias de las Indias', *Cuadernos de Historia* 19 (2009), p. 218; Cañeque, *The King's Living Image*, p. 59.

Audiencia de Charcas judges on three subjects: the legality of war against the Chiriguanaes, how far it was obligatory for *encomenderos* to contribute to any war efforts in the jurisdictions where they exercised their duties as *vecinos*, and the fate of those Chiriguanaes who might be taken captive.[48] Toledo still appears to have been seeking advice about more limited strikes against the border indigenous groups. The Audiencia judges were in an advantageous position as they could not decide on military matters with a viceroy at the helm of Peru, but could offer guidance knowing that the political cost would eventually fall on Toledo. Sheltered from the consequences of problematic *entradas*, the judges gave their full endorsement to the viceroy's plans.

Continuing with those plans, Juan Pérez de Zurita was effectively appointed governor of Santa Cruz de la Sierra, and asked, as part of his instructions, to launch an expedition on the Chiriguanaes border from there.[49] He was going to replace don Diego de Mendoza, who had only taken up his post in 1568.[50] Zurita was given further instructions about the running of Santa Cruz de la Sierra, including the implementation of tighter controls over the local elite, a complete ban on the sale of captive natives—an almost impossible task—and the postponement of any plans for an expedition to nearby Mojos and Itatín. These two sites had only recently been explored by Spaniards, in search of captives and potential mineral deposits. Instead, the *vecinos* of Santa Cruz de la Sierra were going to be asked to contribute to a small *entrada* to the Chiriguanaes, following the viceroy's wishes.

As expected, these plans encountered strong opposition among the local elite which was reluctant to exchange the chances of finding mineral riches and plenty of native labour for promises of honour and glory that might follow their participation in an expedition to the Chiriguanaes. Zurita was overthrown in a revolt led by Diego de Mendoza, frustrating Toledo's project for a small-scale expedition from Santa Cruz de la Sierra.[51] Personal relations between former authorities, prominent *vecinos*, and alliances with the Chiriguanaes all lay behind the defeat of Zurita and Toledo and show how challenging it was to insert the King and his monarchy into a territory ruled by private interest and where recognition of royal authority was weak.

---

48 AGI, Patronato, 235, R2, [1573/1574] Parecer del presidente y oidores de las Audiencias de los Charcas y La Plata, sobre el modo de hacer la guerra a los indios chiriguanaes y castigo que debía imponérseles.

49 'Título e instrucciones al Capitán Juan Pérez de Zurita, para la gobernación de Santa Cruz de la Sierra', 1571, in Maurtua, *Juicio de límites entre el Perú y Bolivia*, Vol. 9, pp. 44, 52–53; Mujía, *Bolivia–Paraguay*, pp. 42–45; 50–52.

50 Don Diego de Mendoza had been elected governor of the district by the *cabildo* of Santa Cruz de la Sierra when he was only 28 years old, succeeding Ñuflo de Chaves. He was son-in-law of both Chaves and Hernando de Salazar, and had been part of the group of Spaniards who founded Santa Cruz de la Sierra. Sanabria, *Crónica sumaria Santa Cruz*, p. 12.

51 García Recio, *Análisis*, pp. 476–77.

In a sense, Toledo and his policy to govern the land in the name of the Crown ran counter to the interests of Santa Cruz de la Sierra's elite, that felt intruded upon by a viceroy whose plans (and Zurita's appointment) challenged the status quo. Their resistance even encompassed an agreement Mendoza made with a Chiriguana faction to fight the viceroy, if needed.[52] The whole situation, a turning point, was a serious blow to Toledo's plans, and is something that has been largely ignored in historiography on the expeditions to the Chiriguanaes. Because of the distance between Santa Cruz de la Sierra and La Plata, and the fact that Chiriguana territory lay in between, it would take Toledo a further two years to bring don Diego to justice.[53]

With his initial plans for expeditions from Santa Cruz de la Sierra and Tucumán in disarray, Toledo was now faced with the impossible task of having to negotiate a large-scale expedition with the involvement of local elites who were shying away from their responsibilities and were reluctant to go along with a costly event unless offered immediate rewards. The task was difficult since these elites were loyal to the King but, until Toledo, they had not felt the real presence of the monarch, his justice, or his law. They were used to officials running Charcas in the name of the monarch, but a viceroy was, in effect, the person nearest to the King himself, and his presence and demands were a novelty for the local elite in Charcas. The viceroy was also constrained by royal policy as he could not be seen to endorse the permanent enslavement of and trade in natives hostile to Spanish presence. Unable to move forward, Toledo decided on a new plan. With the aid of envoys, he would establish direct contact with Chiriguana leaders and bring them to La Plata for discussions, potentially holding them as hostages there. This was not a new strategy: it had been used in other confrontations since the Spanish arrived in the New World. It was part of the early modern war culture that in Europe involved a period of negotiations, diplomatic exchanges, and display, before any resort to arms, perceiving the whole process as a theatrical stage. In this case, it would buy extra time in case a large expedition should eventually be needed or, even better for Toledo, might prompt a compromise with these indigenous peoples, clearing the way for their acceptance of the Catholic faith and settlement. The ultimate goal—as the conclusions of the Junta Magna and Juan de Matienzo's treaty suggest—remained the establishment of two new border towns.

---

52 Martín del Barco Centenera, *Argentina y conquista del Río de la Plata, con otros acaecimientos de los reynos del Perú, Tucumán, y Estado del Brasil* (Lisbon: Pedro Crasbeek, 1602), fol. 120.

53 Letter from Licenciado Pedro Ramírez de Quiñones to the King, 6 May 1575, in Levillier, *La Audiencia de Charcas*, Vol. I, pp. 327–29.

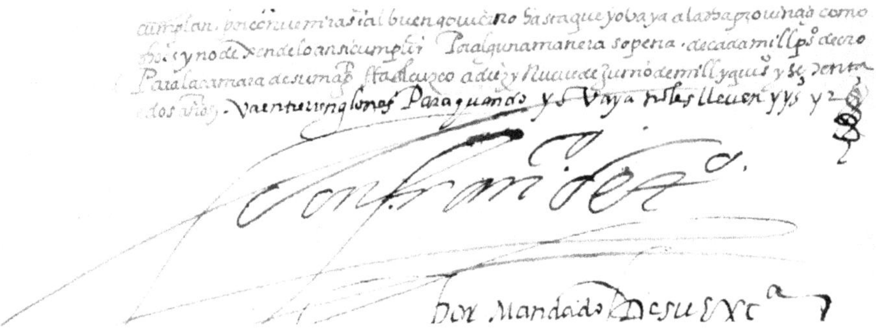

Figure 3.2   Handwritten signature of don Francisco de Toledo, viceroy of
Peru between 1569 and 1581
Source: Used with permission of Archivo y Biblioteca Nacionales de
Bolivia ALP, Min 122.

5. Hostage hunting in the borders

From La Plata, the journey to the border was perilous and long. The way
went across valleys, following rivers that swelled during the rainy season and
narrowed when the dry weather finally set in. The last Spanish district before
the Chiriguana settlements, travelling south from La Plata, was the province
of Chichas, and it was home to the indigenous group of that name analysed
in Chapter Two. Toledo sent a veteran of the war against the Araucanos in
Chile, Captain Agustín de Ahumada, as his envoy to the border, with ten
to twelve men, to gather information and contact the Chiriguanaes.[54] The
viceroy was fond of war veterans and old conquistadors and like many of his
contemporaries he thought of Chile—the 'Flanders of the Indies'—as the
type of border area where armed men would improve their military skills
and accumulate experience they could use along other conflictive borders
of the Catholic Monarchy. Ahumada's presence was received with hostility
and, after some skirmishes, three Chiriguana leaders, not the most important
ones, agreed to travel to La Plata to meet Toledo.[55] A further eight to ten
Chiriguanaes followed in their footsteps, arriving in the city to pay homage
to the viceroy and quieten down the situation. Since the main Chiriguana
leaders had not been drawn to La Plata, Toledo reluctantly decided to resort
to someone from the actual border area who had the knowledge and skills to

54 Ahumada's journey coincided with his role to organise the settlement of the Chichas
in their Toledan towns. Palomeque, 'Los chicha y las visitas toledanas', p. 124.
55 AGI, Patronato, 137, N1, R2, [1598] Luis de Fuentes y Vargas, statement by
Juan Fernández de Castro, image 102; letter from Toledo to the King, La Plata,
30 November 1573, in Levillier, *Gobernantes del Perú*, Vol. 4, p. 198.

approach the peoples living there; the task was entrusted to Captain García Mosquera.

Born in 1538, García Mosquera was the *mestizo* son of Captain Ruy García Mosquera, and a Chiriguana/Guaraní woman. His language skills would certainly help with any enquiry organised by Toledo.[56] Furthermore, through his marriage to Teresa Zavala, daughter of Captain Pedro de Segura Zavala, García Mosquera was also a *vecino* in the border region and part of a network of poor Spaniards, other *mestizos*, and, more importantly, Chiriguanaes, who were all based in Tomina and who could offer the Spanish support for any expedition, in exchange for concessions. García Mosquera and his relatives expected rewards in the form of posts that would give official recognition to their status in the border area and expand their fortunes.[57] However, the captain was caught between two different loyalties. On one hand, he responded to his own Chiriguana allies and factions, who also had their own enemies among other Chiriguana factions, border Spaniards, and *mestizos*. On the other hand, García Mosquera was also close to Spaniards who regularly endured attacks by indigenous groups along the border, a cause he understood very well having been taken captive by local peoples in the past.[58] Although his background made him a firm candidate to help the viceroy, this ambiguity and his *mestizo* origin prompted Toledo to distrust García Mosquera.

Back in La Plata, the viceroy had set up court, waiting for the arrival of García Mosquera with more information and, potentially, new Chiriguanaes. Following his military experience under Charles V, he was waiting for the right opportunity to expand the realm and bring the monarch's presence to the eastern slopes of the Andes. In a reminder of the Spanish strategies in European wars, this was a time for negotiations, that involved pomp and sometimes retreats, as well as regular contact with the enemy and frequent embassies or delegations. Those Chiriguanaes already in La Plata were asked to stay, to guarantee the safe return of the *mestizo* captain. The list of Toledo's 'special' guests included don Francisquillo, a young Chiriguana, who may have changed his name to pay honour to the viceroy, and of whom Toledo

---

56 García Mosquera was the product of 'kinship paradigms from distinct cultures, close social contact, violent encounters on the frontiers and borderlands, minimal European immigration, and the vitality of Indian communities' as experienced in Paraguay. Shawn Michael Austin, *Colonial Kinship: Guaraní, Spaniards, and Africans in Paraguay* (Albuquerque: University of New Mexico Press, 2020), p. 276.

57 BNE, Ms. 3,044, Papeles varios tocantes al gobierno de Indias, fols 315–16, http://bdh-rd.bne.es/viewer.vm?id=0000023047&page=1, accessed 29 April 2024.

58 One witness to a report commissioned by Viceroy Toledo in 1571 mentions García Mosquera as one of many captives the natives were 'fattening up to eat'. Luckily, they all managed to escape. AGI, Patronato, 235, R1, [1571] Informaciones hechas de orden del virrey del Perú, Francisco de Toledo, sobre la conducta y malos procedimientos de los indios llamados Chiriguanaes, images 46–47.

grew fond because of his irreverent manners; the young man became a type of court fool.[59]

In the political theatre that Toledo assembled, his Chiriguana guests were dressed in Spanish clothes and received gifts suitable for a royal court, while being expected to adopt manners and behave accordingly, in an example of performativity.[60] They had to copy pomp and ceremony and behave like emissaries from rulers of noble origin, employing what was seen as appropriate language and manners. In a political culture that privileged performance, the Chiriguana guests were expected to play their role on the viceregal stage. In a context that appreciated values such as reciprocity, friendship, and loyalty the gifts they received—a donation—were exactly those that might fuel connections between patrons and clients—a way of incorporating the Chiriguanaes into the political sphere of Toledo, meaning that the viceroy would expect some reciprocal donation or service from these clients afterwards.[61] Taking into account their own traditions and experience with Andean indigenous peoples, the Spanish frequently perceived lack of reciprocation as betrayal and regularly said that the Chiriguanaes rarely returned favours and gifts and were therefore untrustworthy and unreliable, reinforcing their stereotype that also involved cannibalism and lack of *policía*. After some time, García Mosquera returned to La Plata with a delegation of thirty Chiriguanaes, including two of the groups' main leaders, Marucare and Condorillo, accompanied by Baltasarillo, a Chicha who had been living with the Chiriguana for some time and would act as an interpreter.[62]

Hosting Marucare and Condorillo in his comfortable and luxurious court in La Plata, Toledo slowly turned the Chiriguana guests into prisoners.

59 Lizárraga, *Descripción colonial*, Vol. 2, pp. 116–17. Saignes mentions that Francisquillo was the son of Chiriguana *cacique* Condorillo. Toledo adopted him and Francisquillo travelled with the viceroy on Toledo's return journey to Spain. When they stopped in Panama, Francisquillo decided to return to Potosí and once there he befriended *corregidor* Pedro Osores de Ulloa. After returning to the southeastern Charcas borders, travelling as part of a trade caravan to the Chiriguana territory, Francisquillo murdered the guards and took all the goods, becoming an enemy of the Spaniards. Saignes and Combès, *Historia del pueblo chiriguano*, p. 217.

60 'Performativity is a description of how bodies and selves are controlled and compelled to conform to social standards: performativity is thus not a singular "act", for it is always a reiteration of a norm or a set of norms, and to the extent that it acquires an act-like status in the present, it conceals or dissimulates the conventions of which it is a repetition'. William Egginton, *How the World Became a Stage: Presence, Theatricality, and the Question of Modernity* (Albany: State University of New York Press, 2003), p. 16.

61 Clavero, *Antidora*, p. 100.

62 AGI, Patronato, 235, R4, [1574] Relacion de lo que se hizo en la jornada que el excelentisimo señor virrey del Piru don Francisco de Toledo hizo por su persona entrando a hazer Guerra a los chiriguanaes de las fronteras y cordilleras desta provincial en el año de setenta y quatro, fol. 3r; Lizárraga, *Descripción colonial*, Vol. 2, p. 117.

Spanish security around the indigenous envoys tightened, making them feel uneasy, something they probably communicated to those who were waiting for them in settlements in Chiriguana territory. Rumours, and their leaders' failure to return, eventually prompted the arrival of more Chiriguanaes who, in the manner of a religious procession, carried crosses, showing their willingness to embrace the Catholic faith, and begged to see 'Apo Toledo'.[63] The Chiriguanaes had already performed as 'loyal royal vassals', being hosted by Toledo in La Plata; now this new performance indicated apparent willingness to adopt Christianity, by displaying potential Christian credentials and calling for 'Apo Toledo' as the means to achieve that. The new visitors met the viceroy and told him of the presence of Santiago, a young preacher who had changed their old habits and lifestyle. Sent by Jesus Christ, the missionary had appeared in one of their settlements, Saypurú, two years before, asking them to stop eating human flesh, making war, and having more than one wife. The presence of Christian religious orders in the area was scanty at the time and the story seemed a convenient way to show the Spanish the Chiriguanaes' willingness to adopt Christian traditions. They had come to La Plata to ask for Catholic priests to baptise them and instruct them in religious matters.[64] It seems that the Chiriguana were aware of the stereotypes about them that circulated among the Spanish and were prepared to take advantage of this, to delay any move by Toledo. Although religious authorities in La Plata questioned the whole story, and in effect it seems highly questionable, Toledo still pinned his hopes on the possibility of these natives accepting the Catholic faith and eventually settling and he therefore decided to commission a new journey by García Mosquera to the border area to reassess the situation, something the captain carried out between September and December 1573.[65]

García Mosquera had his own agenda, and it is probable that he used the journey to pass information about Toledo's intentions to the Chiriguanaes. He was trying to position himself in a drama of war that was slowly mounting. After trying to marry him into their groups, probably to secure an ally in Toledo's quarters and obtain a degree of protection as a result,

---

63 In Quechua, *apo* means 'great lord or superior judge, or main *curaca, capay apu,* king'. Diego Gonçalez Holguin, *Vocabulario de la lengua general de todo el Peru llamada lengua quichua, o del inca* (Ciudad de Los Reyes (Lima): Francisco del Canto, 1607), p. 23; Lizárraga, *Descripción colonial*, Vol. 2, p. 120.

64 AGI, Patronato, 235, R3, [1573] Información hecha en la Audiencia de La Plata, de orden del virrey del Perú, Francisco de Toledo, sobre averiguar la aparición de un joven entre los indios chiriguanaes que se dijo ser Santiago Apostol, enviado por Jesús para predicarles y convertirlos a la religión católica; Lizárraga, *Descripción colonial*, Vol. 2, p. 120; letter from Toledo to the King, 30 November 1573, in Levillier, *Gobernantes del Perú*, Vol. 5, p. 201; letter from Licenciado Pedro Ramírez de Quiñones to the King, 6 May 1575, in Levillier, *La Audiencia de Charcas*, Vol. 1, p. 326.

65 Mujía, *Bolivia–Paraguay*, Vol. II, pp. 108–29.

the Chiriguana leaders he met made it clear to García Mosquera that they were prepared to become the monarch's vassals and accept the Catholic faith, but only under certain conditions. They would not allow any Spanish towns or villages near their settlements and neither work for Spaniards on farms nor undertake domestic chores they saw as 'only fit for women', since they perceived themselves to be warriors.[66] Since soldiers would join any Spanish expedition chiefly to gain access to extra land and native labour, this removed the main incentives for them, making Toledo's task impossible.

Meanwhile, in La Plata, following the arrival of García Mosquera from the southeastern Charcas border in December 1573 with the results of his enquiry and more top Chiriguana leaders, Toledo realised that he could keep them under arrest and return to his original plan to establish new border towns.[67] In effect, a month after García Mosquera returned to La Plata, on 22 January 1574 Toledo and Captain Luis de Fuentes y Vargas, a former *corregidor* in the border province of Chichas, who therefore had the knowledge and troops required for the task, signed a *capitulación* for the foundation of San Bernardo de la Frontera de Tarija near Chiriguana lands, clearly against the will of the Chiriguana as they had expressed it to García Mosquera.[68] With his hostages in La Plata and foundation of the first border town under way, Toledo could briefly taste victory, thinking that all this would potentially expand the Catholic monarchy's jurisdiction, strengthening the monarch's presence and his own authority in Charcas and along its borders in the process.

However, in an unpredictable turn to this political opera, a powerful storm hit La Plata in February 1574, washing away the viceroy's plan. Toledo's hostages took advantage of the confusion and escaped during the downpour, in what was a final blow to the viceroy's brief success. Without the Chiriguana leaders, who might have been able to force evangelisation and settlement, and the foundation of San Bernardo de la Frontera de Tarija already under way, Toledo had to rethink his plan and a decision to wage war against the border indigenous populations was made in a matter of days.[69]

6. Negotiating an expedition

As one political and theatrical stage had fallen, another was quickly set up. The organisation of a large-scale expedition required great skills. Toledo had

66 Mujía, *Bolivia–Paraguay*, Vol. II, p. 128.
67 Letter from Toledo to the King, 20 December 1573, in Levillier, *Gobernantes del Perú*, Vol. 5, p. 304.
68 Thierry Saignes, 'Andaluces en el poblamiento del Oriente Boliviano. En torno a unas figuras controvertidas. El fundador de Tarija y sus herederos', in *Actas de las II jornadas de Andalucía y América. Universidad Santa María de La Rábida. Marzo 1982*, Vol. 2, 1983, p. 177; Oliveto, 'Ocupación territorial', p. 166.
69 Lizárraga, *Descripción colonial*, Vol. 2, p. 134.

to consult notables, religious orders, *cabildos*, and the Audiencia de Charcas, again, before he could proceed. There were a few obstacles to overcome. As has been mentioned already, an uncooperative *encomendero* elite who were not prepared to abide by their duties to protect the indigenous peoples assigned to them presented a first challenge. They would only take part if they could obtain from the *entrada* native labour they could trade and/or use. Toledo expressed his frustration in a letter to the King, as follows:

> To draft only one *vecino* from this city as leader of these people [the expedition], even promising the governorship of Condorillo that Manso had [a reference to Andrés Manso's post as governor of the destroyed town of Condorillo and its jurisdiction], they would ask for more concessions than the French king asked from Your Majesty for the peace treaty [of Cateau-Cambrésis in 1559]. They wanted a grant of Indians for three lives. I tried to remind many of them of their duty [to come forward and fight] as *encomenderos*, and in the end I decided to allocate men from my own household [*casa*], as I did when I set up the companies [*compañías*] that went to wage war against the Incas [Vilcabamba] and that took reinforcements to Chile because of the unwillingness [to help] that I found in this land.[70]

A second obstacle was the monarchy's reluctance to let expedition members enslave any local people they could capture, and trade in them. Clear royal instructions and *cédulas reales* set out guidelines on how to carry on expeditions and they banned both the trade in and the enslavement of captives.[71] Faced with such restrictions, Toledo tried to circumvent them by putting

---

70 '[Q]ue para sacar un vezino de aqui por caudillo con esta gente y dándoles la governacion de condorillo que tuvo manso ni estava pidiendo mas capitulaciones que pudiera pedir el rey de Francia a vuestra magestad para hacer una paz y que le diesse un rrepartimiento de yndios en los de acá por tres vidas yo pensava dezir lo que la obligación que tenian como feudatarios ellos y los demás que la tuviesen se la haria cumplir y quando no oviese entre ellos quien quisiese encargarse de la jornada para servir a dios y a vuestra magestad y mostrar que avia persona entre ellos para ser caveza que yo ponia de mi cassa quien lo fuesse como lo avia hecho en las compañias que avia mandado hazer para la guerra de los yngas y socorro del reyno de chyle por la poca voluntad que avia hallado en los de la tierra.' Letter from Toledo to the King, 3 June 1573, in Levillier, *Gobernantes del Perú*, Vol. 5, p. 137. By peace with the French king, Toledo is referring here to the 1559 Peace of Cateau-Cambrésis between the Spanish Crown and France which brought to an end a sixty-five-year struggle for control of Italy. The Spanish Crown was left as the dominant power in the Italian peninsula.

71 'Instrucciones para hacer nuevos descubrimientos y poblaciones', Valladolid, 13 May 1556, in Konetzke, *Colección de documentos para la historia social de la formación de Hispanoamérica*, Vol. 1, pp. 335–39; Cédulas Reales of 1526, 1530, 1532, 1540, 1542, and 1543, in *Recopilación de leyes de los reynos de las Indias*, Vol. 2 (Madrid: Julián Paredes, 1681), Libro VI, Título II, De la libertad de los Indios, p. 194.

the matter to consultation, in a clear example of 'localisation of laws', a mechanism that played a significant role in helping the monarchy retain the loyalty of local elites.[72] Grounded in the tradition of 'I obey, but do not execute' (*obedezco, pero no cumplo*), although laws based on the instructions in the *cédulas reales* could have been collaboratively enacted and might have originated in petitions, those intructions were just for guidance and could be put aside if local circumstances made this necessary and there was a general consensus to do so.[73] Although Toledo never received confirmation from the monarch on this issue, he would follow local advice and let expedition members keep captives for a limited time, insisting merely that to trade in them was something not to be tolerated.

A third obstacle was the expedition's potentially astronomical cost. In theory, each *encomendero* would have to bring along a company of those they could recruit, plus their own clients and relatives, at their own expense. Although access to captives would provide an incentive, for an expedition of the type that Toledo was trying to assemble, with as much display and excess as possible, the few *vecinos* and *encomenderos* who were prepared to fight were not sufficient. The viceroy arranged a series of provisions that formally recognised the status of the *yanaconas* living in farms in Charcas, making their farm owners (*chacareros*) responsible for their well-being, including their defence, adding to the pool of people that could potentially be enlisted.[74] Toledo would also take his own clients and *criados* on the *entrada*, but they had to be rewarded commensurately with their status. Such rewards had to come from the royal coffers, something the viceroy had been trying to avoid up to this point. With silver mining in Potosí booming again, because of the introduction of the amalgamation of silver, Toledo received a windfall

72 Alejandro Agüero, 'Local Law and Localization of Law: Hispanic Legal Tradition and Colonial Culture (16th–18th Centuries)', in *Spatial and Temporal Dimensions for Legal History: Research Experiences and Itineraries* (Frankfurt am Main: Max Planck Institute for European Legal History, 2016); Richard Ross and Philip Stern, 'Reconstructing Early Modern Notions of Legal Pluralism', in *Legal Pluralism and Empires, 1500–1850* (New York, London: New York University Press, 2013), p. 112.

73 Cervantes attributes this approach to how the term *obedecer* was understood at the time, a meaning that was much closer to the Latin root of the word—*obedire*, which comes from *ob audire* or to listen. This meant that obedience was not primarily an act of the will but of the intelligence. Rather than unthinking submission to a command, therefore, the principle of *obedezco, pero no cumplo* allowed obedience to be understood as primarily a learning process, a matter of practical intelligence, where those in command and those who obeyed had come to share a common view. Cervantes, *Conquistadores*, p. 194.

74 'Provisión sobre los indios yanaconas de los Charcas', La Plata, 6 February 1574 in Guillermo Lohmann Villena and María Justina Sarabia Viejo (eds), *Francisco de Toledo: Disposiciones gubernativas para el virreinato del Perú. 1575–1581*, Vol. I (Seville: Escuela de Estudios Hispano-Americanos, 1986), pp. 289–97.

income from the *quintos real*, a tax due to the Crown of one-fifth of all silver extracted, that he could use to cover the initial costs of the expedition.[75]

Aware that he was circumventing royal instructions and *cédulas reales*, and because his questions about policy in this regard were never answered by the monarch, Toledo decided to cover his own back by collecting evidence in a *Quaderno de la Verdad de los Hechos de esta Tierra* ('True Account of the Events of this Land), a suggestive title for a file that was intended to gather all the evidence needed to justify the expedition. The first dossier to form part of this (now largely lost) file was a substantial report written by La Plata *encomendero* and jurist Licenciado Polo Ondegardo in May/June 1574, which tied the expedition to a strategic narrative in which the cannibal trope, among other stereotypes about the Chiriguanaes, suddenly and conveniently reappeared.[76] Polo de Ondegardo was an authority on Charcas and his opinions were held in high regard at the court in Spain; just what Toledo needed. Ondegardo raised the subject of the fate of indigenous peoples taken captive in war, suggesting that enslavement might be an option.

Toledo had consulted the Audiencia de Charcas in May 1573, when he first arrived in La Plata, and its judges had agreed to an eventual war with participation from local *encomenderos* and the possibility of the enslavement of captive Chiriguanaes. One of the firm supporters was Toledo's main ally in the Audiencia, judge Juan de Matienzo, who had already expressed his views on the subject in his political treatise.[77] Because the circumstances had changed dramatically in one year, since de Mendoza's rebellion in Santa Cruz de la Sierra had in effect created a new conflict in Charcas, the viceroy asked for the Audiencia's guidance again, successfully securing the support of the whole bench.[78]

One aspect missing from this theatre so far was the Catholic church. Toledo had to consult the religious orders and church authorities on these matters. Because of their jurisdiction over ecclesiastical matters, the Dean of Charcas Doctor Don Francisco Urquiso was consulted, as were members of religious orders settled in Charcas such as the Dominicans, the Augustinians, the Franciscans, and more importantly, the Mercedarians, an order largely associated with the rescue of captives which would play a substantial role along the southeastern Charcas border for many years after this *entrada*. One order was missing, the Jesuits, who had a difficult relationship with Toledo; the viceroy wanted them to play a more active role in the evangelisation effort by living among indigenous peoples, something that at that point they

---

75 Lizárraga, *Descripción colonial*, Vol. 2, p. 114.

76 AGI, Patronato, 235, R1, Ynformacion del excelentisimo señor visorrey del Peru sobre la cordillera de los chiriguanaes, images 52 to 61.

77 Matienzo, *Gobierno del Perú*, p. 257.

78 AGI, Patronato, 235, R2, [1573/1574], Parecer del presidente y oidores de las Audiencias de los Charcas y La Plata.

were reluctant to do.[79] With the exception of the absent Jesuits, all Catholic officials who were consulted endorsed Toledo's latest plans, agreeing that war against the Chiriguanaes was 'just' and that they could be taken captive by those who took part in the expedition.[80]

On 10 April 1574 Toledo wrote to tell the King that he was going to wage war on the Chiriguanaes at the head of an expedition that would penetrate the dense slopes inhabited by those groups, a dangerous and unknown theatre in which the expedition members had much to lose. As much as the risks involved alarmed the Audiencia, the viceroy insisted that the situation with the Chiriguanaes and the rebellion by de Mendoza had brought the monarchy into some disrepute. He viewed his quintessential role to be the King's alter ego and to take the monarch's presence to every corner of Peru, including the remote border, to confirm the Crown's sovereignty and jurisdiction.[81] He would travel now, at the helm of the body politic of Charcas, at centre-stage, in a true courtly procession, to the Andean slopes.

7. Toledo's journey to the borders

Owing to García Mosquera's knowledge of the land, Toledo appointed him the *entrada*'s guide. The viceroy and his entourage would face a long journey to the Chiriguanaes, one that suspiciously avoided Tomina and could have been significantly shorter. Toledo mistrusted García Mosquera, not without reason, as this new route kept the latter's Tomina network of Chiriguana allies safe.[82]

The plan was for two separate forces, one commanded by Toledo and the other by La Plata *encomendero* don Gabriel Paniagua de Loaysa, whose *encomienda* peoples were settled along the northeastern border of Charcas, an area exposed to Chiriguana raids. Born in Plasencia, Extremadura, don Gabriel had built a vast fortune that relied heavily on *encomienda* labour in Pojo and that was based, at the time, on agriculture and the production of cheap textiles.[83] He was one of only four among the Spaniards who went on the expedition who had the title 'don' (two others were Toledo and don Antonio de Meneses, Toledo's nephew), which reflected his position as the

79 Letter from Toledo to the King, 1 March 1572, in Antonio de Egaña (ed.), *Monumenta peruana (1565–1575)*, Vol. I (Rome: Monumenta Historica Societatis Iesu, 1954), pp. 453–54.

80 AGI, Patronato, 235, R5, [1574] Acuerdo que celebró el virrey con algunos prelados de religiones de la ciudad de La Plata, sobre si convendría hacer guerra a los indios chiriguanaes y declararlos por esclavos; BNE, Ms. 3,044, Papeles varios tocantes al gobierno de Indias, fols 302–03.

81 Letter from Toledo to the King, 10 April 1574, in Levillier, *Gobernantes del Perú*, Vol. 5, pp. 426–27.

82 Saignes and Combès, *Historia del pueblo chiriguano*, p. 195.

83 Presta, *Encomienda, familia y negocios en Charcas colonial*, pp. 104–05.

expedition's captain. Don Gabriel was asked to set out early, following the road to Santa Cruz de la Sierra, to find the Chiriguana leader Vitapué.[84]

The fourth 'don' was Toledo's distant relative and close ally, don Luis de Toledo Pimentel, who was appointed by Toledo Maese de Campo of the expedition. He was a grandson of don Fernando Alvarez de Toledo and a great-grandson of the duke of Alba, don Fadrique Segundo, whose father had been third cousin of Emperor Charles V.[85] After his participation in this *entrada*, don Luis was rewarded with a new post in Cusco, Castellano de la Fortaleza de Sacsahuamán, created by Toledo to honour him and please his relatives in Spain. This post was designed to oversee the protection of the 'city of the Incas' and came with a salary that would be raised from assets seized from Carlos Inca, a descendent of the rulers of Tahuantinsuyu, and his family, who were victims of Toledo's campaign to eradicate any memory of the Incas.[86]

Apart from the *hidalgos* and nobles, corporate bodies such as cities, towns, and villages were also represented in large events and this *entrada* commanded by the most powerful man in the land was no different. Giving it the character of a quasi-religious procession, the *vecinos* of La Plata and Potosí would be able to march in all their gallantry with their own captains at their head. Toledo appointed another political ally, someone close, Pedro de Zárate, to captain the *vecinos* of La Plata who took part in the expedition. This Basque conquistador had been active during the Hernández Girón rebellion (1553–1554) and had a high social and economic status (the product of mining and agriculture and also his marriage to doña Petronila de Castro, who enjoyed the *encomienda* of Omaguaca).[87] This marriage gave Zárate local prestige but also came with *encomendero* duties, which included responding to a call to arms by Toledo. Charcas' other main urban settlement, the Imperial Village of Potosí, the Crown's jewel, was also represented in the *entrada*. Toledo named his *criado* Juan Ortiz de Zárate captain of the town's *vecinos*. One of the viceroy's numerous courtiers (not the Charcas *encomendero* mentioned in Chapter Two), he had arrived in Peru in the same fleet that brought Toledo. Zárate's role at the helm of Potosí's *vecinos* might reflect some involvement with silver mining, an activity that thanks to the viceroy's efforts was booming with

84 Two other Spaniards with the titles of 'don', don Juan de Mendoza and don Francisco de Valenzuela, helped with Toledo's withdrawal from the frontier but did not take part in the expedition. Lizárraga, *Descripción colonial*, Vol. 2, p. 138; AGI, Patronato, 144, R1, [1608] Probanza de don Luis de Mendoza y Rivera.
85 Roberto Levillier, *Biografías de conquistadores de la Argentina. Siglo XVI* (Madrid: Juan Pueyo, 1928), pp. 225–28; Lizárraga, *Descripción colonial*, Vol. 2, p. 134.
86 Lohmann Villena and Sarabia Viejo (eds), *Francisco de Toledo: Disposiciones*, Vol. II, pp. 63–71; Hemming, *The Conquest of the Incas*, p. 434.
87 See Chapter Two in this book. Zanolli, *Tierra, encomienda e identidad*, pp. 112–16; Presta, *Encomienda, familia y negocios en Charcas colonial*, p. 243.

the construction of mills and large-scale use of mercury.[88] Both captains and their networks expected to benefit from their roles and proximity to the viceroy.

Andean chiefs and their subjects marched as key allies of Toledo in this expedition. The list includes Quillaca lord don Juan Colque Guarache, Yampara leader don Francisco Aymoro, Sacaca lord don Fernando Ayavire y Cuysara, and Pocoata *cacique* don Francisco de Ayra, although there were probably others, each representing the 'naciones de Charcas'. In a hierarchical society, they were assigned different roles as His Majesty's indigenous vassals. Their communities contributed greatly with men, supplies, and llamas and, as would occur in other forms of ceremonial, they marched wearing their traditional war garments. Walking in the footsteps of ancestors who had accompanied Diego de Almagro and the Incas before him to the borders, don Juan Colque Guarache travelled as 'captain of the Indians' of the expedition and was allowed to carry firearms. Don Juan was asked to recruit one hundred Indians from *encomiendas* and communities that had been affected by Chiriguana raids to command in the expedition.[89] In agreement with his community, don Fernando de Ayra supplied more than 500 Indians, more than 1,000 llamas loaded with materials, and donated 700 pesos to help with expedition expenses. Because the *entrada* was going to travel across Yampara lands, don Francisco Aymoro was tasked with the job of organising the expedition's supplies.[90] The 'naciones de Charcas' actively collaborated in this event that was seen as an opportunity for these indigenous groups to demonstrate their loyalty to the Crown and for their leaders to confirm their privileged position in the political system.[91]

88 Luis Romera Iruela and María del Carmen Galbís Diez, *Catalogo de pasajeros a Indias durante los siglos XVI, XVII y XVIII*, Vol. 1 (Sevilla: AGI, 1980), p. 287; Lizárraga, *Descripción colonial*, Vol. 2, pp. 138–39. AGI, Charcas, 85, N10, [1607] Informaciones de oficio y parte: Fernando de Irarrazábal y Andía, capitán. Información contenida de 1607. Con parecer de la Audiencia. Hay otra información de 1607 de sus méritos y servicios, y los de su padre Francisco de Irarrazábal y Andía, con una petición y un decreto al final de la misma de 1610, image 47.

89 See Appendix 1, 'Voices of the expedition', with documents. The list includes 24 Yampara Indians, 24 Indians from the Tababuco *encomienda* assigned to Martín de Almendras, 21 Condes and Incas Gualparoca Indians, 20 Moyos-Moyos, Churumatas, Lacaxa, and Suires; and 20 Indians from the *encomienda* of Hernando Sedano. AGI, Charcas 57, [1622] Información de méritos y servicios de don Diego Copatete Guarache, fols 1r–1v.

90 AGI, Charcas, 79, N22, 1592–1593, [1592–1593] Informaciones de oficio y parte: Francisco Aymozo [*sic*], cacique principal y gobernador de los indios yamparaes de Yotala y Quilaquila; AGI, Charcas 53, [1574–1576], Juan Colque Guarache; AGI, Charcas, 56, 1638, Probanza de Francisco Ayra de Ariutu, in Platt, Bouysse-Cassagne, and Harris (eds), *Qaraqara–Charka*, p. 722; AGI, Charcas, 45, Memorial de Charcas, in Platt, Bouysse-Cassagne, and Harris (eds), *Qaraqara–Charka*, p. 840.

91 This highlights the importance of native auxiliaries in these *entradas*. Raquel Guereca

Toledo's expedition was the perfect stage-set for the display of liberality and magnanimity, two courtly values that underpinned the ties between patrons and clients and cemented honour and prestige.[92] It was a 'court on the move', where *encomenderos* were expected to fight as knights, following the values of the nobility. The example was Philip II's court in Madrid and the set was expected to replicate such a court on the Andean slopes. No expense was spared in this 'big joust' on Chiriguana territory.[93] Two years after the event, the president of the Audiencia de Charcas, Lope Diez de Armendáriz, in a long letter to the King revisiting Toledo's time in Peru, wrote:

> the war that the viceroy waged against the Chiriguanaes Indians, as soon as it was agreed, was organised by gathering so many people, wearing clothes and carrying ornaments that were not appropriate for an enterprise that consisted of conquering savage Indians in such a harsh land; [moreover,] for that journey it was not necessary to carry the viceroy in his litter and other embarrassing things that occurred were all done at the expense of Your Majesty; and the Spanish and Indians put everyone at risk because of a lack of supplies; and to punish those barbarians it would only have been necessary to employ captains with expertise in such matters and not the feathers, silks, and trappings that cowardly wars exhibit; thus, this war was of little benefit to Spaniards and Indians, and made the Chiriguanaes more courageous.[94]

Durán, *Milicias indígenas en la América Hispana* (San Antonio, TX: UNAM San Antonio, 2023).

92 Quondam and Torres Corominas, *El discurso cortesano*.

93 Figures for total cost range from 200,000 pesos or 275,000 ducados to 500,000 pesos. This last figure was equivalent to 1,000 town homes in La Plata at the time. For the figure of 200,000 ducados: AGI, Patronato, 137, N1, R2, [1598] Luis de Fuentes y Vargas, fol. 2r; for that of half a million pesos, López Villalva (dir.), *Acuerdos de la Real Audiencia de La Plata de los Charcas*, Vol. 2, 25 November 1574, p. 472; for an estimate of 300,000 pesos, letter from Franciscan Juan de Almagro to Pedro de Segura, 23 October 1583, in Mujía, *Bolivia–Paraguay*, Vol. II, p. 504.

94 '[L]a guerra que hizo el virrey a los yndios chiriguanaes no fue bien acordada de emprenderse por la horden que se hizo con tanto aparato de gente tan atauiada de vestidos y ornatos que no erán decentes ni de efeto para semejante enpresa de conquistar vnos saluages en tierra tan fragosa y aspera y para aquella jornada no auía para que fuese el uirrey en persona especial auiendo de lleuar como lleuo literas y otras cosas de grande enbaraco y haziendo tan ecesiua costa a vuestra magestad y a los españoles y naturales y poniendose a si y a todos en tan gran peligro por la falta que forsosamente auia de tener de mantenimientos y para el castigo de aquellos barbaros bastaua enbiar a algunos capitanes de los mas praticos de esta tierra que fueran con menos gente escogida y exercitada en estas entradas y con el aparejo y horden que se suele tener lo vuieran hecho como se requeria y lo pedia la disposición de la tierra y no· con plumas y sedas y arreos que acostunbran traerse en las guerras de cobardia y asi esta guerra· füe sin prouecho alguno y tan costosa y de tanto daño para españoles y para los yndios que estauan de paz que a sido grande lastima

And indeed, there were plenty of feathers, silk, and trappings, dressing not only the 300 to 400 Spaniards that accompanied the viceroy in his journey, 'la flor del Perú', but also those who went along with them, including numerous African slaves, a number of Catholic priests, around 2,000 horses, and 1,500–3,000 native auxiliaries and their Andean *caciques* who, all lined up, would march into the Chiriguana mountains in a formation that stretched for several miles.[95] Banners, flags, and religious images completed the colourful image. The noise of men and animals on the move was accompanied by drums and Andean musical instruments that brought sound to the animated yet still solemn crowd. As part of the set, Toledo was carried in his own litter, surrounded by men in whom he had extreme confidence, who were known among the other expedition members as 'lions', probably reflecting both the animals in the coat of arms of Castile and these men's alleged ferocity in action. Close to them would be the *paje de guión*, carrying the viceroy's coat of arms, a privilege only conceded to monarchs and their 'living images'.[96] As unreasonable as it sounded to Armendáriz, and he probably echoed many others who shared his thoughts at the time, Toledo, the loyal royal official who had been involved in so many military engagements in Europe, would be carried in great fashion and display, emulating the battlefields of Flanders

ver lo que an padecido todos en esta prouincia y fue enriquecer y dar animo a los chiriguanaes de mas de la autoridad'. Letter from Lope Diez de Armendariz to the King, 25 September 1576, in Levillier, *La Audiencia de Charcas*, Vol. 1, p. 371.

95 For the figures of Spanish and native auxiliaries see Ruy Díaz de Guzmán, *Relación de la entrada a los chiriguanos* (Santa Cruz de la Sierra: Fundación Cultural 'Ramón Darío Gutierrez', 1979 [1615]), p. 75; AGI, Patronato, 131, N1, R3, [1587] Información de los méritos y servicios de Hernando de Cazorla, maese de campo general, hechos en la conquista de Perú, sirviendo particularmente contra Gonzalo Pizarro y en varias batallas contra indios levantados, fol. 10v; AGI, Patronato, 133, R5, [1591] Información de los méritos y servicios de Francisco de Guzmán y Juan de Rivamartín, que sirvieron en Nueva España y después pasaron a Perú hacia 1537 y se hallaron en la conquista de aquel reino y de los indios chiriguanaes, image 194; AGI, Patronato, 137, N1, R2, [1598] Luis de Fuentes y Vargas, fol. 2r; López Villalva (dir.), *Acuerdos de la Real Audiencia de La Plata de los Charcas*, Vol. 2, 25 November 1574, p. 472; Barco Centenera, *Argentina y conquista del Rio de la Plata*, fol. 126. For approximate lists of those who went with Almendras to the Chichas (see Chapter Two), and with Toledo and Lozano Machuca to the Chiriguanaes, see Appendix 2 to this book.

96 AGI, Lima, 213, N4, [1600] Informaciones de oficio y parte: Álvaro Ruíz de Navamuel, secretario de la gobernación del Perú y secretario de la Audiencia de Lima. Consta también la información de Sebastián Sánchez de Merlo, vecino de Lima, secretario de la Audiencia de Panamá, que marchó al Perú con Cristóbal Vaca de Castro, image 138, statement by Friar Gerónimo de Salcedo; AGI, Lima, 212, N19, [1599] Informaciones de oficio y parte: Juan de Reinoso, paje del virrey Francisco de Toledo, vecino de Lima, pacificador de los chiriguanas en Charcas, luchó contra los ingleses en Panamá. Información y parecer de la Audiencia de Lima.

and Naples, to the Andean slopes where his expedition would encounter an exuberant environment and fierce indigenous peoples.

The expedition assembled, over a period of two weeks, in the valley of Yotala, not far from La Plata, from where it began marching on 2 June 1574 in a formation that could be seen from afar (see Figure 0.1 for the route followed by the *entrada*). It stopped first in a farm in the valley of Pocopoco to rebuild supplies, then followed the course of the Pilcomayo River. Although correctly timed, as it reached the river during the dry season, the expedition was slowed down by a voluminous river that had not narrowed sufficiently to let men and animals cross safely, a reminder to Toledo that he was about to penetrate a geography totally alien to the Spanish.[97] It took the expedition a whole month to reach the intersection of the Pilcomayo and Pilaya rivers, from where in July 1574 Toledo finally entered Chiriguana territory.[98] At that point, the viceroy was increasingly frustrated with García Mosquera because of the time and effort involved to reach the border. The captain was guiding the expedition with support from 'friendly' Chiriguanaes.[99] Although they were key to any *entrada*, the participation of Chiriguana factions in such events has been largely overlooked, yet it is a reminder of how politically fractured the Chiriguanaes were, how the Spanish exploited these divisions to their own advantage, and, how different Chiriguana groups manipulated the Spanish to attack rival factions.

At this point, Toledo became aware that perhaps the route followed on advice from García Mosquera had not been the best choice and decided to dismiss him, sending him to Potosí, where he was kept under arrest.[100] García Mosquera's plan to avoid Tomina had paid off and his allies at home were

---

97 AGI, Patronato, 126, R17, [1606] Pedro de Cuéllar Torremocha, fols 64r–64v., statement by Augustinian friar Alonso de Torrejon; AGI, Patronato, 235, R4, [1574] Relación de lo que se hizo en la jornada que el excelentisimo virrey del Piru Don Francisco de Toledo, images 5–6; Oliveto, 'Ocupación territorial', p. 163. Levillier gives a different route, without indicating the source or documents that he used, only mentioning that it can be followed on a map drawn in 1588, and writes that the expedition left late in May 1574, reaching Tarabuco first and from there travelling to Tomina, Villar, Pomabamba, crossing the Pilcomayo River afterwards, entering Chiriguana land through Pilaya and ending thirty leagues from Tarija on 8 August 1574: Levillier, *Nueva Crónica*, p. 32. This route does not match the sites indicated by the documents that were consulted for this book. The 1588 map does not show the actual route followed by this expedition.

98 Lizárraga, *Descripción colonial*, Vol. 2, p. 179.

99 Pifarré mentions, without quoting any source, that Chiriguanaes were also guides. Pifarré, *Historia de un pueblo*, Vol. 2, p. 57.

100 BNE, Ms 3,044, Papeles varios tocantes al gobierno de Indias, http://bdh-rd.bne. es/viewer.vm?id=0000023047&page=1, accessed 29 April 2024. García Mosquera was eventually freed by the Audiencia de Charcas. AGI, Patronato, 235, R4, [1574] Relación de lo que se hizo en la jornada que el excelentisimo virrey del Piru Don Francisco de Toledo, fol. 8; Saignes and Combès, *Historia del pueblo chiriguano*, p. 192.

safe, which was more than the viceroy could say for himself and his men. Toledo was in an insect-infested environment that was home not only to indigenous people who were hostile and elusive, but also to dangerous fauna and poisonous flora. Now relying solely on the experience and knowledge of the Chiriguanaes who had accompanied the expedition, it set up camp either at a site known as Chimbuy or in company of a Chiriguana leader of that name—the sources are not clear on this point.[101] The viceroy's next mission would be to bring to the camp those Chiriguana leaders that had escaped La Plata, or any other with status among the Chiriguana, to compel their submission to royal authority, repeating political rituals that royal armies had traditionally followed elsewhere across the territories of the Catholic monarchy.

In the meantime, don Gabriel Paniagua de Loaysa had left his *encomienda* base in Pojo with a group of 120 men, following the road to Santa Cruz de la Sierra. In contrast to Toledo's formation, don Gabriel carried with him well experienced men, including two leading captains: Hernando de Cazorla and Melchor de Rodas. Veterans of the Peruvian civil wars, both had interests in the border area.[102] Don Gabriel's journey was not easy and there were a few skirmishes, but guidance and possibly support from some Chiriguana factions made the whole adventure less troubled. Still, he and his men never accomplished the task of taking any important prisoners for Toledo.

Although Toledo and his close allies were better sheltered from the harshness of the experience than others, life in the viceroy's camp was a world away from the comforts of La Plata and the court of the King in Madrid. Large tents were erected, banners displayed, and an army of servants was constantly on the move, trying to turn a geography perceived by the Spanish as *aspera* and *fragosa* (rough) into something more agreeable. Daily routines were only interrupted for the occasional mass or other religious celebration hosted by one of the Franciscan or Augustinian priests that accompanied the viceroy. Toledo decided to send Captain Juan Ortiz de Zárate and *maese de campo* don Luis de Toledo Pimentel to find the elusive Chiriguana leaders in their settlements and bring them 'to justice'. Both were unsuccessful, to the viceroy's frustration.[103] In preparation for the arrival of the Spanish, the Chiriguanaes had largely abandoned their settlements, taking refuge in the

101 Levillier, *Gobernación de Tucumán. Probanzas de méritos y servicios*, Vol. 2, p. 569; AGI, Contaduria, 1805, [1575] Gastos de la guerra de los chiriguanaes, fol. 291.

102 AGI, Patronato, 131, N1, R3, [1587] Hernando de Cazorla; ABNB, EC 1618, [1574] Probanza de Melchor de Rodas; Lizárraga, *Descripción colonial*, Vol. 2, p. 138.

103 AGI, Patronato, 126, R18, [1582] Información de los méritos y servicios de Roque de Cuéllar y de su hijo Pedro, en la conquista y pacificación de Perú con el licenciado Gasca, persiguiendo además a los tiranos de aquel reino, image 30, statement by Francisco de Saavedra Ulloa; AGI, Patronato, 235, R4, [1574] Relación de lo que se hizo en la jornada que el excelentisimo virrey del Piru Don Francisco de Toledo, fol. 5v.

dense and impenetrable forests. They were also playing tricks with their visitors, leaving behind cauldrons with human remains to remind the Spanish of their alleged cannibal credentials, or burning down their settlements, making it impossible for the Spanish to feed themselves and their animals.[104]

The expedition was connected to La Plata by a network of messengers and posts. Regular caravans of llamas brought the provisions that the viceregal camp constantly needed. The supply network depended on a small fortress that Captain Pedro de Zárate set up at the intersection of the Pilaya and Paspaya rivers, and the Chiriguanaes were aware of this. They began sporadic attacks on the fortress and even managed to besiege it. At risk of losing such a precious connection, Toledo was forced to send a small group of men to support Zárate and lift the pressure.[105] Without any hostages to take back for justice, and unable to even fight the Chiriguanaes, at this point it became obvious that Toledo's bombastic display in the Andean slopes had moved from epic to tragedy in a matter of months. Overwhelmed by food and water shortages, with native auxiliaries deserting the camp in growing numbers, morale hit a new low. To complicate matters, Toledo contracted an illness and, suffering from a high temperature, was almost delirious.[106]

Alarmed at the circumstances, the Audiencia de Charcas quickly assembled a rescue effort to bring Toledo and the expedition members back, this time using the shorter route through Tomina. A total of 2,000 llamas carrying food supplies accompanied with reinforcements were sent to provide the expedition with some relief. Still at centre-stage, Toledo was placed in his litter, and in the company of his starving and gaunt men started his journey back from the Andean slopes, leaving behind a trail of bodies, dead horses and llamas, and numerous native auxiliaries in captivity at the hands of the Chiriguanaes.[107] Peru's most powerful man was a mere reflection of his pre-expedition self. Toledo had gone to the eastern slopes to defeat 'the

---

104 Lizárraga, *Descripción colonial*, Vol. 2, p. 145.

105 AGI, Patronato, 124, R11, [1580] Información de los méritos y servicios de don Fernando de Zárate en la conquista del reino de Perú, castigo y persecución de los indios chiriguanaes con don Francisco de Toledo. Son dos informaciones. Statement by Pedro de Zárate; Levillier, *Gobernación de Tucumán. Probanzas de méritos y servicios*, Vol. 2, statement by Gutierre Velazquez de Ovando, pp. 568–69.

106 An early seventeenth-century chronicle refers to an ambush by the Chiriguanaes, in which many Spaniards and more than 500 native auxiliaries lost their lives, as the final blow to the expedition. This is not mentioned anywhere else but might have prompted the end of the *entrada*. Díaz de Guzmán, *Relación de la entrada a los chiriguanos*, p. 74.

107 'Relación de la ciudad de Santa Cruz de la Sierra por su gobernador don Lorenzo Suárez de Figueroa' [1586] in Espada, *Relaciones geográficas de Indias: Perú*, Vol. II, p. 166; AGI, Patronato, 237, R7, [1582] Información hecha por la justicia de la villa de Santiago de la Frontera, en virtud de Real Provisión, sobre la conducta y trato que observaban los indios chiriguanaes, fol. 56v; Barco Centenera, *Argentina y conquista del Rio de la Plata*, fol. 127.

cannibals', but he left with these same peoples chasing him. As the curtain closed on the expedition's stage, the viceroy finally reached Tomina where he had to convalesce for many months before he could return to his duties and deal with the legacy of his short jungle adventure; while what was left of the 'flor del Perú' tried to regain strength after its shocking experience. The *entrada* did very little for the reputation of those involved and for the image of the monarchy.

8. The legacy of defeat

At the close of his long Visita General, and in preparation for his return to Spain, Toledo paid a visit to his physician Doctor Sánchez de Renedo in Lima. The years on the move had taken their toll on the viceroy, who looked ill. Sánchez de Renedo stressed, as part of a wider enquiry into his patient's health, 'when his excellency arrived in this city [Lima] from the highland provinces this witness could not recognise him'.[108] The King's living image had lost its lustre. As much as Audiencia de Charcas president Licenciado Pedro Ramírez de Quiñones tried to justify the expedition, explaining that it had helped to set free natives that the Chiriguanaes held captive and improved the knowledge the Spanish had of the area, the effort and expense involved, plus the loss of unaccounted lives, certainly amounted to more than the value of a small group of captives, who could have been set free from the Chiriguanaes in trade, and some limited geographical knowledge of settlements that were occasionally moved.[109] Although the viceroy had travelled into the Chiriguanaes with hopes of restoring confidence in the monarchy, he left with his own reputation and that of the monarchy temporarily in tatters.

While still in Peru, Toledo started hearing public criticism of his actions. This came from an unexpected quarter, in fact from a religious order that under clear instructions from its superiors had not taken part in the expedition: the Jesuits.[110] As part of a large case that involved the Inquisition, papers with derogatory comments about Toledo's viceregal rule were found among the possessions of Jesuit Luis de López during his arrest on charges of raping the sister of Jesuit brother Martín Pizarro. In relation to the expedition, López accused Toledo of waging an unjust war that involved great loss

---

108 AGI, Patronato, 190, R25, [1578] Información recibida a petición del virrey de Perú, don Francisco de Toledo, sobre las enfermedades que padecía en aquel reino, y edad que tenía cuando fue a él, image 4.

109 Letter from Licenciado Pedro Ramírez de Quiñones to the King, 6 May 1575, in Levillier, *La Audiencia de Charcas*, Vol. 1, p. 328.

110 Jesuit father Joseph de Acosta went only up to the Pilcomayo River, which was a limit that separated land seen as the 'land of indigenous peoples at war'—*tierra de Indios de guerra*—from the territory of those who had been settled by the Spanish. León Lopetegui, *El Padre José de Acosta S.I. y las misiones* (Madrid: Consejo Superior de Investigaciones Científicas. Instituto Gonzalo Fernández de Oviedo, 1942), p. 132.

of life among the Spanish, Chiriguanaes, and loyal indigenous peoples. In his papers, López expressed what many others were already thinking and remarking behind Toledo's back. The viceroy penned his answer, stressing a favourable outcome to the expedition—the establishment of new border towns, San Bernardo de la Frontera de Tarija and Santiago de la Frontera de Tomina—and the cessation of regular Chiriguana raids and attacks along the border, though this latter statement was a world away from reality.[111]

Many of the viceroy's *criados* and clients—la flor del Perú—had gone on the *entrada* on the understanding that the merit of being there would be followed by some form of remuneration. As the King's alter ego, Toledo shared royal authority with both Audiencias, that of Lima and Charcas, over the distribution and management of privileges and rewards.[112] Before leaving on his final journey to Spain, the viceroy left a document giving clear instructions over the rewards to be distributed among those loyal to the Catholic monarchy during his period of office, and who should receive them. Although wrongly catalogued, the document dates from 1579, when Toledo still had two years left as viceroy, and includes a list of recipients who had accompanied him to the rough land of the Chiriguanaes. The rewards range from significant privileges—such as the post of Corregidor of Cusco, given to don Gabriel Paniagua de Loaysa—to smaller ones such as permanent posts as members of companies of soldiers such as *Lanzas* or *Arcabuces*, or shares of revenues from vacant *encomiendas*. Privileges such as those granted by Toledo always reflected not only the recent history of the beneficiaries' merits but also their social status and ancestry.[113] As Juan de Matienzo said of such *mercedes*,

> such rewards are like water, that makes things grow; and although it is true that subjects and vassals are obliged to be loyal, to serve and defend their prince and their land, they are also deserving of remuneration and rewards if, in order to defend land and prince, they fought and worked [hard].[114]

111 The document with Lopez's comments can be found in José Sancho Rayon and Francisco de Zabalburu, *Colección de documentos inéditos para la historia de España*, vol. XCIV (Madrid: M. Ginesta y Hermanos, 1889), pp. 479, 494; Sabine Hyland, *The Jesuit and the Incas: The Extraordinary Life of Padre Blas Valera, S.J* (Ann Arbor: University of Michigan Press, 2003), p. 86.

112 Clavero, 'Justicia y gobierno. Economía y gracia', p. 10.

113 AGI, Patronato, 189, R26, [1569 *sic*] [1579] Relaciones de las mercedes hechas por Francisco de Toledo, virrey de Perú, a los sujetos que se expresan en dichas relaciones.

114 '[P]orque este premio es como el agua, que hace crecer todas las cosas; y aunque sea verdad que los súbditos y vasallos son obligados a ser fieles, y servir y defender a su príncipe, y a su tierra, pero todavía son más dignos de remuneración y que se les haga Mercedes sí, por defensión de la tierra e por su príncipe, hobieren peleado y trabaxado'. Matienzo, *Gobierno del Perú*, p. 324.

Many of these men would stay in Charcas and Peru long after Toledo left, yet the rewards took a long time to materialise, if they did at all. In many cases the only record left is a few short paragraphs in a report of merits and services drafted by the relatives and descendants of these men years after the expedition.

Toledo continued to defend his record in the Chiriguana border region, mentioning how the monarchy's policy had been followed with the establishment of new towns. In effect, San Bernardo de la Frontera de Tarija had been founded, only to be moved to a new location after a brief period, one that was far enough from Chiriguanaes settlements to avoid regular raids. Sheltered by García Mosquera and his network, Tomina fared better. The town founded there, Santiago de la Frontera, had a more positive start, yet still faced the occasional conflict with neighbouring Chiriguana factions. In fact, what Toledo's expedition demonstrated was that if the Crown was to extend, implement, and consolidate its jurisdiction on the Charcas southeastern border it had to rely on local knowledge, on captains like Garcia Mosquera and his father-in-law Pedro de Segura Zavala who were part of larger groups that combined *mestizos*, poor Spaniards and even Chiriguanaes. They had the skills and tools to broker agreements in the politically fractured world of these local peoples.

9. The endless possibilities of a localised empire and the limits of a viceroy

This chapter has tried to challenge an image of don Francisco de Toledo, built in the twentieth century, as a law maker, strategist, and state-builder, by rescuing from the past a largely overseen chapter of his administration, his expedition to the Chiriguanaes in 1574. Through an approach that has prioritised the political culture of the time, which was largely imbued with theatrical representations and performativity, the chapter has aimed to portray a different image of Toledo, redimensioning the viceroy's role, which presents an invitation to revise the historiographical treatment of his time as viceroy of Peru. In doing so, this chapter has exposed the limitations Toledo faced, proposing a revision of scholarly views that see royal rule in a top-down manner, with a Crown and a legion of unchallenged royal officials dictating and implementing legislation, suggesting the value of a more bottom-up, localised approach. Toledo had to adapt his plans as he faced new obstacles and was forced to debate and try to build consensus for a costly, large-scale *entrada* against the backdrop of unwilling *encomenderos*, Audiencia de Charcas judges who stood on the side watching the tragedy unfold, a *mestizo* captain with his own agenda, and Chiriguana groups who, despite being taken hostage, always remained in control of the whole situation. Toledo had to negotiate the monarch's presence in Charcas and was forced to make adjustments in line with the needs and aspirations of local elites. In this political environment, as the King's living image approached the humid and dense

eastern slopes, the outcome of the poorly conceived expedition was predictable. Madness was the moment of truth for the delirious viceroy. Toledo was
lucky to escape the Chiriguanaes alive.

His defeat was not just a personal blow; it was the last occasion when a
Peruvian viceroy ventured into Charcas. The Crown would find other ways
of making itself present in these remote borders, without having to tacitly, or
explicitly, consent to exposing the King's alter ego to dangerous conditions,
playing an out-of-date role of conquistador or *adelantado*. With the expansion
of villages and towns along the border, the land would become 'politically
equipped' with *cabildos*, captains, lieutenants, and *corregidores* and the King
would expand his jurisdiction. This was a process that because of the
polycentric and flexible character of the monarchy and its laws, indirectly and
surprisingly, involved the Chiriguanaes who continued to resist, accommodate, and oppose Spanish jurisdiction with interfactional conflicts and the
trade in captive lowlanders, a trade often endorsed by royal agents along the
border who even got involved occasionally. The monarchy accepted that the
border was a land of warring indigenous peoples (*tierra de Indios de guerra*),
and politically incorporated that reality into policies that constantly shifted
from violence through minor expeditions, to attempts to evangelise these
indigenous groups. This was also a status that border people felt proud of,
seeing themselves as heroes capable of enduring the challenges of the area.
As elusive and hostile as they were, in the King's eyes, the Chiriguanaes were
still indigenous peoples and, in exercise of the arrangements between the
monarchy and the Catholic church, it was understood that he had a right to
punish and bring Catholic instruction to these indigenous groups.

Toledo's defeat was seen a personal failure and not a structural problem
of a global monarchy that always struggled to integrate politically fractured
groups such as the Chiriguanaes, who inhabited an environment that apart
from farming offered little other than a life of discomfort for Spaniards and
mestizos prepared to live there. Toledo had been given the task of running
Peru as the King's living image and a long *residencia* or review process would
wait for him in Spain. It would hopefully give those involved in the expedition the chance to vent their grievances. It would also save the monarchy's
name and reputation, allowing the body politic to separate a minister from
the actual monarchy, to separate bad or good government from the political
fiction of a just and loving monarch that it tried so hard to keep going. It
would, finally, foster the illusion that, while royal officials could be good or
bad and came and went, the Catholic monarchy would never cease to exist
and always had the best interest of its vassals at heart, securing its endurance
and resilience for many centuries to come.[115]

Toledo had been preparing his return to Spain from the moment he landed
in Peru in 1569. To please his master King Philip II, he had sent not only

---

115 Herzog, *Ritos de control*, p. 51.

Figure 3.3   Drawing of the death of don Francisco de Toledo, taken from don
Felipe Guamán Poma de Ayala's *Nueva Coronica y Buen Gobierno* of 1615
Source: Royal Danish Library, GKS 223: Guaman Poma, *Nueva corónica y buen gobierno* (c. 1615). Page [458 [460]].

manuscripts, but paintings (*paños*) depicting the rulers of Tahuantinsuyu, bezoar stones, ceramic bowls, and golden idols.[116] As ardently as Toledo pursued a meeting with Philip II, this never happened. The former viceroy of Peru, who was once the most powerful man in that troubled part of the Indies, the strategist and organiser, was kept in Lisbon, as far from the Madrid court as possible, until a short time before his death in Escalona on 21 April 1582. His *residencia* process continued for years.[117]

116 Catherine Julien, 'History and Art in Translation: The *Paños* and Other Objects Collected by Francisco de Toledo', *Colonial Latin American Historical Review* 8, no. 1 (1999): pp. 61–89.

117 Zimmerman, *Francisco de Toledo*, pp. 274–75.

CHAPTER FOUR

Downscaling Politics
A Royal Official Travels to the Borders

'Quien fue para ganar la tierra, también será para gobernarla,
tan bien como otros y aún mejor, por el mejor derecho, práctica
y obligación que para ello tienen.'

'Those who went to conquer the land, could also rule it, as well
or even better than others, because of their use of law, practice
and the duty that they feel for it.'

Don Bernardo Vargas Machuca, 1599[1]

'Y sabe este testigo que en las cosas de la guerra de yndios
[Pedro Segura Zavala] es hombre platico [*sic*] y que les trata muy
bien porque este testigo a venido en su compania por tierra de
guerra.'

'And this witness knows that in matters of warring Indians
[Pedro Segura Zavala] is a practical man as he treats them very
well, because this witness has travelled in his company across
land at war.'

Captain Gaspar de Rojas, 1581[2]

---

1 Don Bernardo Vargas Machuca, *Milicia y descripción de las Indias*, 2 vols (Madrid: Libreria de Victoriano Suárez, 1892 [1599]), Vol. 1, p. 48. Translation by this book's author.
2 AGI, Patronato, 125. R4, [1582] Probanza de Pedro de Segura, image 31. Translation by this book's author.

1. Introduction

In this chapter, the book moves from a viceroy's highly formal journey to the Chiriguanaes, to an expedition undertaken by one of that same viceroy's many *criados*; and from Toledo's 'travelling court' to the permanent stage that was the court around the Audiencia de Charcas. It also shifts from the vast geography that Toledo covered in his Visita General, to the space strictly under the jurisdiction of the Audiencia de Charcas. This chapter offers a more localised study of the political dynamics of post-Toledan Charcas, challenging views developed in the nineteenth century that see the Crown at the time as a centralising and centralised authority.[3] It further asks whether the view that contrasts political centres with peripheries is inappropriate, given the dynamics of the period that clearly emphasise the monarchy's polycentric character. In effect, in this composite monarchy the king was monarch of each political entity individually and had a special connection with each of his possessions and the populations living in them.[4] In this regard, it is argued here that there were as many centres as agents with jurisdiction, and that the implementation of laws and the display of authority were negotiated at a local level. Through the process of confirmation, settlement, and expansion of jurisdiction already described in earlier chapters, the Crown downscaled the political space, handing its agents a high degree of independence, which also sheltered its reputation and image from any criticism that might result from their actions. Any wrongdoing found through a *residencia* process, or a trial, would be the result of 'bad government' (*mal gobierno*), and would have little to do with the Crown itself, which would avoid any adverse judgement.[5] Authority, therefore, was not negotiated between the centre and the periphery, but within and between any of the multiple centres that were part of this global entity, through petitioning, localising laws and regulations, and adapting them to diverse circumstances. It was the outcome of communicative processes recently described as 'empowering interactions'.[6] The concept of 'miniature politics' encapsulates this process and was behind

---

3 On the discussion over centralisation as a critical feature of the 'state' see António Manuel Hespanha, *Vísperas del Leviatán. Instituciones y poder político (Portugal, siglo XVII)*. Trans. Fernando Jesús Bouza Alvarez (Madrid: Taurus, 1989), Introduction; José Javier Ruiz Ibáñez, *Las dos caras de Jano: Monarquía, ciudad e individuo. Murcia, 1588–1648* (Murcia: Universidad de Murcia, 1995), p. 360.

4 Javier Barrientos Grandón, *El gobierno de las Indias* (Madrid: Marcial Pons, 2004), p. 100.

5 Hespanha, *La gracia del derecho*, pp. 100, 105; Colin MacLachlan, *Spain's Empire in the New World: The Role of Ideas in Institutional and Social Change* (Berkeley: University of California Press, 1991), p. 125.

6 Wim Blockmans, André Holenstein, and Jon Mathieu, eds, *Empowering Interactions: Political Cultures and the Emergence of the State in Europe, 1300–1900* (Farnham, Burlington, VT: Ashgate, 2009), p. 25.

the monarchy's adaptability and endurance. This chapter explores in detail the different tensions and multiple agendas behind the groups involved in the discussions and organisation of a new, large-scale, war effort against the Chiriguanaes at a critical time for Peru in general, and Charcas in particular.

The successor to don Francisco de Toledo as Peru's viceroy, don Martín Enríquez de Almanza y Ulloa, died in 1583. His death left the monarchy's wealthiest and most challenging viceroyalty without a head, replicating the situation that had prevailed in the mid-1560s. In Peru, the two Audiencias of Lima and Charcas began to quarrel over their jurisdictions as they had done two decades earlier. However, during those two decades the Audiencia de Charcas had consolidated its position and by the early 1580s, and in the absence of a viceroy, it would have an excellent opportunity to demonstrate this. Because of growing attacks and raids by the Chiriguanaes, partly blamed on the defeat of Toledo's expedition, the Audiencia immediately took control of some viceregal matters, including the organisation of an expedition to the border lands involving three separate forces. Two of the forces would be headed by persons mentioned in Chapter Three: Lorenzo Suárez de Figueroa, who was the governor of Santa Cruz de la Sierra at the time, and Luis de Fuentes y Vargas, the founder and *corregidor* of Tarija. Because of their official positions, they had jurisdiction over two different sections of the border, the first along the eastern side of the Chiriguana border for Santa Cruz de la Sierra and the second south of the border for Tarija, where they each had the duty to protect indigenous peoples and Spaniards from the Chiriguanaes. A third force would be headed by someone with no Charcas border experience, one of Toledo's *criados*, Juan Lozano Machuca. His participation in this punitive campaign has been given a low profile by historiography of the period, yet Lozano Machuca played a key role in supplying the funding that was needed to bring the Audiencia's campaign to fruition.[7] Ambitious and lettered, Lozano Machuca was the perfect viceregal courtier, yet he was certainly not someone suitable to lead a border expedition. A royal official based in Potosí, with access to royal funds and resources from his vast social network, Lozano Machuca saw in an *entrada* an opportunity to gain wealth and status and was well placed to provide the necessary support.[8]

This chapter explains how, at a challenging time along these borders, the Audiencia de Charcas temporarily moved from the largely consultative and subordinate role it had adopted under Viceroy Toledo to a more executive one, as it had done not long after its establishment two decades

7 Pifarré, *Historia de un pueblo*, Vol. 2, p. 79; Saignes and Combès, *Historia del pueblo chiriguano*, p. 56; García Recio, *Análisis*, p. 103.

8 David Alonso García, 'Guerra, hacienda y política. Las finanzas militares en los inicios de la Edad Moderna', in *Los nervios de la guerra. Estudios sociales sobre el ejército de la Monarquía Hispánica (s. XVI–XVIII): Nuevas perspectivas* (Granada: Editorial Comares, 2007), pp. 37–57.

earlier. Chapter Three demonstrated how the judges in the Audiencia de Charcas were consulted over Toledo's decisions and largely endorsed them, in the knowledge that they would be sheltered from any political repercussions. As much as those judges and the Audiencia's president cherished the opportunities offered by the absence of a viceroy, this chapter shows them in the spotlight, again, as had happened in the 1560s. However, in the 1560s the Audiencia de Charcas had only begun to settle its jurisdiction and was able to rely on the local *encomendero* group, something that had become impossible in the 1580s. By then *encomiendas* had ceased to be a major source of wealth, being replaced by a diversified pool of economic activities that included farming and mining, while many *encomiendas* had returned to the Crown, after their initial recipients and any eligible successors had expired. Although the Audiencia struggled with issues similar to those Toledo faced in organising his expedition, without a wealthy and ambitious *encomendero* class to rely upon, it had to make do with more modest support. Toledo, for instance, had been able to draw on the windfall of *quintos reales* from Potosí's silver boom to finance his expedition. The Audiencia would have to resort to a smaller source of revenue: the *caja de granos* of Potosí, a coffer that gathered contributions made by indigenous miners to cover various administrative expenses in the Imperial Village. Lozano Machuca would hand over the keys to that coffer in exchange for participation in an *entrada* that he probably expected to bring him fame and glory. Constant delays bogged down his expedition from the start. In the end, poor preparation and a hostile environment ended the royal official's role at the helm of the *entrada*. It seems that the southeastern border of Charcas did not need any more wars of 'feathers, silks, and trappings'. Instead, it needed 'practical men', as one contemporary put it, with a more down-to-earth approach, who were ready to negotiate and, if necessary, fight.[9] Their political journey would transform these 'soldiers' into *vecinos*, and eventually into royal agents, settling them in remote parts of Charcas.[10]

2. A body without its head

News of the appointment of don Martín Enríquez de Almanza y Ulloa as the sixth viceroy of Peru on 26 May 1580 was probably what a homesick and ill don Francisco de Toledo had been waiting to hear for a long time. Toledo would be able to retire and start a new period of his life, dedicated

---

9 AGI, Patronato, 125, R4, [1582] Pedro de Segura, image 31.
10 This analysis excludes Paraguay, which was run by an *adelantado* between 1540 and 1593, who had been appointed directly by the monarch and over who the Audiencia de Charcas and the viceroy of Perú had very little influence. This created a distinctive political culture in the district. Dario G. Barriera, *Abrir puertas a la tierra: microanálisis de la construcción de un espacio político: Santa Fe, 1573–1640* (Santa Fe: Museo Histórico Provincial Brigadier Estanislao López, 2017), pp. 110, 113.

Figure 4.1   Drawing of don Martín Enríquez de Almanza y Ulloa, viceroy of Peru between 1582 and 1583, taken from don Felipe Guamán Poma de Ayala's *Nueva Coronica y Buen Gobierno* of 1615
Source: Royal Danish Library, GKS 223: Guaman Poma, *Nueva corónica y buen gobierno* (c. 1615). Page [462 [464]].

to meditation and rest in Spain, after twelve long years at the helm of the monarchy's most troublesome and wealthiest district. Enríquez was 72 years old, unwell, and tired, and so extremely disappointed, as he had been longing for a quieter life at home in Valladolid. Toledo could not wait and left Peru three days before the new viceroy's arrival, perhaps fearing that his replacement might never arrive.[11]

Don Martín Enríquez de Almanza was brother of the Marqués de Alqueñizes, a descendant of don Francisco Enrique de Amanza who had been given the title Marqués by the Emperor Charles V, and had years of experience in a viceregal post when he arrived in Peru.[12] His time at the helm of Peru would be brief and during it he only managed to review some of the measures taken by his predecessor; he mainly focused on what he saw as a priority, trying to overcome the rift with the Jesuits that Toledo had created.[13] The King's instructions to Enríquez do not mention the Chiriguana border.[14] However, a royal *provisión* from just before Toledo's 1574 expedition, only acknowledged by the recipient four years later in 1578, confirmed the use of peaceful means to settle and evangelise indigenous groups hostile to the Spanish presence, insisting that *entradas* should be seen as 'pacification efforts'.[15] How such pacification efforts would be conducted remains unclear, yet *provisións* were only for guidance and open to interpretation, although in this case the late acknowledgement suggests this one was probably set aside as another example of 'I obey, but do not execute'.

In New Spain, Enríquez had overseen the continued implementation of the royal policy known as the '*presidio* system' along the border with the Chichimeca, a group of indigenous peoples the Spanish regularly compared with the Chiriguanaes. The system, begun by New Spain's second viceroy, don Luis de Velasco (1550–1564), consisted of fortifying strategically located villages and towns. In Peru, it reached its peak under Enríquez, most likely due to the viceroy's decision to follow the advice in the conclusions of the Junta Magna (discussed in Chapter Three), that recommended the use of fortifications in preference to outright confrontation, in order to keep the land 'in peace' (*quieta*).[16] It seems reasonable to suggest that Enríquez's approach to the Chiriguana border might have been the same, trying to build on

11 Philip Powell, 'Portrait of an American Viceroy: Martín Enríquez, 1568–1583', *The Americas* 14, no. 1 (1957): p. 22.
12 Levillier, *Gobernantes del Perú*, Vol. 9, p. XIII.
13 See Chapter Three in this book.
14 Levillier, *Gobernantes del Perú*, Vol. 9, pp. 10–33.
15 Provisión en que se declara la orden que se ha de tener en las Indias, en nuevos descubrimientos y poblaciones que en ellas se hizieren [1573] in García-Gallo and Encinas, *Cedulario indiano o cedulario de Encinas*, Vol. IV, pp. 232–46; letter from Toledo to the King, 18 April 1578, in Levillier, *Gobernantes del Perú*, Vol. 6, pp. 66–67.
16 Antonio F. García-Abásolo, *Martín Enríquez y la reforma de 1568 en Nueva España* (Sevilla: Excelentísima. Diputación Provincial de Sevilla, 1983), Ch. XIII; Philip W. Powell, '*Presidios* and Towns on the Silver Frontier of New Spain. 1550–1580', *The Hispanic American Historical Review* 24, no. 2 (1944): pp. 181, 187; Cédula dirigida al Virrey del Perú, cerca de la orden que ha de tener y guardar en los nuevos descubrimientos y poblaciones que diere, assi por mar como por tierra, 1568, in García-Gallo and Encinas, *Cedulario indiano o cedulario de Encinas*, Vol. IV, pp. 229–32.

Toledo's limited success with the establishment of two towns: San Bernardo de la Frontera de Tarija and Santiago de la Frontera de Tomina (see Figure 0.1). However, neither Enríquez's policy in New Spain, nor Toledo's two new towns, seem to have placated Chichimecas and Chiriguanaes and both regions were about to experience a period of violence such as they had never seen before.[17]

3. The borders engulfed in jurisdictional conflicts

The foundation of San Bernardo de Tarija was originally planned for March 1574. One month after that date, as settlers were trying to erect their new homes, the first attack by the Chiriguanaes took place, forcing the town's founder, Captain Luis de Fuentes y Vargas, who had arranged the foundation with Viceroy Toledo, to move the settlement to a new site, largely in line with the attackers' wishes. This was 75km from the nearest Chiriguana settlement, and between 25 and 30km from the area they saw as their border with the Spanish.[18] Life in the new settlement that looked more like a fortress—a *presidio*—was hard and half of its residents fled only a few months after the town was moved. This prompted a series of regulations by *corregidor* de Fuentes y Vargas banning any *vecinos* from staying away from Tarija for more than fifty days, on pain of losing ownership of their land: in effect, land was given in return for a commitment by the occupiers to stay and by leaving the site they were in breach of that commitment. With the town now outside their territory, a delegation of the Chiriguana visited the Spanish settlement, opening up a period that constantly shifted between peaceful coexistence and trade, and hostility and war.[19]

The situation in Toledo's northern border town, Santiago de la Frontera de Tomina, was no different. Established by the civil wars veteran Captain Melchor de Rodas, the new settlement's founding date remains a mystery, yet

17 Carlos Lázaro Avila, *Las fronteras de América y los 'Flandes Indianos'* (Madrid: Consejo Superior de Investigaciones Científicas, Centro de Estudios Históricos, Departamento de Historia de América, 1997), p. 61; Luis Alberto García García, *Frontera armada: Prácticas militares en el noreste histórico, Siglos XVII al XIX* (México: Fondo de Cultura Económica: Centro de Investigación y Docencia Económicas, 2021), pp. 47–52.

18 Fray Antonio Comajuncosa and Fray Alejandro Corrado, *El colegio franciscano de Tarija y sus misiones. Noticias históricas recogidas por dos misioneros del mismo colegio* (Quaracchi: Tipografía del Colegio de San Buenaventura, 1884), p. 9; AGI, Patronato, 137, N1, R2, [1598] Luis de Fuentes y Vargas, images 71 and 193; Saignes, 'Andaluces en el poblamiento del Oriente Boliviano', p. 182; BNE, Ms 3,043, Ordenanzas y comisiones para el reino de Granada y obispado de Quito, fol. 176; letter from Juan de Matienzo to the King, 4 January 1579, in Levillier, *La Audiencia de Charcas*, Vol. 1, p. 483; Oliveto, 'Ocupación territorial', p. 190.

19 San Bernardo de la Frontera de Tarija was finally established on 4 July 1574: Julien, Angelis, and Bass Werner de Ruiz, *Historia de Tarija*, p. xx.

knowing that the area was where Toledo first went to rest after his expedition to the Chiriguanaes, it seems likely to have been settled some time after July 1574.[20] Rodas was a controversial character who had frequent problems with the law and a defiant attitude, and his approach to the Chiriguanaes was different from that of Fuentes y Vargas; and for some time it paid off.[21] Chiriguana delegations would come and stay, sometimes for days, engaging in business that would involve the exchange of gifts and goods. Honey, rhea eggs, and fish were swapped for knives, scissors, clothing, and seashells, although a more lucrative trade took place too, as native captives of the Chiriguanaes were also exchanged. Despite this active trade, Santiago de la Frontera de Tomina did not escape the fate of San Bernardo de la Frontera de Tarija and would alternate between periods of relative peace and moments of pronounced hostility.[22]

Through founding such towns, and extending and sharing jurisdiction with characters like Fuentes y Vargas and Rodas, the Crown in effect acknowledged a *de facto* position as some captains already had a presence in the border region with their own political allies, including Spaniards, *mestizos*, and more importantly, factions of the Chiriguanaes. They established partnerships based on mutual trust and an intensive exchange of gifts, partnerships that could also be easily broken. The arrangements in effect connected the Chiriguanaes to a global trade network that, through commercial partners, circulated commodities and valuable items across the Iberian worlds. They also provided the new towns with the native labour that the Spanish constantly demanded, but also exposed them to the constant infighting within the Chiriguanaes. These internal conflicts were imported into the border Spanish settlements, which, as a result, remained precarious and fragile. Because royal posts handed to captains were understood to be commissions, and not bureaucratic jobs as they became centuries later, they were only subject to vague guidelines that were open to interpretation,

20 A document dated 27 July 1574 records the sale of a farm in La Plata to Polo Ondegardo and refers to Melchor de Rodas as *corregidor* of Santiago de la Frontera: ABNB, EP19, Venta de huerta que hace Melchor de Rodas a Polo Ondegardo, fols 322v–323v; Weaver Olson gives 1575 as a date: Weaver Olson, 'A Republic of Lost Peoples', p. 321.

21 Rodas had several long-standing legal cases with other characters including one with Garci de Orellana. The original case file is missing, yet from the Audiencia de Charcas' 'Libro de Acuerdos' it can be guessed that involved a partnership over a mine: López Villalva (dir.), *Acuerdos de la Real Audiencia de La Plata de los Charcas*, Vol. 2, 30 October 1570, p. 143. Another document sheds light on this case, locating the mine, called Chumbe, in Berenguela: ABNB, EP16, Convenio para trueque de mina, 8 de octubre de 1572, fols 195v–197v.

22 ABNB, EC 1618, [1574] Probanza de Melchor de Rodas, fol. 2v; AGI, Patronato, 235, R7, [1582] Información hecha por la justicia de la villa de Santiago de la Frontera, en virtud de Real Provisión, sobre la conducta y trato que observaban los indios chiriguanaes, fols 12v, 12r, 44v.

as stipulated in the commissions' titles, and as far as the monarchy was concerned it was down to the post holders to find the best way to keep the borders at peace. This frequently involved wide-scale abuses and violence. It also meant that if anything went wrong, as it did many times, these captains could be removed or reprimanded on grounds of poor administration, leaving the Crown's reputation intact. Aware of the pressures these captains were under, the Chiriguanaes were also able to play one border captain off against another, and regularly drag them into their own conflicts. Governing the borders was a delicate matter and the region was perceived as a permanent war zone where Spanish presence was limited to the strength of such captains and their alliances, and only manifest along some discontinuous and sometimes overlapping zones that matched their jurisdictions, thereby creating 'miniature political spaces' that did not have clear boundaries.[23]

Some scholars attribute the wave of hostilities along the Chiriguana border in the early 1580s to a ban by the Audiencia de Charcas on trade in local captives and an alleged lack of understanding by the Spanish of the dynamics of inter-faction Chiriguanaes relations that impeded the Spanish when they sought to exploit such politically fragmented peoples to their advantage.[24] This book has shown that such bans never worked and the Spanish along the border were more than aware of the inter-factional dynamics of the Chiriguanaes, with some married to *mestizas* seen as distant Chiriguana relatives. Tensions in the period were in fact high owing to two factors: one was the lack of sufficient labour for the farms that were springing up in fertile valleys along the southeastern Charcas borders. A deadly wave of disease affected populations across the Andes in the early 1580s and this, in turn, impacted on the flow of native workers that were needed both in Potosí and on the farms in the Charcas hinterland.[25] These estates had mushroomed in the valleys of Cochabamba, Mizque, Tomina, Oroncota, and Tarija from the 1560s and they relied heavily not only on captive Indians but also on indigenous peoples escaping from the harsh conditions faced by mineworkers in Potosí.[26] The second issue was the regular raids by Chiriguanaes, which were an impediment to the cultivation and exploitation of land that could be used for agriculture. The period saw the emergence of a new economy in the Andes, one centred around the Toledan and post-Toledan expansion of silver mining, thanks to the introduction of the amalgamation process by the viceroy.[27] This booming mining economy created a demand for valuable

23 Hespanha, *La gracia del derecho*, pp. 100, 102.
24 Scholl, 'At the Limits of Empire', pp. 315–16, 322–23.
25 Cole, *The Potosí Mita*, p. 28; Noble David Cook, 'Epidemias y dinámica demográfica', in *El primer contacto y la formación de nuevas sociedades*, Vol. II (Madrid: Ediciones UNESCO, Ediciones Trotta, 2007), p. 311.
26 Weaver Olson, 'A Republic of Lost Peoples', p. 62.
27 Carlos Sempat Assadourian, *El sistema de la economía colonial. Mercado interno, regiones y espacio económico* (Lima: IEP, 1982), p. 297.

resources found in the border areas, largely timber and maize.[28] Valleys within reach of La Plata and Potosí were good for grazing animals, growing cereals, and logging timber, yet they also lacked sustainable agriculture and labour.[29] A *vecino* in the area probably summarises this better, stressing that by this period the southeastern border was home to

> a large number of cattle farms from which meat is supplied and their pastures used to graze the llamas that carry minerals from Cerro Rico in Potosí to the *yungas*; and from the border also come large volumes of timber and charcoal needed for the smelters that melt down His Majesty's *quintos* and for other metal works; the border's farms provide large quantities of corn, wheat, wine, honey, among other supplies and large quantities of fish.[30]

As hazardous as farming had become, the Spanish needed labour, land, and resources and were prepared to look for ways to gain access to them. However, this also boosted tensions with the Chiriguana, who were reluctant to accept Spanish settlements near their lands and were certainly not prepared to be subjected to farm work. They could, nonetheless, supply labour by exchanging lowland captives with the Spanish, although this was limited by their own willingness to engage in the trade. Toledo's significant defeat only confirmed that they were truly the owners of the border area, as the Spanish were about to learn.

The intensification of the raids by Chiriguana groups took place in two phases. Initially, the attacks centred on travellers on the precarious paths that connected Santa Cruz de la Sierra and La Plata. They would make the journey in company with armed escorts and carried plenty of supplies, aware of the risks involved. Religious orders became more active in the area in the late 1570s, largely a result of Toledo's insistence on more priests coming to live among indigenous peoples. One key religious order with a long tradition of work along the borders of the Catholic Monarchy was the Mercedarians, who

---

28 Jane E. Mangan, *Trading Roles: Gender, Ethnicity, and the Urban Economy in Colonial Potosí*, Latin America Otherwise (Durham, NC: Duke University Press, 2005), p. 30.

29 A document from the late sixteenth century states the species of trees that were regularly cut down: *Tipuana tipu* or *Tipa*; *Soto* or *Schinopsis brasiliensis*; and *Cedros* or cedars. AGI, Patronato, 136, N1, R4, [1596] Información de Méritos y Servicios de Juan Ladrón de Leyba, fol. 70r.

30 'Con gran seguridad gran cantidad de estancias de ganado maior y menor donde se bastece de carne y en los pastos de la dicha frontera pastan la mayor cantidad de carneros de la tierra que bajan el metal del cerro rrico de la villa de potossi a los yungas y de la dicha frontera se proveen de gran cantidad de madera y de carbon para las fundiciones de los reales quintos y demas herrerias y ansimismo se proveen de las chacaras de la dicha frontera de gran cantidad de maiz ttrigo vino miel y otros bastimentos y pescado en gran cantidad': Bibliothèque Nationale de France (from here on, BNF), MS Espagnol 175, letter from Capitán Juan Ladrón de Leyba, undated but possibly from early in the 1590s, fol. 90r.

in Europe were involved in the release of Christians from Muslim captors. Their presence in the southeastern Charcas border area, where they worked closely with Spanish settlers, probably related to the fact that indigenous peoples were regularly kept as captives by the Chiriguanaes. This raises the question how their presence was perceived by the Chiriguanaes and how it could alter the fragile border environment, where tensions over labour and captives were always high. Priests frequently contributed to the establishment of indigenous peoples in permanent settlements, something the Chiriguanaes fiercely opposed; and they were probably perceived as intruders in the world of Chiriguana–Spanish settler relations. Religious orders normally travelled in small groups, which made them vulnerable to attack. This was exactly what happened to the Mercedarian friar Cristóbal de Albarrán who, in 1581, was murdered along with a party accompanying him on a journey back to La Plata.[31] Figure 4.2, painted more than a century later, depicts the martyrdom of the Mercedarian priests.[32]

A second recorded attack took place on a caravan headed by Captain Hernando de Salazar and thirty men who were travelling from La Plata to Santa Cruz de la Sierra. They were escorting doña Elvira Manrique de Lara and her mother doña María de Angulo, the former being the widow of Captain Ñuflo de Chaves, conquistador and founder of Santa Cruz de la Sierra. During the attack doña María lost her life.[33] Elvira and María

31 Albarrán's presence in Charcas had been limited to the area around Asunción and Santa Cruz de la Sierra, where he had focused on evangelising the Guaraní/Chiriguanaes. Nolasco Pérez, *Religiosos de la merced*, pp. 298–99.

32 This painting, in the Mercedarian convent in Cusco, depicts Albarrán's martyrdom, as the event was re-interpreted in subsequent centuries, based on a new perception of Spanish America's borders that Alejandro Cañeque has called 'the wild paganism martyrdom borders'. Documents from the time of Albarrán's death suggest that he was murdered while making a journey; the actual circumstances, whether he was preaching among indigenous peoples in the area at the time or simply passing through, are less clear. The painting is now in Cusco because it was the provincial hub of the Mercedarians, from where their activities between Cusco and Tucumán were overseen. AGI, Patronato, 235, R9, [1583] Autos y diligencias hechas por la Audiencia de La Plata, sobre los daños, muertes y robos que los indios chiriguanaes cometían en aquellas fronteras, y guerra que contra ellos se ha pregonado. Contienen estos autos las capitulaciones y asiento que se tomó con el capitán Miguel Martínez [*sic*], sobre la población de la villa de San Miguel de la Laguna y lo que en ella sucedió, fols 1v, 37v, 43v, 49r; British Library (from here on, BL), Ms 13,977, Memoria de las casas y conventos y doctrinas que tiene la horden de Nuestra Señora de Nuestra Merced en las Yndias del Peru, [undated, probably from early in the seventeenth century], fol. 99; Alejandro Cañeque, *Un imperio de mártires: Religión y poder en las fronteras de la Monarquía Hispánica* (Madrid: Marcial Pons Historia, 2020), p. 22.

33 On Chaves see Chapter Two in this book. Hernando de Salazar was married to one daughter of Francisco de Mendoza (1515–1547), deputy governor of Paraguay. The

Figure 4.2   Anonymous painting representing the martyrdom of Albarrán and
other Mercedarian friars
Source: Used with permission of the La Merced convent in Cusco, with
thanks to Mercedarian friar Elthon Pacheco and Carlos Piccone Camere.

had been kept away from Santa Cruz de la Sierra where, as described in
Chapter Three, don Diego de Mendoza, who was a relative, had rebelled in
Toledo's time. Now, with don Diego executed and Toledo back in Spain, the
Audiencia de Charcas allowed their passage to Santa Cruz de la Sierra. In the
fatal attack, the Chiriguanaes also took 300 horses, and goods worth more
than 25,000 pesos, an enormous sum at the time.[34] The horses and goods
seized were more than enough to make this group an attractive target for
the Chiriguanaes, who probably knew which people were travelling as part of
the caravan and what was being transported. The attack certainly magnified
the threat that the Chiriguanaes posed to the Spanish residents along the
border, sending a clear message about who was in control of the area. This
was a heavy blow to the local elite—the family in question was one of the
most respected and best-known across Charcas. This assault prompted not
a painting, but a poem. Written by Extremadura-born cleric and traveller

other daughter, who married Captain Ñuflo de Chaves, was doña Elvira Manrique
de Lara. This explains Salazar's presence escorting the caravan. On Salazar: AGI,
Charcas, 94, N19, [1589] Probanza de Hernando de Salazar, fols 236v–296v.
34 AGI, Patronato, 235, R9, [1583] Autos y diligencias, fols 36v, 43v, 47v, 50v.

Martín del Barco Centenera early in the seventeenth century, it describes this event and how it was perceived by contemporaries:

In that sad hour the dearest loss of all
Was doña María Angulo whose corpse,
Struck by a hundred shafts and lances fell
In the main's thick; living, this lovely lady
Was cause of intrigues and rebellions,
By passions caused; too fond of power was she,
In manner overbearing, so that all
She had dissensions with, or enmities.[35]

With the Chiriguanaes clearly in control of the paths between La Plata and Santa Cruz de la Sierra, from 1582 onwards a new phase of attacks followed, this time raids targeting farms along the Andean piedmont valleys. One of such incidents gives a glimpse of the world of 'miniature politics', showing the involvement of Spanish captains with Chiriguana factions and how feuds between different captains, mainly over jurisdiction, frequently created more conflict.

Captain Melchor de Rodas was succeeded as *corregidor* of Tomina on 12 June 1582 by Captain Pedro de Segura Zavala, the father-in-law of Captain García Mosquera, who was mentioned in Chapter Three as Toledo's guide in his *entrada* to the Chiriguanaes in 1574.[36] Segura Zavala and García Mosquera were therefore part of the same family group settled in Tomina, the area where Santiago de la Frontera de Tomina had been founded by Rodas a few years earlier. Both men had family links with the Guaraní/Chiriguanaes. Segura Zavala was married to Jinebra Martínez de Irala, *mestiza* daughter of Captain Domingo Martínez de Irala, who had been governor of the Río de la Plata. García Mosquera was *mestizo* himself—his mother had been Chiriguana/Guaraní. Both men were seeking the consolidation of their authority along the border, using their connections with the Chiriguanaes, which Rodas, who was a favourite of Toledo, had opposed until then. This was a struggle over who was best positioned to evoke the presence of the monarch in the borders based on their background and skills.

---

35 Martín del Barco Centenera, *The Argentine and the Conquest of the River Plate* (Buenos Aires: Instituto Cultural Water Owen, 1965), Canto XXV, p. 432. The original is:
'Fenece aqui la triste su triste hora,
Cubierta de mil flechas y harpones,
Doña Maria de Angulo causadora
De motines, rebueltas, y pasiones,
Amiga de mandar, y tan señora,
Que con todos tramava dissensiones'.
Barco Centenera, *Argentina y conquista del Rio de La Plata*, fol. 210r.
36 AGI, Patronato, 190, R44, [1582] Minuta de los corregimientos que había en 1582, fol. 1.

The political change in Tomina from Rodas to Segura Zavala proved challenging for both the Spanish and their Chiriguanaes allies. Following a raid by the latter, and unable to find those responsible, Segura Zavala decided to wait for Chiriguana to visit Santiago de la Frontera de Tomina, hoping to arrest them and threaten to keep them hostage, until those responsible for robbing and pillaging farms in the area returned the captives and goods they had taken. He was clearly under pressure from Spanish farmers who wanted their looted possessions back. However, it was not his Chiriguana allies who were arrested but another group, who were visiting Rodas. In the documentary record those arrested are presented using stereotypical views that the Spanish tended to construct around the Chiriguanaes, yet nothing is said about Segura Zavala's own allies and relatives, who are kept hidden from the narrative—in effect, in the kitchen, as they are only mentioned as gathering there to exchange goods. The whole incident is very revealing of the types of political dynamics that characterised border areas: these were not based on identity, as all captains, including Rodas, had allies among Chiriguana factions, but on political agency. The boundaries were also blurred. Segura Zavala spoke the Chiriguana language fluently and his loyalties were mixed, as were those of Rodas. This was not just a conflict between Chiriguanaes and Spaniards, but one over jurisdiction, involving on one hand Segura Zavala and his network, and Rodas and his allies on the other; but until now it has been presented as a dispute between Chiriguanaes and settlers. Rodas and Segura Zavala were fighting over which leader was the most powerful, to most effectively expand the jurisdiction of the monarchy along the border. Disputes over jurisdiction included different Chiriguana factions, who were probably aware of the political dynamics. Fearing an escalation of the conflict, the Audiencia de Charcas finally stepped in, just to keep the land *quieta*, and commissioned an official inquiry into the matter.[37] As Toledo's hostages had the decade before, the imprisoned Chiriguanaes eventually escaped.

In a report on his merits and services in later years, Melchor de Rodas referred to this event as an example of how to make a bad situation worse, accusing Segura Zavala of wrongly imprisoning Chiriguanaes. Rodas was obviously referring to his own allies. Reading around and beyond the Chiriguanaes–Spaniards divide, the episode offers a glimpse of the problems caused by often juxtaposed jurisdictions that extended beyond the Spanish villages into Chiriguana lands. In effect, although not *corregidor* of Santiago de la Frontera de Tomina at the time, Rodas was still someone of importance as the village's founder and, in his view, the arrest of his Chiriguana allies was an affront and added tension to a situation that was already complicated because of the raids. Aware of this, the Audiencia realised that it had to step

---

37 AGI, Patronato, 235, R7, [1582], Información por Santiago de la Frontera; ABNB, EC 1618, [1574] Melchor de Rodas, fol. 2a.

in, not only to contain the Chiriguanaes, but also to ease the tension between different Spaniards, each with his own claim to jurisdiction over the border because of either their status as founder of the town (Rodas), or their seniority in the area and family ties (Segura Zavala).

Concerned at the deteriorating situation along the southeastern Charcas border, in December 1582 the president of the Audiencia de Charcas, Licenciado Cepeda, wrote to Viceroy Enríquez. Clearly preparing for some form of punitive action, Cepeda suggested that the Chiriguanaes should be given the status of local people 'subject to servitude' (*sujetos a servidumbre*), based on his own findings of their actions along the border. This would transform them into enemies of the monarchy and of Christianity, and justify *entradas* against them, at no cost to the monarch. The new status of these indigenous people would create an incentive for Spaniards to launch attacks, seize captives, and secure extra farm labour.[38] His advice, like that proffered by the Audiencia judges during the Toledo administration a decade earlier, was offered only for guidance. Unfortunately, Enríquez's answer, if it ever existed, is missing from the records. The viceroy passed away shortly afterwards, leaving the Audiencia de Charcas to handle the issue, as had occurred two decades before. Without the constraints that viceroys faced, because of their concerns over how their decisions would be perceived among their patrons and the court in Madrid, Audiencia members were less politically exposed in relation to any measure they could take. Conversely, they were more politically compromised at home, where many of their loyalties lay. Without Enríquez, it would be down to the Audiencia to tackle the Chiriguanaes in its own manner and organise an expedition that would try to avoid a repeat of Toledo's tragic 1574 *entrada*.

4. The court meets the lowland natives

In 1583 Chiriguana raids against farms intensified. They reached Presto and Tarabuco and as close to La Plata as 50km. Despite knowing how concerned the Chiriguanaes were about new Spanish villages along the border, but probably aware that these urban settlements would break up the jurisdiction further among captains in the area and ease tensions among them, the Audiencia de Charcas decided to press ahead with the instructions in the Junta Magna, by founding fortified towns and cities to contain the Chiriguana. Accordingly, it proposed to negotiate with Segura Zavala's son-in-law Captain García Mosquera and Miguel Martín, a *vecino* of Tomina and close ally of Melchor de Rodas, the foundation of two new towns to be called Rio de los Sauces and San Miguel de la Frontera or San Miguel de La Laguna—the present-day Padilla in Bolivia (see Figure 0.1).

---

38 Letter from the President of the Audiencia de Charcas, Licenciado Cepeda, to the King, 27 December 1582, in Levillier, *La Audiencia de Charcas*, Vol. 2, p. 37.

Negotiations with both characters ensued. García Mosquera asked for men, weapons, cattle, and supplies. Martín was more ambitious. He claimed the existence of silver deposits in the future jurisdiction of San Miguel de la Laguna (or Frontera) and secured a concession for the village's *vecinos* to trade their maize in Potosí tax-free. Maize was a crop of vast importance in border areas because of its connection to the prosperous market in Potosí producing *chicha*.[39] Despite García Mosquera's best intentions, and the hopes of his extended family, the negotiations for his village failed.[40] In contrast, Martín managed to succeed, in what was a blow to Segura Zavala and his network. However, many prominent La Plata *vecinos* reacted to the news by protesting that Martín's new village would pose a risk to the already established town of Santiago de la Frontera de Tomina, due to the overlapping of jurisdictions. Those who had not had the time and resources to occupy and establish their farms in this region would lose their properties altogether. Furthermore, the new town would take indigenous labour away from Santiago de la Frontera de Tomina.[41] Despite these complaints, and emphasising its role as mediator, the Audiencia de Charcas decided to press ahead and approve Martín's settlement, to secure a balance of power between the networks headed by Segura Zavala and by Rodas along that section of the border, and to contain the Chiriguanaes. On the ground, with *vecinos* in La Plata having land in the area and Chiriguanaes present, both groups opposing the new town, the Audiencia's decision would prove disastrous.

As had happened a decade earlier under Toledo, an enquiry, and the subsequent establishment of new urban settlements, eventually set the ground for war against the Chiriguanaes. In charge, the Audiencia quickly summoned the body politic of Charcas for consultation about how to move forward. The list of those consulted includes individuals already discussed in this book such as Juan de Zurita, the former governor of Santa Cruz de la Sierra; the current governor of Santa Cruz de la Sierra, Lorenzo Suárez de Figueroa; and don Gabriel de Paniagua de Loaysa, the prominent *vecino* and *encomendero*. Remembering Toledo's disastrous *entrada*, those involved in the consultations recommended that any attack against the Chiriguanaes should be undertaken on several fronts. It was also suggested that any

---

39 AGI, Patronato, 235, R9, [1583] Autos y diligencias, fols 80v–81r, 85r–87v, 91r. *Chicha* is a beverage, sometimes fermented and hence alcoholic.
40 A letter from the Audiencia official Juan de Liano mentions, without disclosing the identity of those involved, that three people clearly opposed García Mosquera's plans. It begs the question whether one of these was Melchor de Rodas. AGI, Patronato, 235, R9, [1583] Autos y diligencias, fol. 82.
41 Mujía, *Bolivia–Paraguay*, Vol. II, p. 576.

indigenous person seized should be taken captive and kept as 'yanacona perpetuo',[42] and that any campaign should be carried out in the summer.[43]

As far as war matters were concerned, the Audiencia was trying to distinguish its approach as more pragmatic than Toledo's. It was prepared to listen to the advice of those who knew the border very well and act accordingly. By doing this, it was able to demonstrate the King's presence in Charcas in a manner that was less obtrusive than deploying the King's living image. Toledo's presence in Charcas had at times clearly overwhelmed the local elite who perceived his style of government as far too centred around his position. During his time in the district the city of La Plata had, in effect, two courts, that of the Audiencia and that of the viceroy. The Audiencia, in contrast, had deep roots in its district and was much better positioned to engage and involve different political groups without antagonising them. In this battle over the best way to make the monarchy present in the district, the Audiencia would win. From Toledo onwards, Peru's viceroys would largely stay in Lima.

As Toledo had reluctantly done ten years earlier, when he approached the Chiriguanaes by sending García Mosquera to their settlements, the Audiencia de Charcas reached out to the indigenous peoples by inviting their leaders to come to La Plata. Two leaders travelled all the way from the border to express their views as part of the wider enquiry into the need for an expedition. Any *entrada* would be conceived as punitive, as retribution for the regular raids on Spanish farms, the captivity of other native people, the murder of Catholic priests and Spaniards, the destruction of property, as well as for the alleged refusal of the Chiriguana to accept the Catholic faith and work on Spanish farms. Those Chiriguanaes that turned up for discussions in October 1583 expressed the same views as their predecessors who had been interviewed by García Mosquera on their home territory and by Toledo in La Plata. They were reluctant to accept the presence of the Spanish near their own settlements or to work for them as they were free and had interests of their own.

They were interrogated in particular about the presence of Catholic church ornaments and other religious items among them and whether they had been engaged in conflict with the Chané, probably the Audiencia seeking confirmation for the stereotypes 'apostates' and 'cannibals'. While the Audiencia saw such discussions, as had Toledo a decade earlier, as part of the build-up to war that involved missions, negotiations, and exchanges, the Chiriguanaes saw it as an opportunity to assess the situation and delay any punitive expedition. They would also receive gifts and obtain information on any potential plans which they could use to prepare for armed confrontation; which at that point was inevitable.[44]

42 This was an ambiguous status: *yanaconas* were free and *perpetuo* seems to indicate some permanent guardianship by the Spanish.
43 AGI, Patronato, 235, R9, [1583] Autos y diligencias.
44 The ornaments and materials about which they were asked had probably been taken from the expedition of Francisco Ortiz de Vergara from the Rio de la Plata to Peru:

To continue with the assessment, and using guidelines similar to those followed by Toledo a decade earlier, the Audiencia de Charcas met *encomenderos* having grants located near the border that had been attacked by the Chiriguanaes. The raids were regularly targeting farms, some of them belonging to the Toledan *reducciones* of San Lucas, Caiza, and Puna. The *caciques* of these areas were also asked to take part in the enquiry. At the time the Audiencia were also concerned at the growing number of indigenous people who had left Andean *reducciones* towns to reside in border areas and were regularly helping the Chiriguanaes. They hoped to be able to bring these people back within the royal jurisdiction, somehow.[45] It was also in their interest to contain the raids and bring peace to the area as much as it was in the interest of other border residents. It is also reasonable to suggest that such residents would probably be asked to contribute to, and perhaps take part in, any *entrada* against the Chiriguanaes accordingly. Through the answers to their questions, the Audiencia learned about a new development: the Chiriguanaes had managed to co-opt the Laxaca peoples, who were now joining in their raids. This was alarming news and prompted immediate action by the Audiencia, which on 8 December 1583 declared war against the Chiriguanaes.[46]

Throughout this process, the Audiencia de Charcas largely replicated the protocol Toledo had followed previously, sharing responsibility for the *entrada* with those who had been consulted and perhaps would participate in the event. This would reduce any political risk that could follow a negative outcome. Furthermore, demonstrating its decision to stick to royal guidance, the Audiencia de Charcas invoked the *provision* that had been handed to Toledo in 1568 to declare war against the Chiriguanaes, showing that the laws and legal provisions in this period were far from orders and were simply

Relación hecha al Consejo de Indias por Francisco Ortiz de Vergara, del viaje que hizo del Rio de la Plata al Perú (1565) in Luis Torres de Mendoza, *Colección de documentos inéditos relativos al descubrimiento, conquista y organización de las antiguas posesiones españolas de América y Oceanía sacados de los archivos del reino y muy especialmente del de Indias*, Vol. 4 (Madrid: Imprenta de Frias y Cia, 1865), p. 388; AGI, Patronato, 235, R9, [1583] Autos y diligencias, fols 17v–18v.

45 AGI, Patronato, 136, N1, R4, [1596] Title of *Caudillo* for Juan Ladrón de Leyba, La Plata, 18 March 1584, fols 4v–5r.

46 The Lacaxa were part of a larger indigenous group, the Moyos-Moyos, and had settled in the southeastern Charcas border area at least from the time of the grants of *encomienda* handed out by La Gasca in the 1540s. The fact that they were the objects of *encomienda* might mean that they were settled and could be worked for the benefit of the *encomenderos* receiving the grants. It seems that by the 1580s they had evaded the control of their *encomenderos* and were now under the influence of the Chiriguanaes. Ana María Presta and María de las Mercedes del Río, 'Un estudio etnohistórico en los corregimientos de Tomina Yamparaes: casos de multietnicidad', in *Espacio, etnias, frontera. Atenuaciones políticas en el sur del Tawantinsuyu. Siglos XV–XVIII* (Sucre: ASUR, 1995), pp. 212–13. Oliveto, 'De mitmaqkuna incaicos en Tarija', p. 18; AGI, Patronato, 235, R9, [1583] Autos y diligencias, fols 52v–75v.

matters of advice, always needing acknowledgement, but to be executed if and when needed and to be adapted to the circumstances, in accordance with all members of the body politic.

The agreement in the end was for a large-scale campaign operating on three fronts. Luis de Fuentes y Vargas, Corregidor of Tarija, would lead the *entrada* from his jurisdiction. Lorenzo Suárez de Figueroa, having responsibilities over Spaniards and indigenous peoples living near the Santa Cruz de la Sierra border, would do the same from Santa Cruz de la Sierra. Finally, royal official Juan Lozano Machuca would head an *entrada* starting from Potosí, passing through Tomina, all the way to the border area. Additionally, the Audiencia de Charcas arranged for further towns to be founded, to strengthen Spanish presence along the border: in the old Tahuantinsuyu fortress of Samaipata, and a new settlement called San Juan de la Frontera de Paspaya.[47] Located close to Santa Cruz de la Sierra, Samaipata had been built by the Incas to contain the Chiriguanaes (see Chapter One). The town in Paspaya, to be situated between San Bernardo de la Frontera de Tarija and Santa Cruz de la Sierra, would play the same role as it was not far from the Chiriguana settlements (see Figure 0.1). Because these new towns were negotiated after the Audiencia de Charcas declared war against the Chiriguanaes, their residents would be allowed to carry out regular raids on Chiriguana settlements and take captives they could use as labour on their farms and in their villages.[48] The presence of Juan Lozano Machuca, an official of the royal exchequer and former *criado* of Viceroy Toledo, seems out of place, but his privileged access to funding, built through a career that by the early 1580s spanned well over a decade, provides some clues to the role that he played in this campaign.[49]

5. A man of the quill

Born in Ciudad Real, in Castilla-La Mancha, in or around 1539, to Juan Lozano Machuca and Quiteria Gómez, Juan Lozano Machuca grew up as part of a noble household, that of the Duque de Béjar, Francisco de Zúñiga y Sotomayor (1523–1591), to whom he was secretary. Zúñiga y Sotomayor

---

47 AGI, Patronato, 235, R10, [1586] Testimonio de los autos formados en la Audiencia de La Plata, sobre la guerra que debía hacerse a los indios chiriguanaes. Acompaña la descripción de aquella tierra y de la provincia de Santa Cruz de la Sierra, fols 12v, 8v–9v.

48 AGI, Patronato, 136, N1, R4, [1584] Juan Ladrón de Leyba, fols 9r–17r.

49 As an official in the Cajas Reales in Potosi, Lozano Machuca was aware of the challenging situation along the border, going by a letter these officials received from the Audiencia de Charcas asking for a loan of 8,000 pesos to cover the costs of any campaign against the Chiriguanaes. The loan was approved on 12 July 1583. Archivo Histórico de Potosí (from here on, AHP), Cajas Reales 7, fols 79v–81v in Julien, Angelis, and Bass Werner de Ruiz, *Historia de Tarija*, pp. 231–34.

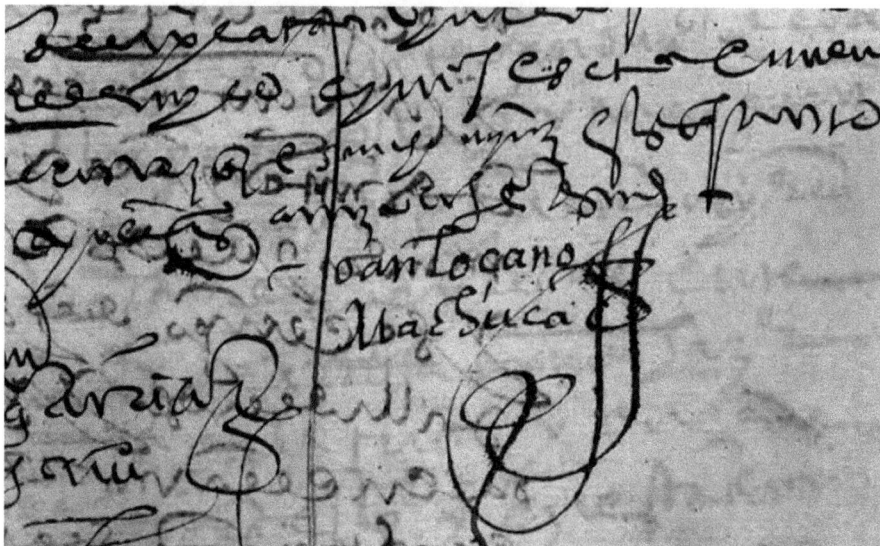

Figure 4.3   Handwritten signature of Juan Lozano Machuca
Source: Used with permission of Archivo y Biblioteca Nacionales de
Bolivia CaCh 11.

was the uncle of the Duque de Medina Sidonia, Alonso Pérez de Guzmán
y Sotomayor (1550–1615), the commander or Admiral of the Seas of the
Spanish Armada of 1588.[50] With such connections and experience, Lozano
Machuca secured a post as *chanciller*, or keeper of the Royal Seal, in the
Audiencia de San Francisco de Quito on 15 June 1567.[51] In preparation for
this job, the Consejo de Indias reviewed the paperwork on Lozano Machuca's

50 AGI, Patronato, 122, R2, N9, [1578] Informaciones de los méritos y servicios del
general Juan Lozano Machuca, que fue nombrado en comisión para levantar gente
en Valladolid, Toro, Zamora, Salamanca, Medina del Campo, Toledo, y otras partes,
con cuya gente pasó al socorro de Chile y ayudó a su conquista, y estando allí fue
nombrado sucesor del general Juan Lozada tras su Muerte, statement by Juan de
Vega, image 59; Diego Rosales, *Historia general de el reyno de Chile. Flandes Indiano*,
Vol. II (Valparaiso: Imprenta del Mercurio, 1878 [1674]), p. 198; Robert Hutchinson,
The Spanish Armada (London: Weidenfeld & Nicolson, 2014), p. 276.

51 The job of *chanciller* involved the safekeeping and use of the Royal Seal, which when
attached to documents conveyed that what was contained in them had royal endorsement. The person in charge was also responsible for the filing of royal *provisions* and
other Audiencia records. AGI, Quito, 35, N24, [1567–1571] Expediente de confirmación del oficio de canciller de la audiencia a Juan Lozano Machuca; Julio Alberto
Ramírez Barrios, 'En defensa de la autoridad real: Oficiales de la pluma de la Real
Audiencia de Lima durante la rebelión de Gonzalo Pizarro (1544–1548)', *Revista de
Historia del Derecho* 63 (2022): pp. 65–67.

background and experience and on 9 July 1567 he received the title Notario de Indias.[52] The post secured Lozano Machuca, his two single sisters Petronila Gómez Machuca and Estefanía Lozana, and two *criados*, Alonso Gómez and Isabel García, passage on board the same fleet that took Viceroy Toledo to Peru in 1569.[53] A man of letters who grew up in the patronage of wealthy nobility, Lozano Machuca could only expect a prosperous life ahead in the viceroyalty of Peru as a member of a viceregal court centred around Peru's fifth viceroy.

His post in the Audiencia de San Francisco de Quito did not probably offer substantial social and economic benefits for an ambitious character such as he, given the fact that the Audiencia, established on 29 August 1563, had limited resources.[54] The perfect opportunity to move on came when the Consejo de Indias commissioned Lope García de Castro to carry out a *visita* and *residencia* of the Audiencia de Charcas which resulted in the suspension of the *factor* and *veedor* of Charcas, Juan de Anguciaga, and the temporary appointment of Lorenzo de Cantoral in his place. With experience of notarising the *visita*, Lozano Machuca returned to Spain and in 1573 he was rewarded with the permanent post of *factor* and *veedor* of Charcas.[55]

This job entailed assisting with the melting of and trade in metal and the exchange of goods received in general and as Indian tribute, for gold and silver. It gave Lozano Machuca the opportunity to build wealth and connections, but was nonetheless a post that required a guarantee (*fianza*) that took Lozano Machuca three years to gather. The necessary funds came from several Charcas officers, *encomenderos*, and miners, some close to Viceroy Toledo, which is evidence of the extended social network Lozano Machuca had managed to build through his background and status.[56] Responsible for

52 AGI, Indiferente, 425, L24, [1567] Real provisión de notaría de las Indias para Juan Lozano Machuca, fol. 345v.
53 Romera Iruela and Galbís Diez, *Catalogo de pasajeros a Indias durante los siglos XVI, XVII y XVIII*, Vol. 1 (Sevilla: AGI, 1980), pp. 272–73.
54 The post of *chanciller* was more prestigious than remunerative. Julio Alberto Ramírez Barrios, *El sello real en el Perú Colonial: poder y representación en la distancia* (Lima, Sevilla: Fondo Editorial, Pontificia Universidad Católica de Perú, Editorial Universidad de Sevilla, 2020), p. 327.
55 AGI, Contratación, 5792, L1, [1573] Nombramiento de Juan Lozano Machuca como factor y veedor de Charcas, fols 170–171v; AGI, Charcas, 79, N14, [1590] Informaciones de oficio y parte: Núñez Maldonado. Traslado de 1600 de una información de 1590. Con parecer de la Audiencia de 1599, fol. 3r; AGI, Charcas, 418, L1, Título de factor y veedor de la provincia de los Charcas, en lugar de Juan de Anguciana, suspendido a raíz de la visita que a él, y demás oficiales reales, tomó el licenciado Castro, del Consejo de Indias, fols 257r–259r; letter from the President of the Audiencia de Charcas don Lope Diez de Armendáriz to the King, 25 September 1576, in Levillier, *La Audiencia de Charcas*, Vol. 1, p. 359.
56 Francisco López de Caravantes, *Noticia General del Perú*, Vol. 6, Biblioteca de

royal accounts and the associated paperwork, Lozano Machuca was typical of the lettered elite that existed in the major cities across the Catholic monarchy. He was part of a growing cadre of royal officials who, although they were appointed to different posts and jurisdictions, maintained social networks that brought geographically distant places such as Potosí, Lima, Quito, Panamá, Seville, and Madrid close. They were mainly courtiers and as such tried to combine 'the quill' and 'the sword' following the image of the virtuous noble, someone who was prepared to fight, yet who was also exemplary in upholding knightly values such as honour and prudence and promoted Christian virtues.[57]

However, even though as a *hidalgo* Lozano Machuca had received training in the art of war, his record of involvement in military tasks was far from positive. His first experience, transporting reinforcements for the war against the Araucanos in Chile, ended in mutiny. This *socorro* (back-up/rescue expedition) carried 120 men from various locations in the interior of Spain, first to Seville, and from there to Panamá, Peru, and Chile.[58] Panamá Audiencia judge Alonso Criado de Castilla, who saw the mutiny unfold, wrote that Lozano Machuca 'was perceived as someone without any experience with military discipline, because of his experience in the world of the quill'.[59] In effect, the notary found it difficult to bring the two worlds together.

Autores Españoles (Madrid: Ediciones Atlas, 1989, [1630–1631]), p. 46. Juan Lozano Machuca's guarantors were Melchor Juárez de Valer and his father Pedro Juárez de Valer, who was secretary of the Audiencia de Charcas and legal overseer of unclaimed or litigious assets, a role known as *depositario*; prominent and wealthy miner Carlos Corzo and through him Corzo's brother in Seville, Juan Antonio Corzo, who would hold assets on behalf of Lozano Machuca in Spain; Alonso Barriales; *encomendero* Gaspar de Solis; and Juan Pérez: AGI, Indiferente, 2086, N83, [1573] Expediente de concesión de licencia para pasar a Nueva Toledo, a favor de Juan Lozano Machuca, escribano, factor y veedor de la Real Hacienda de Nueva Toledo (Charcas), con tres criados, uno de ellos casado, y tres esclavos, image 7; ABNB, Cédulas Reales, Cédula 105, 12 January 1574, Para que Juan Lozano Machuca, que va por factor y veedor de la provincia de Los Charcas, pueda dar las fianzas que se le ha mandado que de para el uso de su oficio en las ciudades de La Plata, Cusco y La Paz, y en Potosí; y cumpla con ello no embargante que esta mandado las de en la ciudad de Los Reyes in José Enciso Contreras, *Cedulario de la Audiencia de La Plata de Charcas (Siglo XVI)* (Sucre: ABNB, 2005), p. 320; letter from the President of the Audiencia de Charcas, Licenciado Cepeda, to the King, 28 February 1585, in Levillier, *La Audiencia de Charcas*, Vol. 2, p. 204.

57   Angel Rama and John Charles Chasteen, *The Lettered City*, Post-Contemporary Interventions (Durham, NC: Duke University Press, 1996); Quondam and Torres Corominas, *El discurso cortesano*, p. 37.

58   AGI, Patronato, 122, R2, N9, [1578] Juan Lozano Machuca. On *socorros* see Ruiz Ibáñez, *Las dos caras de Jano*, pp. 84–99.

59   Notaries, and other jobs that required high literary skills as well as a good knowledge of paperwork and bureaucracy, were seen as 'jobs of the quill' (*oficios de pluma*). Víctor

A new commission he received afterwards showed the difficulties he found in venturing away from urban centres into a different world along borders or even *tierras de Indios*, lands inhabited by indigenous peoples. Lozano Machuca is known for a report he allegedly wrote about the Lipes and their eponymous region which is today in Potosí. He was commissioned to conduct a *visita* to their territory but, knowing that Potosí miner Pedro Sande was a frequent visitor to the region, the *factor/veedor* decided to delegate the task to him, only writing the final report.⁶⁰ Lozano Machuca, resident of one of the world's largest populated centres at the time, Potosí, found life outside that type of urban space inhospitable and dangerous. It was certainly a world away from his earlier life in the Iberian peninsula.

At the peak of his career, in the late 1570s, the pleasant-faced, tall, thin official who wore a prominent red-tinged beard and was recognisable by a scar across one hand—as he is described in a document—asked to travel back to Spain, with plans to return to Potosí after some time.⁶¹ Opposition to this move was expressed by Licenciado Diego López de Zúñiga, who was carrying out a *visita* to the Audiencia de Charcas at the time, and insisted that someone like Lozano Machuca, because of his knowledge of royal accounts and laws, should remain in Potosí.⁶² The Audiencia de Charcas disagreed, probably due to Lozano Machuca's connections with Toledo, and accepted the *factor*'s request to let him travel, approving a temporary replacement.⁶³

Gayol, '"Por todos los dias de nuestra vida..." Oficios de pluma, sociedad local y gobierno de la monarquía', in *Los oficios en las sociedades indianas* (México: UNAM, 2020), pp. 301–29; AGI, Panama, 13, R16, N70, [1577] letter from Doctor Alonso Criado de Castilla, judge of the Audiencia de Panamá, fol. 6.

60 The report is in AGI, Charcas 35 and was published by José María Casassas, 'Carta del factor de Potosí Juan Lozano Machuca (al virrey del Perú don Martín Enríquez) en que da cuenta de cosas de aquella villa y de las minas de los Lipes (Año 1581)', *Estudios Atacameños. Arqueología y Antropología Surandinas*, no. 10 (1992): pp. 30–34; José Luis Martínez Cereceda, *Gente de la tierra de guerra: Los lipes en las tradiciones andinas y el imaginario colonial* (Lima, Santiago, Chile: Fondo Editorial, Pontificia Universidad Católica del Perú; Dirección de Bibliotecas, Archivos y Museos de Chile, 2011), p. 46.

61 AGI, Indiferente, 2086, N83, [1573] Expediente de Juan Lozano Machuca; AGI, Charcas 35, letter from Juan Lozano Machuca to the King, 12 February 1578, fols 166r–166v.

62 Letter from don Diego López de Zúñiga to the King, in Levillier, *Gobernantes del Perú*, Vol. 9, p. 98.

63 The Audiencia in La Plata agreed to him leaving between January and February 1584. His replacement was going to be Ventura Gutiérrez, a royal accountant based in Costa Rica. López Villalva (dir.), *Acuerdos de la Real Audiencia de La Plata de los Charcas*, Vol. 3, 21 November 1583, 398; AGI, Charcas, 16, R22, N96, [1583] letter from Juan Lozano Machuca, 8 January 1583.

However, before he could leave Lozano Machuca embarked upon a campaign to the border of the Chiriguanaes; he would never see his homeland again.[64]

6. An expedition in the making

As preparations for a campaign were under way, in January 1584 news arrived in La Plata of the destruction of Miguel Martín's town, San Miguel de la Frontera or La Laguna. Martín's settlement had an auspicious start: Chiriguana groups supplied labour to help build the town. As had happened with San Bernando de la Frontera de Tarija and Santiago de la Frontera de Tomina, following an initial period of peaceful relations and exchanges, violence broke out. Scholars have different views on this, with some arguing that too much trust was placed in the Chiriguanaes, and others suggesting that the *vecinos* of the new town expanded into land they were supposed to leave alone.[65] On the surface, both seem likely reasons. However, in the past both Martín and García Mosquera had been involved in the Spanish side of the trade in local captives, exchanging weapons for captives with the Chiriguanaes in the area, and probably as supplies of weapons and gifts dwindled, so did Chiriguana support for a town in land so close to their settlements.[66] Furthermore, Martín was aware of an imminent campaign against the Chiriguanaes and the groups probably took this as a sign of betrayal, since he and his men were supposed to be border allies, to protect them.[67] The attack on his town was devastating, the worst incident since the destruction of Santo Domingo de la Nueva Rioja (or Condorillo) and La Barranca, the settlements established by captains Andrés Manso and Ñuflo de Chaves, two decades earlier.[68] The Audiencia put preparations for the expedition on hold only briefly and decided to press ahead with the policy of founding new towns along the border. It pushed to rebuild San Miguel de la Frontera (or La Laguna), a task arranged with Segura Zavala's rival Melchor de Rodas in order to keep the area's political balance in check,

---

64 A letter from the Audiencia de Lima judge Licenciado Estebán Marañón mentions the possibility that Machuca might decide to stay in Charcas. Whether Marañón knew the actual reasons for this and preferred not to disclose them in this letter is not clear. Marañón had Gutiérrez as his guest in Lima. Letter from Licenciado Esteban Marañón, Lima, 16 August 1581 in Enrique Otte and Guadalupe Albi Romero, eds, *Cartas privadas de emigrantes a Indias, 1540–1616* (Sevilla: Consejería de Cultura, Junta de Andalucía: Escuela de Estudios Hispano Americanos de Sevilla, 1988), p. 400.

65 Scholl, 'At the Limits of Empire', p. 358; Pifarré, *Historia de un pueblo*, Vol. 2, p. 77.

66 Scholl, 'At the Limits of Empire', p. 339; Weaver Olson, 'A Republic of Lost Peoples', p. 322.

67 Mario Graña Taborelli, 'Speaking the Language of Friendship: Partnerships in the Political Construction of the Late Sixteenth-Century South-East Charcas Frontier', *Bulletin of Latin American Research* 42, no. 5 (2023): pp. 721–33.

68 See Chapter Two.

given that Martín had been an ally of Rodas. The Audiencia was also aware that it needed someone like Rodas on board for its war effort against the Chiriguanaes.[69]

More urgency to launch the campaign was now expressed. While Toledo had been able to fund the initial cost of his expedition from a windfall of extra *quintos reales*, the Audiencia de Charcas did not have access to similar resources, and did not want to be seen as organising another *entrada* of 'feathers, silks, and trappings'. Juan Lozano Machuca saw this as an opportunity and submitted a *capitulación* and *asiento* to the Audiencia in June 1584, applying for an expedition that would contribute to the encirclement and punishment of the Chiriguanaes.[70] He committed himself to raise a force of 250 men with all the necessary supplies, spending the enormous sum of 50,000 pesos. The *factor* and *veedor* would have resorted to borrowing from his network of contacts, as he had done when he raised the *fianza* to guarantee his post. The Audiencia promised him the titles of governor, *Justicia Mayor*, and captain with rights over the distribution of land, native labour, and all other jurisdictional matters. More importantly, it also arranged for the founding of a new town to be called Concepción y Río de los Sauces, which would provide Lozano Machuca prestige and status.[71]

Within the Audiencia's jurisdiction, the Cajas Reales were based in Potosí and because of his official position Lozano Machuca could provide the Audiencia with a unique opportunity to request funds and have such a request granted. The *factor* agreed to hand the Audiencia de Charcas the initial funds required for the *entrada*, which came from the Caja de Granos in Potosí. These were funds raised from indigenous miners who contributed half a real per day to pay the wages of their Protector de Indios (a royal official responsible for representing indigenous people in trials); their Capitanes de Mita (Andean chiefs in charge of drafting sufficient local people to meet Potosí's need for miners); and mine inspectors or *veedores*. The contribution from the Caja de Granos would account for almost half of the total royal

69 In effect, at the time San Miguel de La Frontera was destroyed, Rodas donated some land to Martín, supporting his ally's strength. ABNB, EP3, fols 447r–447v; Mujía, *Bolivia–Paraguay*, Vol. II, p. 615.

70 The original documents would have been kept by the Audiencia and copies issued to Juan Lozano Machuca and sent to the Consejo de Indias. The copies sent to Spain should be in the AGI, where they should be with the other papers of Lozano Machuca in AGI, Charcas 35. However, that file contains only a reference to the documents, not the documents themselves: AGI, Charcas 35, letter from Juan Lozano Machuca to the King, 28 February 1584, fols 313v–314r. Only a small section of these *capitulaciones* and *asientos* has survived as part of the report on merits and services drafted for Pedro de Cuellar Torremocha: AGI, Patronato, 126, R17, [1606] Información de Pedro de Cuéllar Torremocha (1582), fols 73r–75v.

71 AGI, Charcas, 79, N14, [1590] Núñez Maldonado, fol. 1v.

funds assigned to this campaign.[72] Lozano Machuca also handed over 1,200 pesos from the royal coffers to complete the funds needed to start preparations.[73] Given these funds and Lozano Machuca's prestige and connections, the Audiencia de Charcas felt obliged to endorse his expedition and plan for a new border town.

However, aware of his military record, the Audiencia pushed him to agree that all decisions in relation to the *entrada* would be made in close consultation with his lieutenant and *maese de campo*, captains Francisco Arias de Herrera and Pedro de Cuellar Torremocha, respectively.[74] Both men, described as *hombres pláticos*, were a world away from the background and life of Lozano Machuca. Arias de Herrera had begun his military career in Spanish wars against the Ottomans, first during the attack on Velez de la Gomera in 1564, and later in the siege of Malta in 1565 and the battle of Lepanto in 1571, all victories for the monarchy. After battling the Ottomans, he was commissioned to travel to China, to secure the release of a Spanish vessel that had been captured, and from there to New Spain where, at the request from Viceroy Enríquez, he was engaged to fight the Chichimecas along the colony's northern borders. An experienced warrior and someone used to border life, Arias de Herrera arrived in Peru as part of Enríquez's entourage. Following the viceroy's passing, he unsuccessfully requested commissions from the Audiencia de Charcas and in the end moved to Potosí to look for opportunities in this prosperous mining town. While there, and almost ready to travel back to Spain via Tucumán and Brazil, Arias de Herrera received a letter asking him to join Lozano Machuca's expedition as lieutenant.[75] The other captain, Pedro de Cuellar Torremocha, was more familiar with the southeastern Charcas border since he had been *corregidor* in Tomina. Cuellar Torremocha was close to Pedro Segura Zavala and García Mosquera and all three were part of a network of respected captains and their allies who were interested in the expansion of the monarchy's jurisdiction

72 Additional funding would come from half of an *encomienda*—Huaqui—granted to Alonso Ramirez de Sosa, a *vecino* in La Paz; and the military salary of Captain Fernando Diez. Both had died, meaning the funds were available at the time. Letter from the Audiencia de Charcas to the King, in Levillier, *La Audiencia de Charcas*, Vol. 2, p. 181.

73 BNE, Ms 3,044, Papeles varios tocantes al gobierno de Indias, obtained at http://bdh-rd.bne.es/viewer.vm?id=0000023047&page=1, accessed 15 May 2024; Luis Capoche, *Relación general de la villa imperial de Potosí*, Vol. CXXII, Biblioteca de Autores Españoles (Madrid: Atlas, 1958 [1585]), pp. 145–46.

74 AGI, Patronato, 126, R17, [1606] Información de Pedro de Cuéllar Torremocha (1582), fols 73v–75v.

75 AGI, Patronato, 127, N2, R4, [1584] Información de los méritos y servicios del capitán Francisco Arias de Herrera, que sirvió en la conquista y pacificación de Perú y particularmente en el sosiego de los indios chichimecas, también en la toma del Peñón, batalla de Lepanto, habiendo ido dos veces a la China y con socorros a las islas Filipinas, images 23, 31.

over the eastern borders of Charcas and who saw themselves as the people best fitted to achieve this task.[76] The Audiencia was thus hoping that the trio would combine military skills (Arias de Herrera) and local knowledge (Cuellar Torremocha), with Lozano Machuca's financial and administrative support, thereby avoiding a repeat of Toledo's 1574 expedition, while providing a back-up plan in case Lozano Machuca's leadership faltered.

7. A royal official's last journey

Lozano Machuca's expedition was supposed to leave on 15 June 1584, but it was still being prepared in September. The departure had been coordinated with the *entradas* from Santa Cruz de la Sierra and Tarija, so that the Chiriguanaes would be encircled from three separate fronts, and any delays would therefore put the whole strategy at risk. The reputation of the Audiencia de Charcas hung in the balance and its judges called captains de Cuellar Torremocha and Arias de Herrera for meetings demanding explanations. They both stated that Lozano Machuca had 'gone cold' on the expedition, waiting for the arrival of a new viceroy.[77] This was not the news the Audiencia was hoping to hear, and a decision was made to put Lozano Machuca under pressure to start marching immediately.

The expedition eventually left for the site of the future village of Concepción y Río de los Sauces via Tomina, part of the jurisdiction of Segura Zavala (see Figure 0.1), who provided support and through his connections with local Chiriguana factions probably secured its safe passage.[78] As with previous *entradas*, the force involved a large contingent of indigenous Andeans, including Yampara peoples who had been assigned by the Audiencia to do various jobs in La Plata, and people supplied by the *capitanes de mita*, all headed by the leading *capitan de mita* at the time.[79] They took with them 1,200 llamas. Along with the indigenous leaders, Mercedarians also accompanied this expedition, through friar Diego de Reynoso, confirming the order's connection with borders and local captives.[80] Although who guided the

76   AGI, Patronato, 126, R17, [1606], Información de Pedro de Cuéllar Torremocha (1582), fols 73v–75v.

77   ABNB, ALP, CACh-38, [1585] Auto de la Audiencia de La Plata y declaración del capitán Arias de Herrera, teniente general, sobre su sentir de la pretendida entrada y guerra a la Cordillera del general Juan Lozano Machuca contra los indios chiriguanaes, fol. 2v.

78   AGI, Charcas, 80, N17, [1600] Informaciones de oficio y parte: Pedro de Mendoza Quesada, capitán. Traslado de 1600 [SUP] de una información de 1598, image 32; AGI, Charcas, 79, N14, [1590], Núñez Maldonado, fol. 18r. 31 January 1590.

79   Capoche, *Relación general de la villa imperial de Potosí*, pp. 134, 142–43.

80   Reynoso had worked in Chile before moving to Charcas. Mercedarians travelled across different borders carrying with them their valuable knowledge and experience. AGI, Charcas, 80, N17, [1600] Mendoza Quesada, image 32; Fray Policarpo

expedition is unknown, the presence of García Mosquera, the same guide initially used by Toledo a decade earlier, speaks for itself. The Chiriguanaes, who were close allies of this guide and his extended family, were probably involved in the *entrada*. García Mosquera, who enjoyed seniority both in the area and the expeditionary force, had his own agenda and at this stage his participation probably reflected his own ambitions and those of his network to improve their status and potentially secure new land in another corner of the region.

Apart from the initial delay, up to that point things ran smoothly. However, once the expeditionary forces arrived at the proposed site for the new village, the argument about Lozano Machuca's lack of military skills resurfaced, and the royal official faced his second mutiny. Growing dissatisfaction over the way the *entrada* was being managed lay at the core of the claims of those who decided to rebel against the expedition leader.[81] Other sources claim that problems had been caused by the initial delays: that when the men began marching, the dry season had ended and intense rain held up the expedition's progress.[82] As had happened with Toledo, the Spanish were encountering an unfamiliar environment, one they perceived as hostile, on their journey to the border. Other problems arose, too. Lozano Machuca had not abided by his side of the arrangements, bringing only half of the 250 men he had promised.[83] Alerted, the Audiencia de Charcas called him back to La Plata to provide explanations. Once there, the official was put in prison.[84] In October 1584, and to prevent further problems following claims that the disillusioned men of Lozano Machuca's expedition were planning to move on to Tucumán where they would demand rewards from the authorities there, the Audiencia appointed the more pragmatic and experienced de Cuellar Torremocha temporary leader of the expedition. Cuellar Torremocha assumed his new role in a ceremony at the old Inca fortress of Cuscotoro with García Mosquera as one of the witnesses. Soon after, a new town was founded, but under a different name than that planned by Lozano Machuca: to honour the new leader's birthplace (Torremocha), Concepción Torremocha de los Sauces was established. The new settlement only lasted a few months before being

Gazulla, *Los primeros mercedarios en Chile. 1535–1600* (Santiago de Chile: Imprenta La Ilustración, 1918), p. 155.

81 AGI, Lima, 212, N8, [1598] Informaciones de oficio y parte: Cristóbal de Baranda, capitán, alguacil mayor de Charcas y Potosí, pacificador de los chiriguanas y pacificador en Chile como alférez de la compañía del capitán Fernando de Córdoba y Figueroa. Información y parecer de la Audiencia de Lima, image 3.

82 Capoche, *Relación general de la villa imperial de Potosí*, p. 134.

83 AGI, Patronato, 126, R17, [1606] Información de Pedro de Cuéllar Torremocha (1582), fol. 51v.

84 AGI, Charcas, 79, N14, [1590] Núñez Maldonado, fol. 1v.

abandoned under constant attacks from the Chiriguanaes and because the land was unsuitable for farming.⁸⁵

In the meantime, Lozano Machuca had been released under the condition that he made up for the men he had not provided for his *entrada*. As he was travelling back to the new village, aiming to resume his post as the expedition's leader, he fell ill of 'dolor de costado' (pleurisy)⁸⁶ and after three days of agony passed away in the town of Chaqui. He was only 46 years old and was buried in La Plata.⁸⁷

The courtier, the man of the quill, Lozano Machuca, was only behind this expedition because of his connections and the financial arrangements he could secure for the Audiencia de Charcas so that he could turn an event that would normally be expensive (as Chapter Three showed) into one that would not represent a substantial cost to the monarchy. The Audiencia also took extra precautions, demanding consensus between Lozano Machuca and his two subordinates on any decisions in relation to the expedition, thereby reducing the leader's authority, in a manner that possibly also undermined him. Lozano Machuca had his own agenda and, learning of the forthcoming arrival of a new viceroy in Peru, someone who would engage with him differently, possibly handing him new posts and rewards reflecting his merits and connections, may have decided to procrastinate, and delay the *entrada* for as long as he could. In fact, Peru's next viceroy, don Fernando de Torres y Portugal (1585–1592) was already in Panamá about to embark on his trip to Lima.

Lozano Machuca's defeat was Cuellar Torremocha's triumph, as he seized control of the expedition he had only been marginally involved in helping to organise. It was also a victory for Segura Zavala and García Mosquera, two veteran settlers with good connections with both the Audiencia de Charcas and the Chiriguanaes, who now were able to add yet another border town

85 AGI, Patronato, 126, R17, [1606] Información de Pedro de Cuéllar Torremocha (1582), fol. 72r.

86 '*Dolor de costado* has been variously translated as 'chest pain', or 'pain in the side', but perhaps the most appropriate definition is 'pain in the ribcage'. The term reflects upper respiratory discomfort, as with severe infections involving the lungs and chest cavity, when pain that is difficult to locate exactly pierces one when the thorax expands and contracts as the lungs inhale and exhale. The pain might be reported in the back, the chest, the side, the ribs. The English used the world pleurisy to describe the same affliction': Noble David Cook, *Born to Die: Disease and New World Conquest, 1492–1650*, New Approaches to the Americas (Cambridge, New York: Cambridge University Press, 1998), p. 104.

87 Lozano Machuca passed away on 23 February 1585. AGI, Charcas, 35, letter from the Real Hacienda officials to the King, 23 February 1585, fol. 332r; letter from the Audiencia de Charcas to the King, 26 February 1585, in Levillier, *La Audiencia de Charcas*, Vol. 2, p. 200. Scholl states that Machuca was murdered by the Chiriguanaes: Scholl, 'At the Limits of Empire', p. 374. AGI, Charcas, 79, N14, [1590] Núñez Maldonado, fol. 11r.

to the jurisdiction of the Corregimiento of Tomina. Finally, it was also a success for the Audiencia de Charcas, which managed to step in and take on executive functions, normally the jurisdiction of a viceroy, in a manner that compared favourably with Toledo's expedition, and which demonstrated that the tribunal was well equipped, both legally and politically, to handle political challenges. The episode also highlights the more practical approach the Audiencia de Charcas took to the complexities and reality of the southeastern borders, increasingly preferring to leave the running of such remote regions in the hands of captains with local and political know-how. This was, in the Audiencia's view, a more secure way of extending the Catholic monarchy's jurisdiction over the Charcas borders.

8. Epilogue: The downscaling of politics as the basis for the empire's resilience and endurance

Both Toledo and his *criado*, Juan Lozano Machuca, were blamed for the failure of their expeditions. Toledo returned to Spain and had to stay away from Madrid until almost the end of his life. Lozano Machuca was accused, put in prison, and forced to abide by the arrangements made by others. The Audiencia de Charcas, however, was able to move on totally unscathed, demonstrating that it was well equipped and prepared to handle emergencies and was in control of how it exercised jurisdiction. The Audiencia was the focus of local political activity. Its judges knew everyone's affairs and had learned from the viceroy's mistakes and how to manipulate different groups and agendas, thereby saving the monarchy's reputation and finances in the process. It was in a much better position than a viceroy to perform 'miniature politics'.

By agreeing commissions or jobs with key individuals in line with their merits and background, the Crown was able to expand geographically, without having to compromise its own reputation. This approach guaranteed the endurance and resilience of the monarchy across its vast geography. This was not centralism, in fact the opposite: the sharing of authority that made each vassal feel part of a larger entity encompassing a wide diversity of peoples under its monarch and the Catholic faith. In this polycentric polity, as a result negotiation did not take place between a core or centre and the periphery, but within and between many centres, between royal agents and vassals, involving petitioning and the localisation of laws and regulations, adapting them to the particular circumstances of place and time. This element provided the whole system of government with immense flexibility.

'Miniature politics' required the Crown to provide its agents a great degree of independence as well as significant trust, understood as obedience and allegiance.[88] Independence involved knowing that they would do the

---

88 Alicia Esteban Estríngana, ed., *Servir al rey en la monarquía de los Austrias: Medios, fines y logros del servicio al soberano en los siglos XVI y XVII* (Madrid: Sílex, 2012).

right thing to keep the land *quieta*, trouble-free. Obedience was the basis for patronage, through the recognition of authority and political obligation. Perceived by their contemporaries as 'practical men' (*hombres pláticos* [*sic*]), with solid knowledge of border life and strong connections with the Chiriguanaes, the likes of Segura Zavala, García Mosquera, Martín, Cuellar Torremocha, and Rodas were entrusted with the running of their towns and jurisdictions as loyal vassals. Their success or failure would not be the Crown's responsibility, it would be theirs as independent agents. This level of miniaturisation of politics also resulted in a miniaturisation of conflicts that largely originated and were resolved locally. Miniaturisation did not mean disintegration, however. By respecting the autonomy and customs of its villages, towns, and cities, the Crown strengthened its own authority, fostering their loyalty as custodians of its own political values. This approach mirrored the world of the Chiriguanaes who were influenced by and influenced the political stance of these urban centres. Their personal connections with the leaders of these towns and the relational character of the expansion of jurisdiction in the borders made the ties with these Spanish populations unstable. The fact that Santo Domingo de La Nueva Rioja (Condorillo), La Barranca, San Miguel de la Frontera (La Laguna), and even Concepción Torremocha de los Sauces, are today absent from Bolivia's maps, is testament to this.

Conclusion

Final but not Definitive Comments

This book has explored, through the political culture of the Catholic monarchy, three expeditions pursued by the Spanish into the borders of Charcas and Tucumán in the second half of the sixteenth century. These *entradas* mark three different moments in the process of settlement and the expansion of royal jurisdiction in Charcas.

The journeys of *encomendero* Martín de Almendras between 1564 and 1565 took place at a time when a young Audiencia de Charcas was trying to extend and settle its authority, which brought conflict with the Audiencia de Lima and the governor of Chile. Against the backdrop of a viceroyalty without a viceroy, an ambitious *encomendero* group, and indigenous uprisings occurring in Tucumán and along the southeastern Charcas border, the Audiencia de Charcas moved swiftly to restore order and extend its jurisdiction, first over the Chichas and Chiriguanaes, and then in the most conflictive and remote Tucumán, where the Crown's presence was more tenuous and where jurisdiction was highly contentious. In effect, the province was torn between Chile and Charcas, and the Audiencia de Lima that was exercising power in the absence of a viceroy sided with the former as a means to limit the latter. On the ground, and for some time, the alleged death of Francisco de Aguirre, the governor of Tucumán, was seen by the Audiencia de Charcas as a great opportunity to expand its jurisdiction by sending a new governor. News that Aguirre was still alive and in office did not deter Martín de Almendras or the plan of the Audiencia de Charcas to move forward to seize the province in its name, yet in the end it was not Almendras who brought Tucumán back within the Charcas sphere of influence, but his men who arrested Aguirre and sent him to La Plata, saving the province for the Audiencia de Charcas. The expeditions show that jurisdiction was contested and had to be legitimised and fought for, even against other Spaniards and their jurisdictions. Frequently juxtaposed, a jurisdiction had to be settled and this had to be done not only on paper but also with the help of armed men on the ground, and through theatrics. The Crown had nothing to lose as the downscaling of jurisdiction and the sharing of authority kept such conflicts largely at a local level, preventing large-scale problems that might threaten the status quo and jeopardise government. The mantra 'keeping the land quiet' was of tantamount importance for the monarchy and its elites.

The highly ornamented and elaborated *entrada* of don Francisco de Toledo, the fifth viceroy of Peru, to the Chiriguanaes in 1574 marked a second moment in the early history of Charcas. In contradiction of earlier historiography that, based on the image of nation-states created in the early nineteenth century, sees Toledo as a law reformer, planner, and organiser, or the mastermind behind a strong 'colonial state', the expedition shows a viceroy who went into Charcas with a plan that had to be changed many times and negotiated with different parties. The viceroy had a very authoritative and fixed approach to exerting influence and making the monarch present in Peru, one which frequently clashed with local elites generally accustomed to rule the land, and to a weak and highly negotiable royal presence. In travelling to the dense Andean slopes inhabited by the Chiriguanaes Toledo was largely surrounded by his courtiers, and after facing challenges, was lucky to leave the lowlands alive. The expedition shows a jurisdiction that had matured in the decade before the fifth viceroy's rule and that was more localised and increasingly relied on knowledgeable agents, such as captains, to represent royal authority, rather than the presence of royal dignitaries like the 'King's living image'. There was no room for high royal officials in a region like Charcas that had become aware of its possibilities and limitations as a district within the global monarchy. Challenging historiographic views that see the Catholic monarchy as archaic, absolutist, inefficient, and bureaucratic, this expedition shows that its political system combined a high dose of localism, pragmatism, and consensus, all characteristics that Toledo at times found challenging.

The final expedition examined in this book was carried out by Juan Lozano Machuca in 1584 and shows two key components in the Catholic monarchy's resilience and adaptation: the miniaturisation of politics and its polycentrism. The *entrada* was part of a larger armed effort against the Chiriguanaes that took place on three war fronts. The event was the perfect opportunity for the Audiencia de Charcas to demonstrate that it could take on military functions of a viceregal nature and negotiate, organise, and execute an expedition against the rebels with little cost to the Crown and with an enduring impact along the border. This is the complete opposite to Toledo's costly *entrada*. Lozano Machuca, an *hidalgo* close to Toledo and a royal officer, helped to secure the funds that were needed to pursue the expedition. However, it was not he who would emerge triumphant from this event but those 'practical' members of his crew who brought the expedition to completion. The Audiencia gave credit and power to those individuals with strong local connections who were able to keep the land trouble-free. In effect, this pragmatic approach made the monarchy resilient and flexible, as laws and strategies were changed, discussed, and scrutinised at a small scale. Those implementing decisions were always 'good' or 'bad' agents, keeping the monarchy at a distance from their actions and thus its reputation safe.

This book has also shifted the discussion on jurisdiction that has largely been approached from a legal perspective to the symbolic and ritual sphere, as it demonstrates the importance of 'presence' associated with the concept. Jurisdiction aimed to make a distant authority present, yet, ambiguously, whenever such presence was achieved, its absence was simultaneously acknowledged. In the dramaturgy of the political in Spanish American societies, jurisdiction was embodied, exerted, performed, staged, ritualised, and displayed. It was anchored in space through towns and cities, and their churches, convents, and *cabildo* buildings, which symbolised possession and radiated political and religious power across a discontinuous area. Over distances, jurisdiction was measured in terms of journeys, of how many days it would take someone to travel from one point to the next. When such journeys acquired political meaning, such as during *visitas* or *entradas*, there was also a political and religious liturgy to follow which turned them into processions, never dissimilar to those frequently organised to mark religious festivals and/or civic occasions, which often included punishment and violence. Rituals and ceremonies made jurisdiction feel real and close to those involved. They reaffirmed loyalties and replayed political fictions, both needed in remote lands such as the Charcas borders.

With the borders in focus, this book analyses the transformation of geographical and cultural areas into political boundaries during the sixteenth century, including the situation in the last decades of Tahuantinsuyu. With its vast armies, a complex road network, and a sophisticated warehouse system, Tahuantinsuyu's original approach to managing the southeastern Charcas borders was one that combined fortresses and exchanges, that largely relied on alliances with indigenous groups who were recompensed with privileged roles and status in return for participation in the polity's expansion. In line with Tahuantinsuyu's political cycles, such partnerships had to be renewed with every new Inca and were already under strain at the time of the regime's collapse.

The space vacated by Tahuantinsuyu was not occupied by the Spanish, but by the Chiriguanaes, who were able to expand during the chaos that followed. The Crown's aggregational and integrational expansionism, which transformed land into territories, sharing authority among agents with sometimes conflicting and juxtaposed jurisdictions, integrated and accommodated the fragmented world of Chiriguana factions within its own political culture. Such expansionism relied heavily on local elites, who adapted and petitioned for rules and regulations to meet their needs and those of their political allies, including the indigenous groups with whom they coexisted. However, this fragmentation also exposed border towns and their *vecinos* to chronic infighting which thwarted the first attempts to establish Spanish settlements near Chiriguana land. Further attempts, undertaken in a more organised manner, would be more successful, yet living conditions in border villages, which resembled fortified settlements, always remained fragile and vulnerable. The border was seen as an area with no law, no justice, and therefore no King and no religion. It was not a space empty of people, as it would be seen in later years, for there were always, at least in the Spanish imagination, crowds of indigenous souls waiting to be evangelised, to be placed under the jurisdiction of the Catholic monarchy. Devoid of law and justice, it became a space for outcasts, somewhere to hide among or close by unconquerable indigenous peoples. The land and its inhabitants were classed 'at war', a status the Crown could do little to change in Charcas throughout its long history and one it inadvertently reinforced because of its own political constraints and inability to establish permanent jurisdiction along the border, something that, when achieved, was always ephemeral. The borders were where the monarchy placed its wars, to quieten the rest of its realms. By sending its men to fight along the edges, it kept its other possessions in peace.

From an ideological point of view, this study contributes to rebuilding the narratives that were used as strategies to justify armed action and unleash violence and coercion against indigenous peoples seen as unconquerable and hostile, with the purpose of securing privileges, status, and honour, in a political system based on an 'economy of rewards and *mercedes*'. Such strategic narratives were centred on the potential loss of Porco and Potosí, stereotypical views of the Chiriguanaes based on carefully constructed and circulated 'hegemonic knowledges' that emphasised the childlike status of indigenous peoples and their 'natural inclination to sin and vice', and, lastly, the potential loss of Tucumán, all of which justified continuous war and enslavement. Such narratives show how local elites saw themselves and wanted to be perceived as part of the Catholic monarchy, whose principles and defence they carried out, always awaiting the King's approval and rewards.

Through a fiction carefully crafted over time, the elites of Charcas saw themselves as the guardians of these borders. In their imagination their presence guaranteed the monarchy the mineral wealth it needed, keeping its new vassals, its indigenous peoples, in peace and order. However, guardians can only exist if there is something or somebody to be guarded against, and the Chiriguanaes fitted the stereotype of savages that local elites recurrently conveyed in strategic narratives to justify any expedition against them. Although this symbiotic relation between the Chiriguanaes and local elites might seem to have trapped both sides in a recurrent cycle of violence and trade from which neither side could escape, this whole process was constantly changing and was quite fluid. The way that different border groups and Chiriguana factions articulated with each other and with the Audiencia, and through it with other realms of the Monarchy, is likely to have varied over time. The conflicts in Tomina in the early 1580s between captains García Mosquera and Segura on one side, and Rodas on the other, that involved their Chiriguana factions, which were explored only superficially in Chapter Four, provide a glimpse of this. The arrangements between Chiriguanaes and the Spanish are also likely to have intensified the incursions of the former against other lowland groups in search of captives. The arrangements probably changed the whole perception that the Chiriguanaes had of other indigenous peoples. Such dynamics have not been studied yet and require further investigation, because of their complexity and their importance, since the Catholic monarchy's presence in the borders relied on them.

In summary, all three expeditions show how, as Charcas grew in importance for the monarchy, so did the ambitions of its own elite. The creation of an Audiencia was a key stage in this shift. The Audiencia was seen as the ideal institution to channel and make the monarch present in a district where royal presence had been weak and where *vecinos* were largely self-reliant and independent. A region 'politically equipped' more densely, with numerous towns and cities, and a thriving civic and religious life, combined with mineral wealth and resources, including a settled indigenous population, would always weigh favourably for the Audiencia and its elites. However, this process of consolidating Charcas must not be mistaken for a journey towards 'political independence' or a sign of 'proto-national patriotism'. It was simply the transition that most districts in the Catholic monarchy hoped to make as part of their own political journeys.

This book should hopefully be a small contribution to a growing scholarship that highlights that it is anachronistic to analyse the monarchy through the prism of the nation-states that succeeded it. The downscaling of politics, that relied on localisation of laws, as well as a high degree of flexibility and authority-sharing, moved the stage to the local sphere and presents an image that challenges traditional views of a centralised, slow-to-react, almost monolithic, inefficient monarchy prone to red tape. Its unique approach combined with a political culture that thrived on litigation and petitioning, local values and customs, and consensus as the basis for the common good, made the monarchy largely resilient for three centuries. The same culture made honour, obedience, and hierarchies a cult, transporting a bulk of medieval traditions across the vast Iberian worlds. This was mocked by the nineteenth-century liberal states that began their own search for a newly imported modernity that quite never found its home in Latin America. Indeed, the sixteenth-century Catholic monarchy is still alive and not just in its manuscripts, works of art, and buildings. The region's soul searching must continue, but the journey should necessarily include the regime's early history to make it meaningful.

Glossary of Terms

Acuerdos:	Any resolutions or 'agreements' made by the Audiencia. The room where debates on these matters took place was also known as Acuerdos.
Adelantado:	A senior military title.
Alcalde Ordinario/Mayor:	Magistrate attached to a *cabildo*.
Audiencia:	A governmental/judicial body of the Catholic monarchy with jurisdiction over a vast area around a main town or city and by extension the region within its jurisdiction.
Beneméritos:	Old conquistadors, honoured for particular services.
Cabildo:	Town council.
Cacique:	Leader of an indigenous group (Hispanised Arawak).
Cajas Reales:	Royal coffers. They were frequently situated in major cities.
Camarero:	Chamberlain.
Campero:	Organiser of military camp.
Capac Ñam:	The main Inca official road.
Capitulaciones y asientos:	Contracts for the exploration and pacification of new areas and the establishment of cities and towns.
Cédula:	Decree.
Cédula real:	Royal decree.
Consejo de Indias:	The Castilian body responsible for overseeing the Indies (or Spanish America) and the Philippines.
Corregidor:	Spanish official with administrative and judicial authority.

Corregimiento:	Jurisdiction of a *corregidor*.
Criado:	Normally someone who was raised as part of a large family. It can also mean someone familiar with social and political connections; or even (in some circumstances) a servant.
Depositario:	Legal post to oversee unclaimed assets or assets subject to litigation.
Encomendero/a:	Holder of an *encomienda*.
Encomienda:	Grant to an individual as a personal reward for merits or services that gave the recipient the right to exact from defined groups of indigenous people tribute in kind or cash and, until 1549, labour services; in return the *encomendero/a* undertook to provide Christian instruction to and protect the group(s) so granted.
Encomienda en depósito:	Grant kept aside for a time when the indigenous group granted could be reached and conquered.
Entrada:	Military or religious expedition into unexplored or unpacified territory.
Gobernación:	Jurisdiction of a governor.
Gobernador:	Governor.
Hidalgo:	A nobleman whose title was not hereditary.
Huaca:	Andean deity.
Indios de Guerra:	Warlike, as opposed to 'friendly', indigenous peoples.
Justicia Mayor:	Post with responsibilities for the delivery of justice.
Licenciado:	Title given to a person with a bachelor's degree or a licentiate.
Maese de campo:	Camp-master.
Mayordomo:	Head of household, typically one of some substance.
Mercedes:	Royal rewards.
Mestizaje:	Racial mixing; hence *mestizo, mestiza*.
Mita:	Andean rotational labour draft.
Mitayo:	Male adult compulsorily serving under a *mita*.
Mitimaes:	Andean colonists removed from their original settlements to occupy land as colonists of Tahuantinsuyu.

Naciones:	A denomination used by the Spanish to refer to groups of indigenous people who possibly shared similar cultural patterns.
Oidor:	Spanish judge and member of an Audiencia.
Paje de guión:	Person responsible for bearing the coat of arms of a noble person.
Policía:	Used as a state of being: kept in *policía* (in good order), meaning abiding by Christian customs and respecting royal authority. *Policía* could be achieved through founding villages and towns.
Presidio:	Garrison, fort.
Probanza de méritos y servicios:	Report on a person's personal merits and services to the Crown, ordinarily drafted with the help of a notary and/or lawyer for the purpose of obtaining privileges or rewards from the Crown.
Procurador:	Representative, lawyer, attorney.
Puna:	Dry highland grasslands characteristic of the southern Andes.
Quinto:	Tax of one-fifth the value of an item. Generally paid on silver, among other goods.
Quipo:	Knotted cords used in Andean cultures to store information. Those with the ability to read *quipos* are called *quipocamayos*.
Reducción:	Settlement formed by the amalgamation of several smaller settlements or created by drawing together indigenous people.
Reducido:	Indigenous person forced to relocate to a settlement.
Relación:	An account.
Relaciones geográficas:	Geographical accounts.
Reparto de encomienda:	Distribution of *encomienda* grants.
Requerimiento:	Legal document read to indigenous peoples about to be subject to military intervention.
Residencia:	Judicial review of the conduct of a Spanish official.
Tambo:	Inca lodging-house, sometimes used to store *quipos*.
Tasa:	Tribute.
Traslado:	Copy of a document or part of a document, frequently made to provide further evidence as part of a legal process.

Vecino:	Citizen of a town.
Veedor:	Inspector.
Visita:	Tour of inspection of an area, conducted by a royal official called a *visitador*.
Yanacona:	Indigenous servant.

Bibliography and Sources

1. Unpublished sources

Archivo y Bibliotecas Nacionales de Bolivia (ABNB)

ABNB, 1674, EC25, [1573] Visita de Agustín de Ahumada a los Chichas.

ABNB, ALP, CACh-38, [1585] Auto de la Audiencia de La Plata y declaración del capitán Arias de Herrera, teniente general, sobre su sentir de la pretendida entrada y guerra a la cordillera del general Juan Lozano Machuca contra los indios chiriguanaes.

ABNB, EC1618, [1574] Probanza de Melchor de Rodas.

ABNB, EP3, fols 447r–447v, Donación de tres fanegadas de tierra para sembrar maiz en Mojotorillo en terminus de Santiago de la Frontera de Tomina de Melchor de Rodas a Miguel Martín. 13 de enero de 1584.

ABNB, EP16, fols 195v–197v, Convenio para trueque de mina. 8 de octubre de 1572.

ABNB, EP18, fols 399v–399r, Poder especial que otorga Catalina Ñusta, india, viuda mujer de Juan Bautista Morisco, a Alonso Gutiérrez, para que en nombre suyo pueda cobrar de Fray Pedro Gutiérrez, capellán del virrey Francisco de Toledo trescientos y más pesos de plata corriente, los cuales le mandó dar por el tiempo que le sirvió en la entrada a los indios chiriguanaes, [1578].

ABNB, EP19, fols 322v–323v, Venta de huerta que hace Melchor de Rodas a Polo Ondegardo [1574].

ABNB, EP20, fols 319r–320r, Poder de León de Ayance y Gasión de Torres de Mendoza, a Diego de Zárate, vecino de la ciudad de La Paz, para compra de ganado y ropa, o plata para Chiriguanaes [1584].

ABNB, EP39, fols 77r–78r, [1586].

ABNB, EP 48, fols 400r–401r, Venta de ocho piezas de indios, cinco varones y tres mujeres, sacados de la jornada de los chiriguanaes, que hace el capitán Juan Valero, residente en la ciudad de La Plata, a favor de Antonio Pantoja de Chávez, los cuales, por auto de la audiencia de La Plata, tiene por esclavos y yanaconas perpetuos y se los vende al precio de novecientos cincuenta pesos de plata ensayada y marcada. Escribanía pública de Blas López de Solórzano, 25 de noviembre de 1585, La Plata.

Archivo General de Indias (AGI)

AGI, Charcas, 16, R22, N96, [1583] Letter from Juan Lozano Machuca, 8 January 1583.

AGI, Charcas, 21, R1, N2, [1600] Relación cierta de Diego Felipe de Alcaya.

AGI, Charcas, 31, R1, N2, [1600] Relación cierta de Diego Felipe de Alcaya.

AGI, Charcas, 35, [1578] Letters from Lozano Machuca to the King.

AGI, Charcas, 35, [1561–1614] Cartas y expedientes de oficiales reales.

AGI, Charcas, 53, [1574–1576] Información de méritos y servicios de don Juan Colque Guarache.

AGI, Charcas, 57, [1622] Información de méritos y servicios de don Diego Copatete Guarache.

AGI, Charcas, 58, [1656] Información de servicios de Diego Moreno Contreras.

AGI, Charcas, 78, N20, [1583] Probanza de Cristóbal Ramirez de Montalvo.

AGI, Charcas, 78, N34, [1585] Probanza de Antonio Alderete Riomayor.

AGI, Charcas, 79, N11, [1592] Probanza de Lope Vazquez Pestana.

AGI, Charcas, 79, N14, [1590] Informaciones de oficio y parte: Núñez Maldonado. Traslado de 1600 de una información de 1590. Con parecer de la Audiencia de 1599.

AGI, Charcas, 79, N22, [1592–1593] Informaciones de oficio y parte: Francisco Aymozo [*sic*], cacique principal y gobernador de los indios yamparaes de Yotala y Quilaquila.

AGI, Charcas, 79, N25, [1593] Probanza de Francisco de la Cuba.

AGI, Charcas, 80, N17, [1600] Informaciones de oficio y parte: Pedro de Mendoza Quesada, capitán. Traslado de 1600 de una información de 1598.

AGI, Charcas, 81, N11, [1601–1610] Informaciones de oficio y parte: Julio Ferrufiño, contador y juez oficial de La Paz. Traslado de 1610 con informaciones de 1601–1606–1610. Dos ejemplares de traslados de 1606 con informaciones de 1601–1606. Otro traslado de 1601 con información y parecer del mismo año.

AGI, Charcas, 84, N10, [1605] Probanza de Fernando de Toledo Pimentel.

AGI, Charcas, 85, N5, [1606] Probanza de Juan Alonso de Vera y Zárate.

AGI, Charcas, 85, N10, [1607] Informaciones de oficio y parte: Fernando de Irarrazábal y Andía, capitán. Información contenida de 1607. Con parecer de la Audiencia. Hay otra información de 1607 de sus méritos y servicios, y los de su padre Francisco de Irarrazábal y Andía, con una petición y un decreto al final de la misma de 1610.

AGI, Charcas, 86, N17, [1610] Probanza de Diego de Zárate Irarrazábal y Andía.

AGI, Charcas, 87, N19, [1618] Informaciones Gabriel Paniagua de Loaisa.

AGI, Charcas, 93, N1, [1646] Probanza de Francisco de Maturana Trascapo.

AGI, Charcas, 94, N19, [1589] Probanza de Hernando de Salazar.

AGI, Charcas, 418, L1, [1563] Registro de oficio y partes: reales cédulas y provisiones, etc., conteniendo disposiciones de gobierno y gracia para las autoridades y particulares del distrito de la Audiencia de Charcas.

AGI, Charcas, 418, L1, Título de factor y veedor de la provincia de los Charcas, en lugar de Juan de Anguciana, suspendido a raíz de la visita que a él, y demás oficiales reales, tomó el licenciado Castro, del Consejo de Indias.

AGI, Contaduria, 1805, [1575] Gastos de la guerra de los chiriguanaes.

AGI, Contratación, 5792, L1, [1573] Nombramiento de Juan Lozano Machuca como factor y veedor de Charcas.

AGI, Indiferente, 425, L24, [1567] Real provisión de notaría de las Indias para Juan Lozano Machuca.

AGI, Indiferente, 1086, L6, [1577] Registro de Peticiones.

AGI, Indiferente, 2086, N83, [1573] Expediente de concesión de licencia para pasar a Nueva Toledo, a favor de Juan Lozano Machuca, escribano, factor y veedor de la Real Hacienda de Nueva Toledo (Charcas), con tres criados, uno de ellos casado, y tres esclavos.

AGI, Justicia, 1125, N5, R1, [1551] El capitán Cristóbal Barba, con el adelantado Juan Ortiz de Zárate, ambos vecinos de la ciudad de La Plata, sobre el derecho a los indios moyos.

AGI, Justicia, N1, R2, [1565–1571] Jerónimo de Alanís, mercader, vecino de la ciudad de La Plata contra los herederos del Capitán Martín de Almendras, sobre el pago de 8.000 pesos.

AGI, Lima, 207, N8, [1578] Probanza de Francisco de Valenzuela.

AGI, Lima, 207, N13, [1581] Probanza de Juan Ortiz de Zarate.

AGI, Lima, 207, N25, [1575] Probanza de Pedro Gutiérrez Flores.

AGI, Lima, 208, N24, [1589] Probanza de Diego de Aguilar.

AGI, Lima, 209, N1, [1589] Probanza Rodrigo Campuzano de Sotomayor.

AGI, Lima, 212, N8, [1598] Informaciones de oficio y parte: Cristóbal de Baranda, capitán, alguacil mayor de Charcas y Potosí, pacificador de los chiriguanas y pacificador en Chile como alférez de la compañía del capitán Fernando de Córdoba y Figueroa. Información y parecer de la Audiencia de Lima.

AGI, Lima, 212, N19, [1599] Informaciones de oficio y parte: Juan de Reinoso, paje del virrey Francisco de Toledo, vecino de Lima, pacificador de los chiriguanas en Charcas, luchó contra los ingleses en Panamá. Información y parecer de la Audiencia de Lima.

AGI, Lima, 213, N4, [1600] Informaciones de oficio y parte: Alvaro Ruíz de Navamuel, secretario de la gobernación del Perú y secretario de la Audiencia de Lima. Consta también la información de Sebastián Sánchez de Merlo, vecino de Lima, secretario de la Audiencia de Panamá, que marchó al Perú con Cristóbal Vaca de Castro.

AGI, Lima, 213, N9, [1601] Probanza Juan Bautista Gallinato.

AGI, Lima, 214, N5, [1602] Probanza de Gaspar Flores.

AGI, Lima, 218, N2, [1611] Probanza de Antonio Zapata.

AGI, Lima, 241, N9, [1648] Informaciones de oficio y parte: Alonso Troncoso Lira y Sotomayor, capitán de infantería española, vecino de las fronteras de Tomina.

AGI, MP, Buenos Aires 12, [1588] Esta es la cordillera en que habita la nación chiriguana, que por la parte del Este confina con la provincia de los Charcas en distancia de 170 leguas de longitud [sic] Norte Sur, y de longitud por lo más angosto 20.

AGI, Panamá, 13, R16, N70, [1577] Carta del doctor Alonso Criado de Castilla, oidor de la Audiencia de Panamá, en que da cuenta de los siguientes puntos: disminución del comercio en aquel reino por los robos y asaltos de corsarios, en particular de los ingleses luteranos, aliados con los negros cimarrones, que entraron por Nombre de Dios hasta el río de las Balsas, por donde salieron al Golfo de San Miguel en la Mar del Sur; conveniencia de reducir a los indios del asiento de Choruca a uno de los pueblos que tienen doctrina; valuación de las mercaderías por debajo de los precios en que se venden después, en especial las perlas; cuentas que se han tomado a Baltasar de Sotomayor y otros oficiales antiguos; problemas de invernar la flota en aquellas partes; fraudes que se cometen en los pleitos de acreedores por parte de los mercaderes de aquel reino; juzgado de bienes de difuntos y cosas que interesan para su buena administración, cobranza, depósito, y entrega a los interesados; diligencias que hizo con la gente que vino con el capitán Losada para el socorro de Chile, la cual no aceptó a Juan Lozano Machuca, factor de la Plata, que sucedió en el cargo al citado capitán tras su fallecimiento; aprobación de su matrimonio con Casilda de Vera, hija del licenciado Diego de Vera.

AGI, Panamá, 61, N67, [1578] Informaciones de Diego de Frias Trejo.

AGI, Patronato, 120, N2, R6, [1575] Probanza de Diego de Valera.

AGI, Patronato, 122, R2, N9, [1578] Informaciones de los méritos y servicios del general Juan Lozano Machuca, que fue nombrado en comisión para levantar gente en Valladolid, Toro, Zamora, Salamanca, Medina del Campo, Toledo, y otras partes, con cuya gente pasó al socorro de Chile y ayudó a su conquista, y estando allí fue nombrado sucesor del general Juan Lozada tras su muerte.

AGI, Patronato, 124, R9, [1580] Información de los méritos y servicios de los generales Pedro Álvarez Holguín y Martín de Almendras, desde el año de 1536 en la conquista y pacificación de Perú, habiéndose hallado en el cerco de la ciudad de Cuzco perseguidos por Mango Inca, cuyos servicios hicieron en compañía de los capitanes Hernando y Juan Pizarro. Constan asimismo los servicios hechos por Diego de Almendras, hermano del general Martín de Almendras.

AGI, Patronato, 124, R10, [1580] Información de Garci Martin de Castaneda.

AGI, Patronato, 124, R11, [1580] Información de los méritos y servicios de don Fernando de Zárate en la conquista del reino de Perú, castigo y persecución de los indios chiriguanaes con don Francisco de Toledo. Son dos informaciones.

AGI, Patronato, 125, R4, [1582] Probanza de Pedro de Segura.

AGI, Patronato, 126, R6, [1582] Méritos y Servicios de Diego Pantoja de Chaves.

AGI, Patronato, 126, R11, [1582] Probanza de Alonso de Peñafiel.

AGI, Patronato, 126, R17, [1606] Información de los méritos y servicios de Pedro de Cuéllar Torremocha, maese de campo, en la conquista de Perú, con el presidente Gasca, sirviendo contra Gonzalo Pizarro.

AGI, Patronato, 126, R18, [1582] Información de los méritos y servicios de Roque de Cuéllar y de su hijo Pedro, en la conquista y pacificación de Perú con el licenciado Gasca, persiguiendo además a los tiranos de aquel reino.

AGI, Patronato, 127, N1, R12, [1584] Información de los méritos y servicios de Juan Pérez de Zorita en la conquista y pacificación de Perú y persecución de Francisco Hernández Girón, habiendo servido también en las guerras de Italia, Argel, y Tremecén.

AGI, Patronato, 127, N1, R17, [1583] Probanza de Toribio Bernaldo y Rodrigo de Arce.

AGI, Patronato, 127, N2, R4, [1584] Información de los méritos y servicios del capitán Francisco Arias de Herrera, que sirvió en la conquista y pacificación de Perú y particularmente en el sosiego de los indios chichimecas, también en la toma del Peñón, batalla de Lepanto, habiendo ido dos veces a la China y con socorros a las islas Filipinas.

AGI, Patronato, 131, N1, R3, [1587] Información de los méritos y servicios de Hernando de Cazorla, maese de campo general, hechos en la conquista de Perú, sirviendo particularmente contra Gonzalo Pizarro y en varias batallas contra indios levantados.

AGI, Patronato, 131, N2, R3, [1588] Probanza de Rodrigo de Orellana.

AGI, Patronato, 132, N1, R4, [1589] Información de Juan Gutierrez de Beas.

AGI, Patronato, 132, N2, R7, [1590] Probanza de Alonso de Paredes.

AGI, Patronato, 132, N2, R8, [1590] Información de Juan Mejía Miraval.

AGI, Patronato, 133, R5, [1591] Información de los méritos y servicios de Francisco de Guzmán y Juan de Rivamartín, que sirvieron en Nueva España y después pasaron a Perú hacia 1537 y se hallaron en la conquista de aquel reino y de los indios chiriguanaes.

AGI, Patronato, 136, N1, R4, [1596] Información de méritos y servicios del capitán Juan Ladrón de Leyba.

AGI, Patronato, 137, N1, R2, [1598] Información de los méritos y servicios del capitán Luis de Fuentes y Vargas, corregidor y poblador de la villa de San Bernardo de la Frontera de Tarija y conquistador de otros pueblos de Perú.

AGI, Patronato, 137, N1, R4, [1598] Probanza de Luis Hernández Barja.

AGI, Patronato, 141, R1, [1603] Probanza de Juan de Villegas.

AGI, Patronato, 144, R1, [1608] Probanza de Luis de Mendoza y Rivera.

AGI, Patronato, 146, N3, R1, [1613] Probanza de Juan de la Reinaga Salazar.

AGI, Patronato, 147, N4, R3, [1618] Probanza de don Pedro de Portugal y Navarra.

AGI, Patronato, 149, N1, R1, [1627] Méritos y Servicios. Lorenzo de Cepeda y Hermanos.

AGI, Patronato, 189, R 26, [1569 sic] [1579] Relaciones de las mercedes hechas por Francisco de Toledo, virrey de Perú, a los sujetos que se expresan en dichas relaciones.

AGI, Patronato, 190, R23, [1577] Representación de Diego de Porras sobre el origen y estado de las compañías de lanzas y arcabuceros en Perú. Acompaña una relación de lo que han supuesto los tributos en Perú, destinados al pago de dichas lanzas y arcabuces.

AGI, Patronato, 190, R25, [1578] Información recibida a petición del virrey de Perú, don Francisco de Toledo, sobre las enfermedades que padecía en aquel reino, y edad que tenía cuando fue a él.

AGI, Patronato, 190, R44, [1582] Minuta de los corregimientos que había en 1582.

AGI Patronato, 235, R1, [24 octubre 1571] Chiriguanaes. Ynformacion que se hizo por mandado del excelentisimo señor visorrey del Peru sobre la cordillera de los chiriguanaes por su persona que su excelencia ymbio y lo que piden los dichos yndios que se haga con ellos para salir de paz.

AGI, Patronato, 235, R1, [1571] Informaciones hechas de orden del virrey del Perú, Francisco de Toledo, sobre la conducta y malos procedimientos de los indios llamados Chiriguanaes.

AGI, Patronato, 235, R2, [1573/1574] Parecer del presidente y oidores de las Audiencias de los Charcas y La Plata, sobre el modo de hacer la guerra a los indios chiriguanaes y castigo que debía imponérseles.

AGI, Patronato, 235, R3, [1573] Información hecha en la Audiencia de La Plata, de orden del virrey del Perú, Francisco de Toledo, sobre averiguar la aparición de un joven entre los indios chiriguanaes que se dijo ser Santiago Apostol, enviado por Jesús para predicarles y convertirlos a la religión católica.

AGI, Patronato, 235, R4, [1574] Relacion de lo que se hizo en la jornada que el excelentisimo señor virrey del Piru don Francisco de Toledo hizo por su persona entrando a hazer Guerra a los chiriguanaes de las fronteras y cordilleras desta provincial en el año de setenta y quatro.

AGI, Patronato, 235, R5, [1574] Acuerdo que celebró el virrey con algunos prelados de religiones de la ciudad de La Plata, sobre si convendría hacer guerra a los indios chiriguanaes y declararlos por esclavos.

AGI, Patronato, 235, R7, [1582] Información hecha por la justicia de la villa de Santiago de la Frontera, en virtud de Real Provisión, sobre la conducta y trato que observaban los indios chiriguanaes.

AGI, Patronato, 235, R9, [1583] Autos y diligencias hechas por la Audiencia de La Plata, sobre los daños, muertes y robos que los indios chiriguanaes cometían en aquellas fronteras, y guerra que contra ellos se ha pregonado. Contienen estos autos las capitulaciones y asiento que se tomó con el capitán Miguel Martínez, sobre la población de la villa de San Miguel de la Laguna y lo que en ella sucedió.

AGI, Patronato, 235, R10, [1586] Testimonio de los autos formados en la Audiencia de La Plata, sobre la guerra que debía hacerse a los indios chiriguanaes. Acompaña la descripción de aquella tierra y de la provincia de Santa Cruz de la Sierra.

AGI, Patronato, 237, R7, [1582] Información hecha por la justicia de la villa de Santiago de la Frontera, en virtud de Real Provisión, sobre la conducta y trato que observaban los indios chiriguanaes.

AGI, Patronato, 255, N4, G3, R1, [1591] Diego Garcia de Paredes.

AGI, Quito, 35, N24, [1567–1571] Expediente de confirmación del oficio de canciller de la audiencia a Juan Lozano Machuca.

Biblioteca Nacional de España (BNE)

BNE, Ms. 2,927, Libro de cédulas y provisiones del Rey Nuestro Señor para el gobierno de este reino y provincia, justicia y hacienda y patronazgo real, casos de Inquisición y eclesiasticos y de indios y de bienes de difuntos y de otras materias, que se han enviado a esta Real Audiencia de La Plata.

BNE, Ms. 3,043, Ordenanzas y Comisiones para el Reino de Granada y Obispado de Quito.

BNE, Ms. 3,044, Papeles varios tocantes al gobierno de Indias.

BNE, Ms. 6,643, El héroe, Baltasar Gracián.

Bibliothèque Nationale de France (BNF)
MS Espagnol 175, fols 90–91v, Mémorial du capitaine 'Joan Ladron de Leyba, corregidor y justicia maior de la frontera de Pazpaia', pour obtenir que le capitaine Alvaro de Paz Villalobos ne s'entremette pas dans son gouvernement.

British Library
British Library, Ms. 13,977, Memoria de las casas y conventos y doctrinas que tiene la horden de Nuestra Señora de Nuestra Merced en las Yndias del Peru.

2. Published primary sources

Acosta, José de. *Historia natural y moral de las Indias*. Sevilla: Casa de Juan Leon, 1590.
Anon. *Las Siete Partidas del Sabio Rey Don Alonso El Nono, Nuevamente Glosadas por El Licenciado Gregorio López del Consejo Real de Indias de Su Magestad*. Vol. 1. Salamanca: Andrea de Portonari, 1555.
Anon. *Recopilación de leyes de los reynos de las Indias*, Vol. 2. Madrid: Julián Paredes, 1681.
Arsans de Orzúa y Vela, Bartolomé. *Historia de la villa imperial de Potosí*. Providence, RI: Brown University Press, 1965 [1705].
Barco Centenera, Martín del. *Argentina y conquista del Rio de la Plata, con otros acaecimientos de los reynos del Perú, Tucumán, y Estado del Brasil*. Lisbon: Pedro Crasbeek, 1602.
Barco Centenera, Martín del. *The Argentine and the Conquest of the River Plate*. Buenos Aires: Instituto Cultural Water Owen, 1965.
Barriga, Victor M. *Los mercedarios en el Perú en el siglo XVI. Documentos del Archivo General de Indias. 1518–1600*. Vol. 3. Arequipa: Establecimientos Graficos La Colmena SA, 1942.
Barriga, Victor M. *Mercedarios ilustres en el Perú. El padre fray Diego de Porres, misionero insigne en el Perú y en Santa Cruz de la Sierra*. Vol. II. Arequipa: Establecimientos Graficos La Colmena SA, 1949.
Betanzos, Juan de, María del Carmen Martín Rubio, Horacio Villanueva Urteaga, and Demetrio Ramos Pérez, eds. *Suma y narración de los incas*. Madrid: Atlas, 1987 [1551].
Calancha, Antonio de la. *Chronica moralizada del orden de San Augustin en el Perú con sucesos exemplares vistos en esta monarchia*. Barcelona: Pedro Lacaballeria, 1638.
Candela, Guillaume. *Entre la pluma y la cruz: El clérigo Martín González y la desconocida historia de su defensa de los indios del Paraguay: Documentos inéditos (1543–1575)*. Asunción, Paraguay: Editorial Tiempo de Historia, 2018.
Capoche, Luis. *Relación general de la villa imperial de Potosí*. Vol. CXXII. Biblioteca de Autores Españoles. Madrid: Atlas, 1958 [1585].
Casassas, José María. 'Carta del factor de Potosí Juan Lozano Machuca (al virrey del Perú don Martín Enríquez) en que da cuenta de cosas de aquella villa y de las minas de los Lipes (Año 1581).' *Estudios Atacameños. Arqueología y Antropología Surandinas*, no. 10 (1992): 30–34.

Cieza de León, Pedro. *Crónica del Perú*. Cuarta Parte. Vol. 2. Lima: Pontificia Universidad Católica del Perú, 1994 [1551].

Comajuncosa, Antonio, and Corrado Alejandro. *El colegio franciscano de Tarija y sus misiones. Noticias históricas recogidas por dos misioneros del mismo colegio*. Quaracchi: Tipografía del Colegio de San Buenaventura, 1884.

Díaz de Guzmán, Ruy. *Relación de la entrada a los chiriguanos*. Santa Cruz de la Sierra: Fundación Cultural 'Ramón Darío Gutierrez', 1979 [1515].

Díaz de Guzmán, Ruy. *Argentina: Historia del descubrimiento y conquista del Río de la Plata*. Buenos Aires: Editorial de la Facultad de Filosofía y Letras, Universidad de Buenos Aires, 2012 [1612].

Egaña, Antonio de, ed. *Monumenta peruana (1565–1575)*. Vol. I. Rome: Monumenta Historica Societatis Iesu, 1954.

Enciso Contreras, José. *Cedulario de la Audiencia de La Plata de Charcas (siglo XVI)*. Sucre: ABNB, 2005.

Espada, Marcos Jiménez de la. *Relaciones geográficas de Indias: Perú*. Vol. II. Ministerio de Fomento, Madrid: Impreso en la Casa Real, 1885.

Garay, Blas. *Colección de documentos relativos a la historia de América y particularmente a la historia de Paraguay*. Vol. 2. Asunción: Talleres Nacionales de Martín Kraus, 1901.

García-Gallo, Alfonso, and Diego de Encinas. *Cedulario indiano o cedulario de Encinas*. Vol. IV. Madrid: Boletín Oficial del Estado, 2018 [1596].

Garcilaso de la Vega, El Inca. *Primera parte de los commentarios reales*. Lisbon: Oficina de Pedro Crasbeeck, 1609.

Gonçalez Holguin, Diego. *Vocabulario de la lengua general de todo el Peru llamada lengua quichua, o del inca*. Ciudad de Los Reyes (Lima): Francisco del Canto, 1607.

Guamán Poma de Ayala, Felipe, *El primer nueva corónica y buen gobierno*. México: Siglo Veintiuno, 2006 [1615].

Gutiérrez de Santa Clara, Pedro. *Historia de las guerras civiles del Perú (1544–1548)*. Vol. 2. Madrid: Librería General de Victoriano Suárez, 1904.

Julien, Catherine J. *Desde el Oriente: Documentos para la historia del oriente boliviano y Santa Cruz La Vieja, 1542–1597*. Santa Cruz de la Sierra: Fondo Editorial Municipal, 2008.

Julien, Catherine, Kristina Angelis, and Zulema Bass Werner de Ruiz. *Historia de Tarija. Corpus documental*. Vol. VI. Tarija: Editora Guadalquivir, 1997.

Konetzke, Richard. *Colección de documentos para la historia social de la formación de Hispanoamérica. 1493–1810*. Vol. 1 (1493–1592). Madrid: Consejo Superior de Investigaciones Científicas, Instituto Francisco de Vitoria, 1953.

Levillier, Roberto. *La Audiencia de Charcas. Correspondencia de presidentes y oidores. 1561–1579*. Vols 1 and 2. Madrid: Colección de Publicaciones Históricas de la Biblioteca del Congreso Argentino, 1918.

Levillier, Roberto. *Gobernación de Tucumán. Correspondencia de los cabildos en el siglo XVI*. Madrid: Sucesores de Rivadeneyra, 1918.

Levillier, Roberto. *Gobernación del Tucumán. Papeles de gobernardores en el siglo XVI*. Madrid: Sucesores de Rivadeneyra, 1920.

Levillier, Roberto. *Gobernación de Tucumán. Probanzas de méritos y servicios de los conquistadores. Documentos del Archivo de Indias (1583–1600)*. Vol. 2. Madrid: Sucesores de Rivadeneyra, 1920.

Levillier, Roberto. *Audiencia de Lima. Correspondencia de presidentes y oidores (1549–1564)*. Vol. I. Madrid: Juan Pueyo, 1922.

Levillier, Roberto. *Gobernantes del Perú. Cartas y papeles. Siglo XVI.* Vols 3, 4, 6, 9. Madrid: Sucesores de Rivadeneyra, 1921–1924.

Lizárraga, Reginaldo de. *Descripción colonial. Libros uno y segundo.* Buenos Aires: Librería de la Facultad, 1916 [1605].

Lohmann Villena, Guillermo and Sarabia Viejo, María Justina, eds. *Francisco de Toledo: Disposiciones Gubernativas Para El Virreinato Del Perú. 1575–1581.* Vols I and II. Seville: Escuela de Estudios Hispano-Americanos, 1986.

López de Caravantes, Francisco. *Noticia general del Perú.* Vol. 6. Biblioteca de Autores Españoles. Madrid: Ediciones Atlas, 1989 [1630–1631].

López de Velasco, Juan. *Geografía y descripción universal de las Indias.* Madrid: Establecimiento Tipográfico de Fortanet, 1894 [1571–1574].

López Villalva, José Miguel (dir.). *Acuerdos de la Real Audiencia de La Plata de los Charcas (1561–1568).* Vols 1 and 2. Sucre: Corte Suprema de Justicia de Bolivia, Archivo y Biblioteca Nacionales de Bolivia, Embajada de España en Bolivia, Agencia Española de Cooperación Internacional para el Desarrollo, 2007.

Loredo, Rafael. 'Relaciones de repartimientos que existían en el Perú al finalizar la rebelión de Gonzalo Pizarro.' *Revista de La Universidad Católica de Perú* VIII, no. 1 (1940): 51–62.

Loredo, Rafael. *Los Repartos; Bocetos para la nueva historia del Perú.* Lima: no identified publisher, 1958.

Mariño de Lovera, Pedro. *Crónica del reino de Chile.* Vol. VI. Colección de Historiadores de Chile y Documentos Relativos a la Historia Nacional. Santiago de Chile: Imprenta del Ferrocarril, 1865 [1594].

Matienzo, Juan de. *Gobierno del Perú.* Paris, Lima: IFEA, 1967 [1567].

Maurtua, Victor. *Juicio de límites entre el Perú y Bolivia. Prueba peruana presentada al gobierno de la República Argentina.* Vols 1, 2, and 9. Barcelona: Imprenta de Henrich y Cia, 1906.

Medina, José Toribio. *Colección de documentos inéditos para la historia de Chile.* Vols VI and VII. Santiago de Chile: Imprenta Elzeviriana, 1896.

Melendez, Fray Ivan. *Tesoros verdaderos de las Yndias en la historia de la gran provincia de San Juan Bautista del Peru.* Vol. 3. Rome: Imprenta de Nicolas Angel Tinassio, 1681.

Miraflores, Marqués, and Miguel Salva. *Colección de documentos inéditos para la historia de España.* Vol. L. Madrid: Imprenta de la Viuda de Calero, 1867.

Mujía, Ricardo. *Bolivia–Paraguay. Exposición de los títulos que consagran el derecho territorial de Bolivia, sobre la zona comprendida entre los rios Pilcomayo y Paraguay, presentada por el doctor Ricardo Mujía, enviado extraordinario y ministro plenipotenciario de Bolivia en el Paraguay. Anexos.* Vol. II. La Paz: Empresa Editora 'El Tiempo', 1914.

Murua, Martín de. *Historia general del Perú. De los orígenes al último inca.* Madrid: Cambio16, 1992 [1606].

Nuñez Cabeza de Vaca, Alvar. *Relación de los naufragios y comentarios.* Madrid: Libreria General de Victoriano Suárez, 1906 [1542].

Otte, Enrique, and Guadalupe Albi Romero, eds. *Cartas privadas de emigrantes a Indias, 1540–1616.* Sevilla: Consejería de Cultura, Junta de Andalucía: Escuela de Estudios Hispano Americanos de Sevilla, 1988.

Pachacuti Yamqui Salcamaygua, Joan de Santa Cruz. *Relación de antiguedades deste reyno del Piru: Estudio etnohistórico y lingüístico.* Edited by Pierre Duviols and César Itier. Lima: Institut français d'études andines, 1993 [1613].

Pärssinen, Martti, and Jukka Kiviharju, eds. *Textos andinos: corpus de textos khipu incaicos y coloniales. T. 2:* Acta Ibero-Americana Fennica 6. Madrid: Inst. Iberoamericano de Finlandia, 2004.

Pizarro, Pedro. *Descubrimiento y conquista del Perú.* Vol. VI. Lima: Imprenta y Librería San Martí Ca, 1917 [1571].

Platt, Tristán, Thérèse Bouysse-Cassagne, and Olivia Harris, eds. *Qaraqara–Charka: Mallku, inka y rey en la provincia de Charcas (siglos XV–XVII): Historia antropológica de una confederación aymara.* 1. ed. Lima Perú: La Paz, Bolivia: Instituto Francés de Estudios Andinos (IFEA); Plural Editores; University of St Andrews; University of London; Fundación Cultural del Banco Central de Bolivia; Inter-American Foundation, 2006.

Rayon, José Sancho, and Francisco de Zabalburu. *Colección de documentos inéditos para la historia de España.* Vol. XCIV. Madrid: M. Ginesta y Hermanos, 1889.

Real Academia Española. *Diccionario de la lengua castellana en que se explica el verdadero sentido de las voces su naturaleza y calidad con las phrases o modo de hablar, los proverbios y refranes y otras cosas convenientes al uso de la lengua.* Vol. I. Madrid: Imprenta de la Real Academia Española, 1726.

Romera Iruela, Luis, and María del Carmen Galbís Diez. *Catalogo de pasajeros a Indias durante los siglos XVI, XVII y XVIII.* Vol. 1. Sevilla: AGI, 1980.

Rosales, Diego. *Historia general de el reyno de Chile. Flandes indiano.* Vol. II. Valparaiso: Imprenta del Mercurio, 1878 [1674].

Rowe, John. 'Probanza de los incas nietos de conquistadores.' *Histórica* IX, no. 2 (1985): 193–245.

Sarmiento de Gamboa, Pedro. *Historia de los incas.* Madrid: Miraguano Editores, 2001 [1572].

Torres de Mendoza, Luis. *Colección de documentos inéditos relativos al descubrimiento, conquista y organización de las antiguas posesiones españolas de América y Oceania sacados de los archivos del reino y muy especialmente del de Indias.* Vol. 4. Madrid: Imprenta de Frias y Cia, 1865.

Vargas Machuca, Don Bernardo. *Milicia y descripción de las Indias.* Vol. 1. Madrid: Libreria de Victoriano Suárez, 1892 [1599].

3. Secondary sources

Abercrombie, Thomas Alan. 'The Politics of Sacrifice: An Aymara Society in Action.' PhD dissertation, The University of Chicago, 1986.

Abercrombie, Thomas A. *Pathways of Memory and Power: Ethnography and History among an Andean People.* Madison: University of Wisconsin Press, 1998.

Adorno, Rolena. *The Polemics of Possession in Spanish American Narrative*. New Haven, CT: Yale University Press, 2007.

Agüero, Alejandro. 'Las categorías básicas de la cultura jurisdiccional.' In Marta Lorente Sariñena, ed. *De justicia de jueces a justicia de leyes: Hacia la España de 1870*, Vol. VI. Cuadernos de Derecho Judicial. Madrid: Consejo General del Poder Judicial, 2006.

Agüero, Alejandro. *Castigar y perdonar cuando conviene a la república. La justicia penal de Córdoba del Tucumán, siglos XVII y XVIII*. Madrid: Centro de Estudios Políticos y Constitucionales, 2008.

Agüero, Alejandro. 'Ciudad y poder político en el Antiguo Régimen. La tradición castellana.' In Víctor Tau Anzoátegui and Alejandro Agüero, eds. *El derecho local en la periferia de la Monarquía Hispana. Río de La Plata, Tucumán y Cuyo. Siglos XVI–XVIII*. Buenos Aires: Editorial Dunken, 2013.

Agüero, Alejandro. 'Local Law and Localization of Law: Hispanic Legal Tradition and Colonial Culture (16th–18th Centuries).' In Massimo Meccarelli, María Julia Solla Sastre, Thomas Duve, and Stefan Vogenauer, eds. *Spatial and Temporal Dimensions for Legal History Research: Experiences and Itineraries*, 101–29. Frankfurt am Main: Max Planck Institute for European Legal History, 2016.

Alconini Mujica, Sonia. *Southeast Inka Frontiers: Boundaries and Interactions*. Gainesville: University Press of Florida, 2016.

Altman, Ida. *Emigrants and Society: Extremadura and America in the Sixteenth Century*. Berkeley: University of California Press, 1989.

Alvarez, Salvador. 'La guerra chichimeca.' In Thomas Calvo and Aristarco Regalado Pinedo, eds. *Historia del reino de Nueva Galicia*, 211–62. Jalisco: Universidad de Guadalajara, 2016.

Arkush, Elizabeth N. *Hillforts of the Ancient Andes: Colla Warfare, Society, and Landscape*. Gainesville: University Press of Florida, 2011.

Arze Quiroga, Eduardo. *Historia de Bolivia. Fases del proceso hispano-americano: Orígenes de la sociedad boliviana en el siglo XVI*. La Paz-Cochabamba: Los Amigos del Libro, 1969.

Assadourian, Carlos Sempat. *El sistema de la economía colonial. Mercado interno, regiones y espacio económico*. Lima: IEP, 1982.

Austin, Shawn Michael. *Colonial Kinship: Guaraní, Spaniards, and Africans in Paraguay*. Albuquerque: University of New Mexico Press, 2020.

Aznar Vallejo, Eduardo. 'The Conquests of the Canary Islands.' In Stuart B. Schwartz, ed. *Implicit Understandings: Observing, Reporting and Reflecting on the Encounters between Europeans and Other Peoples in the Early Modern Era*, 134–56. Cambridge: Cambridge University Press, 1994.

Bakewell, P. J. *Miners of the Red Mountain: Indian Labor in Potosí, 1545–1650*. Albuquerque: University of New Mexico Press, 1984; *Mineros de la montaña roja: el trabajo de los indios en Potosí, 1545–1650*. Madrid: Alianza Editorial, 1989.

Barnadas, Josep M. *Charcas. Orígenes históricos de una sociedad colonial. 1535–1565*. La Paz: CIPCA, 1973.

Barragán Vargas, Mario E. *Historia temprana de Tarija*. Tarija, Bolivia: Grafica Offset Kokito, 2001.

Barrientos Grandón, Javier. *El gobierno de las Indias*. Madrid: Marcial Pons, 2004.

Barrientos Grandón, Javier. '"Méritos y servicios": Su patrimonialización en una cultura jurisdiccional (s. XVI–XVII).' *Revista de Estudios Histórico-Jurídicos* XL (2018): 589–615.

Barriera, Dario G. *Abrir puertas a la tierra: microanálisis de la construcción de un espacio político: Santa Fe, 1573–1640*. Santa Fe (Argentina): Museo Histórico Provincial Brigadier Estanislao López, 2017.

Barriera, Dario. *Historia y justicia: Cultura, política y sociedad en el Río de La Plata*. Buenos Aires: Prometeo Libros, 2019.

Benton, Lauren A. 'Making Order out of Trouble: Jurisdictional Politics in the Spanish Colonial Borderlands.' *Law & Social Inquiry* 26, no. 2 (2001): 373–401.

Benton, Lauren A. *Law and Colonial Cultures: Legal Regimes in World History, 1400–1900*. Cambridge, New York: Cambridge University Press, 2002.

Blockmans, Wim, André Holenstein, and Jon Mathieu, eds. *Empowering Interactions: Political Cultures and the Emergence of the State in Europe, 1300–1900*. Farnham, Burlington, VT: Ashgate, 2009.

Boccara, Guillaume. 'Génesis y estructura de los complejos fronterizos euro-indígenas. Repensando los márgenes americanos a partir (y mas allá) de la obra de Nathan Wachtel.' *Memoria Americana* 13 (2005): 21–52.

Bouysse-Cassagne, Thérèse. *La Identidad aymara. Aproximación histórica (siglo XV, siglo XVI)*. La Paz: Hisbol/IFEA, 1987.

Bouza Alvarez, Fernando J. *Palabra e imagen en la corte: Cultura oral y visual de la nobleza en el Siglo de Oro*. Madrid: Abada Editores, 2003.

Brendecke, Arndt. *Imperio e información: funciones del saber en el dominio colonial español*. Trans. Griselda Mársico. Madrid: Iberoamericana Vervuert, 2016.

Bridikhina, Eugenia. *Theatrum mundi. Entramados del poder en Charcas colonial*. Lima: Institute Français d'Études Andines, 2015.

Burns, Kathryn. *Into the Archive: Writing and Power in Colonial Peru*. Durham, NC: Duke University Press, 2010.

Calvo, Thomas, and Aristarco Regalado Pinedo. *Historia del reino de la Nueva Galicia*. Jalisco: Universidad de Guadalajara, 2016.

Cañeque, Alejandro. *The King's Living Image: The Culture and Politics of Viceregal Power in Colonial Mexico*. New York: Routledge, 2004.

Cañeque, Alejandro. *Un imperio de mártires: Religión y poder en las fronteras de la Monarquía Hispánica*. Madrid: Marcial Pons Historia, 2020.

Cañizares-Esguerra, Jorge. 'Typology in the Atlantic World: Early Modern Readings of Colonization.' In Bernard Bailyn and Patricia L. Denault, eds. *Soundings in Atlantic History: Latent Structures and Intellectual Currents, 1500–1830*, 237–64. London: Harvard University Press, 2009.

Cardim, Pedro, Tamar Herzog, José Javier Ruiz Ibáñez, and Gaetano Sabatini, eds. *Polycentric Monarchies: How Did Early Modern Spain and Portugal Achieve and Maintain a Global Hegemony?* Eastbourne: Sussex Academic Press, 2012.

Castillo, David. 'Gracián and the Art of Public Representation.' In Nicholas Spadaccini and Jenaro Talens, eds. *Rhetoric and Politics: Baltasar Gracián and the New World Order*, 191–209. Minneapolis: University of Minnesota Press, 1997.

Centenero de Arce, Domingo. '¿Una monarquía de lazos débiles? Circulación y experiencia como formas de construcción de la Monarquía Católica.' In Juan Francisco Pardo Molero and Manuel Lomas Cortés, eds. *Oficiales reales. Los ministros de la Monarquía Católica (Siglos XVI–XVIII)*. Valencia: Universitat de Valencia, 2012.

Cervantes, Fernando. *Conquistadores: A New History*. London: Penguin Books, 2021.

Chiva Beltrán, Juan. *El triunfo del virrey*. Madrid: Universitat Jaume I. Servei de Comunicació i Publicacions, 2012.

Clavero, Bartolomé. *Antidora: Antropología católica de la economía moderna*. Milan: Giuffré, 1991.

Clavero, Bartolomé. 'Justicia y gobierno. Economía y gracia.' In Javier Moya Morales, Eduardo Quesada Dorador, and David Torres Ibáñez, eds. *Real Chancillería de Granada: V Centenario 1505–2005*, 121–48. Granada: Junta de Andalucía, Consejería de Cultura, 2006.

Colajanni, Antonino. 'El virrey Toledo como "primer antropólogo aplicado" de la edad moderna. Conocimiento social y planes de transformación del mundo indígena peruano en la segunda mitad del siglo XVI.' In Laura Laurencich-Minelli and Paulina Numhauser Bar-Magen, eds. *El silencio protagonista. El primer siglo jesuita en el virreynato del Perú. 1567–1667*, 51–95. Quito: Abya-Yala, 2004.

Colajanni, Antonino. *El virrey y los indios del Perú: Francisco de Toledo (1569–1581), la política indígena y las reformas sociales*. Quito: Abya Yala, 2018.

Cole, Jeffrey A. *The Potosí Mita, 1573–1700: Compulsory Indian Labor in the Andes*. Stanford, CA: Stanford University Press, 1985.

Combès, Isabelle. *Etno-historias del Isoso: Chané y chiriguanos en el Chaco boliviano (siglos XVI a XX)*. La Paz: Institut français d'études andines, 2005.

Combès, Isabelle. 'Grigotá y Vitupue. En los albores de la historia chiriguana (1559–1564).' *Bulletin de l'Institut Français d'Études Andines* 41, no. 1 (2012): 57–79.

Combès, Isabelle. 'De luciferinos a canonizables: Representaciones del canibalismo chiriguano.' *Boletín Americanista*, 2, LXIII, no. 67 (2013): 127–41.

Cook, Noble David. *Born to Die: Disease and New World Conquest, 1492–1650*. Cambridge, New York: Cambridge University Press, 1998.

Cook, Noble David. 'Epidemias y dinámica demográfica.' In Franklin Pease and Frank Moya Pons, eds. *El primer contacto y la formación de nuevas sociedades*, Vol. II. Madrid: Ediciones UNESCO, Ediciones Trotta, 2007.

Córdoba Ochoa, Luis Miguel. 'Guerra, imperio, y violencia en la Audiencia de Santa Fe, Nuevo Reino de Granada. 1580–1620.' PhD dissertation, Universidad Pablo de Olavide, 2013.

Costa, Pietro. *Iurisdictio. Semantica del potere politico nella pubblicistica medievale (1100–1433)*. Milan: Giuffré, 2002 [1969].

Covey, R. Alan. *How the Incas Built Their Heartland: State Formation and the Innovation of Imperial Strategies in the Sacred Valley, Peru*. History, Languages, and Cultures of the Spanish and Portuguese Worlds. Ann Arbor: University of Michigan Press, 2006.

D'Altroy, Terence N. *The Incas*. Malden, MA: Blackwell, 2002.

Deardorff, Max. *A Tale of Two Granadas: Custom, Community, and Citizenship in the Spanish Empire, 1568–1668*. Cambridge: Cambridge University Press, 2023.

Deeds, Susan M. *Defiance and Deference in Mexico's Colonial North: Indians under Spanish Rule in Nueva Vizcaya*. Austin: University of Texas Press, 2003.

Del Busto, José Antonio. *La hueste perulera*. Lima: Pontificia Universidad Católica del Perú, Fondo Editorial, 1981.

Díaz Ceballos, Jorge. *Poder compartido: Repúblicas urbanas, monarquía y conversación en Castilla de Oro, 1508–1573*. Madrid: Marcial Pons Historia, 2020.

Duviols, Pierre. *La lutte contre les réligions autochtones dans le Perou colonial. 'L'extirpation de l'idolatrie' entre 1532 et 1660*. Lima: IFEA, 1971.

Egginton, William. *How the World Became a Stage: Presence, Theatricality, and the Question of Modernity*. Albany: State University of New York Press, 2003.

Elliott, John. *Imperial Spain, 1469–1716*. Harmondsworth: Penguin, 1970.

Elliott, John. 'A Europe of Composite Monarchies.' *Past and Present*, no. 137 (November 1992): 48–71.

Escribano Páez, José Miguel. *Juan Rena and the Frontiers of Spanish Empire, 1500–1540*. New York: Routledge, 2020.

Espinoza Soriano, Waldemar. 'El Reino Aymara de Quillaca-Asanaque, Siglos XV y XVI.' *Revista del Museo Nacional de Lima* XLV (1981): 175–274.

Espinoza Soriano, Waldemar. 'La Confederación Quillaca-Asanaque. Siglos XV y XVI.' In Espinoza Soriano, *Temas de Etnohistoria Boliviana*. La Paz: Producciones CIMA, 2003.

Estríngana, Alicia Esteban, ed. *Servir al rey en la monarquía de los Austrias: Medios, fines y logros del servicio al soberano en los siglos XVI y XVII* (Madrid: Sílex, 2012).

Faudree, Paja. 'Reading the "Requerimiento" Performatively: Speech Acts and the Conquest of the New World.' *Colonial Latin American Review* 24, no. 4 (2015): 456–78.

Flüchter, Antje. 'Structures on the Move: Appropriating Technologies of Governance in a Transcultural Encounter.' In Antje Flüchter and Susan Richter, eds. *Structures on the Move: Technologies of Governance in a Transcultural Encounter*, 1–30. Heidelberg, New York, London, Dordrecht: Springer, 2012.

Folger, Robert. *Writing as Poaching: Interpellation and Self-Fashioning in Colonial Relaciones de Méritos y Servicios*. Leiden, Boston, MA: Brill, 2011.

García, David Alonso. 'Guerra, hacienda y política. Las finanzas militares en los inicios de la Edad Moderna.' In Antonio Jiménez Estrella and Francisco Andújar Castillo, eds. *Los nervios de la guerra. Estudios sociales sobre el ejército de la Monarquía Hispánica (s. XVI-XVIII): Nuevas perspectivas*, 37–57. Granada: Editorial Comares, 2007.

García-Abásolo, Antonio F. *Martín Enríquez y la reforma de 1568 en Nueva España*. Sevilla: Excelentísima. Diputación Provincial de Sevilla, 1983.

García García, Luis Alberto. *Frontera armada: Prácticas militares en el noreste histórico, Siglos XVII al XIX*. México: Fondo de Cultura Económica: Centro de Investigación y Docencia Económicas, 2021.

García Hernán, David. *La cultura de la guerra y el teatro del Siglo de Oro*. Madrid: Sílex, 2006.

García Recio, José María. *Análisis de una sociedad de frontera: Santa Cruz de La Sierra en los siglos XVI y XVII*. Publicaciones de La Excma. Diputación Provincial de Sevilla. Sección Historia. V Centenario Del Descubrimiento de América, no. 9. Sevilla: Excma. Diputación Provincial de Sevilla, 1988.

Garrido, Francisco, and Erick Figueroa. 'Establishing Colonial Rule in a Frontier *Encomienda*: Chile's Copiapó Valley under Francisco de Aguirre and His Kin, 1549–1580.' *Latin American Research Review*, August 2023, 1–17.

Garriga, Carlos. 'Orden jurídico y poder político en el Antiguo Régimen.' *Revista de Historia Internacional* 16 (2004): 13–44.

Garriga, Carlos. 'Patrias criollas, plazas militares. Sobre la América de Carlos IV,' In Eduardo Martiré, ed. *La América de Carlos IV*, Vol. 1. Cuadernos de Investigaciones y Documentos. Buenos Aires: Instituto de Investigaciones de Historia del Derecho, 2006.

Garriga, Carlos. 'Concepción y aparatos de justicia: Las reales audiencias de las Indias.' *Cuadernos de Historia* 19 (2009): 203–44.

Gayol, Víctor. '"Por todos los dias de nuestra vida..." Oficios de pluma, sociedad local y gobierno de la monarquía.' In Felipe Castro Gutiérrez and Isabel M. Povea Moreno, eds. *Los oficios en las sociedades indianas*, 301–29. México: UNAM, 2020.

Gazulla, Fray Policarpo. *Los primeros mercedarios en Chile. 1535–1600*. Santiago de Chile: Imprenta La Ilustración, 1918.

Giudicelli, Christophe. 'Encasillar la frontera. Clasificaciones coloniales y disciplinamiento del espacio en el área diaguito-calchaquí. Siglos XVI–XVII.' *Anuario IEHS*, no. 22 (2007): 161–211.

Gómez Rivas, León. *El virrey del Perú don Francisco de Toledo*. Serie Ia. Monografías, no. 37. Toledo: Instituto Provincial de Investigaciones y Estudios Toledanos, Diputación Provincial, 1994.

González Pujana, Laura. *Polo de Ondegardo: un cronista vallisoletano en el Perú*. Valladolid: Universidad de Valladolid, Instituto de Estudios de Iberoamérica y Portugal, 1999.

Graña, Mario Julio. 'Autoridad y memoria entre los killakas. Las estrategias discursivas de don Juan Colque Guarache en el sur andino. S. XVI.' *Historica* XXIV, no. 1 (2000): 23–47.

Graña, Mario Julio. '"Bastardo, mañoso, sagaz y ladino." Caciques, pleitos y agravios en el sur andino. Don Fernando Ayavire y Velasco contra Don Juan Colque Guarache. Charcas, Siglo XVI.' *Anuario 2000* (2001): 541–77.

Graña, Mario Julio. 'La verdad asediada. Discursos de y para el poder. Escritura, institucionalización y élites indígenas surandinas. Charcas. Siglo XVI.' *Andes. Antropología e Historia*, no. 12 (2001): 123–39.

Graña Taborelli, Mario. 'Speaking the Language of Friendship: Partnerships in the Political Construction of the Late Sixteenth-Century South-East Charcas Frontier.' *Bulletin of Latin American Research* 42, no. 5 (2023): 721–33.

Graubart, Karen B. *Republics of Difference: Religious and Racial Self-Governance in the Spanish Atlantic World*. New York: Oxford University Press, 2022.

Griffiths, Nicholas. *The Cross and the Serpent: Religious Repression and Resurgence in Colonial Peru*. Norman: University of Oklahoma Press, 1996.

Guereca Durán, Raquel. *Milicias Indígenas en La América Hispana*. San Antonio, TX: UNAM San Antonio, 2023.

Guevara-Gil, Armando, and Frank Salomon. 'A "Personal Visit": Colonial Political Ritual and the Making of the Indians in the Andes.' *CLAHR* 3, nos 1–2 (1994): 3–36.

Gustafson, Bret. 'Were the Chiriguano a Colonial Fabrication? Linguistic Arguments for Rethinking Guaraní and Chané Histories in the Chaco.' In Silvia Hirsch, Paola Canova, and Mercedes Biocca, eds. *Reimagining the Gran Chaco: Identities, Politics, and the Environment in South America*, 53–72. Gainesville: University Press of Florida, 2021.

Hanke, Lewis. *The Spanish Struggle for Justice in the Conquest of America*. Philadelphia: University of Pennsylvania Press, 1949.

Hanke, Lewis. *Los virreyes españoles en América durante el gobierno de la casa de Austria. Peru*. Vol. 1. Biblioteca de Autores Españoles. Madrid: Ediciones Atlas, 1978.

Haring, Clarence Henry. *The Spanish Empire in America*. New York and Burlingame, CA: First Harbinger Books, 1963.

Hemming, John. *The Conquest of the Incas*. London: Macmillan, 1970.

Herzog, Tamar. *Ritos de control, prácticas de negociación: Pesquisas, visitas y residencias y las relaciones entre Quito y Madrid (1650–1750)*. Madrid: Fundación Ignacio Larramendi, 2000.

Herzog, Tamar. *Frontiers of Possession: Spain and Portugal in Europe and the Americas*. Cambridge, MA: Harvard University Press, 2015.

Hespanha, António Manuel. *Vísperas del Leviatán. instituciones y poder político (Portugal, siglo XVII)*. Trans. Fernando Jesús Bouza Alvarez. Madrid: Taurus, 1989.

Hespanha, António Manuel. *La gracia del derecho. Economia de la cultura en la Edad Moderna*. Madrid: Centro de Estudios Constitucionales, 1993.

Hespanha, António Manuel. *Caleidoscópio do antigo regime*. São Paulo: Alameda, 2012.

Hespanha, António Manuel. 'The Legal Patchwork of Empires.' Review of *Legal Pluralism and Empires, 1500–1850*, by Lauren Benton and Richard J. Ross. *Rechtsgeschichte* 22, 2014: 303–14.

Hespanha, António Manuel. *A ordem do mundo e o saber dos juristas: imaginários do antigo direito europeu*. Lisbon: independently published, 2017.

Hutchinson, Robert. *The Spanish Armada*. London: Weidenfeld & Nicolson, 2014.

Hyland, Sabine. *The Jesuit and the Incas: The Extraordinary Life of Padre Blas Valera, S.J.* Ann Arbor: University of Michigan Press, 2003.

Jara, Alvaro. *Guerra y sociedad en Chile. La transformación de la guerra de Arauco y la esclavitud de los indios*. Santiago de Chile: Editorial Universitaria, 1971.

Jiménez Estrella, Antonio. 'Las relaciones de servicios y la capitalización de la memoria de los antepasados y familiares de los militares de la monarquía hispánica en el siglo XVII.' *Tiempos Modernos*, no. 47 (2023): 314–37.

Julien, Catherine. 'Colonial Perspectives on the Chiriguana (1528–1574).' In María Susana Cipolletti, ed. *Resistencia y Adaptación Nativa en las Tierras Bajas Latinoamericanas*, 17–76. Quito: Abya-Yala, 1997.

Julien, Catherine. 'History and Art in Translation: The *Paños* and Other Objects Collected by Francisco de Toledo.' *Colonial Latin American Historical Review* 8, no. 1 (1999): 61–89.

Julien, Catherine. 'Kandire in Real Time and Space: Sixteenth-Century Expeditions from the Pantanal to the Andes.' *Ethnohistory* 54, no. 2 (2007): 245–72.

Jurado, María Carolina. 'Autoridades étnicas menores y territorios. El impacto de la fragmentación colonial en las bases del poder en Macha (Norte de Potosí) S.XVI–XVII.' PhD dissertation, Universidad de Buenos Aires, 2010.

Jurado, María Carolina. '"Descendientes de los primeros". Las probanzas de méritos y servicios y la genealogía cacical. Audiencia de Charcas, 1574–1719.' *Revista de Indias* 74, no. 261 (2014): 387–422.

Klein, Herbert S. *Historia de Bolivia*. La Paz: Libreria Editorial 'Juventud', 1997.

Konetzke, Richard. *América Latina*, Vol. II, *La época colonial*. Trans. Pedro Scaron. México: Siglo Veintiuno, 1977.

Lamana, Gonzalo. *Pensamiento colonial crítico: textos y actos de Polo Ondegardo.* Lima, Cusco: IFEA Instituto Francés de Estudios Andinos; CBC Centro Bartolomé de las Casas, 2012.

Langer, Erick Detlef. *Expecting Pears from an Elm Tree: Franciscan Missions on the Chiriguano Frontier in the Heart of South America, 1830–1949*. Durham, NC: Duke University Press, 2009.

Lantigua, David. *Infidels and Empires in a New World Order: Early Modern Spanish Contributions to International Legal Thought.* Cambridge, New York: Cambridge University Press, 2020.

Lázaro Avila, Carlos. *Las fronteras de América y los 'flandes indianos'.* Colección Tierra Nueva e Cielo Nuevo 35. Madrid: Consejo Superior de Investigaciones Científicas, Centro de Estudios Históricos, Departamento de Historia de América, 1997.

Levillier, Roberto. *Francisco de Aguirre y los orígenes del Tucumán, 1550–1570.* Madrid: Imprenta de Juan Pueyo, 1920.

Levillier, Roberto. *Biografías de conquistadores de la Argentina. Siglo XVI.* Madrid: Juan Pueyo, 1928.

Levillier, Roberto. *Nueva crónica de la conquista del Tucumán. 1563–1573.* Vol. II. Buenos Aires: Editorial 'Nosotros', 1931.

Levillier, Roberto. *Don Francisco de Toledo. Supremo organizador del Perú. Su vida, su obra (1515–1582).* Buenos Aires: Colección de Publicaciones Históricas de la Biblioteca del Congreso Argentino, 1935.

Levin Rojo, Danna, and Cynthia Radding Murrieta, eds. *The Oxford Handbook of Borderlands of the Iberian World.* Oxford Handbooks. New York: Oxford University Press, 2019.

Lisi, Francesco Leonardo. *El tercer concilio limense y la aculturación de los indígenas sudamericanos: estudio crítico con edición, traducción y comentario de las actas del concilio provincial celebrado en Lima entre 1582 y 1583.* Salamanca: Universidad de Salamanca, 1990.

Lockhart, James. *The Men of Cajamarca: A Social and Biographical Study of the First Conqueror of Peru.* Austin: University of Texas Press, 1972.

Lockhart, James. *Spanish Peru, 1532–1560: A Colonial Society*. Madison: University of Wisconsin Press, 1974.

Lohmann Villena, Guillermo. 'Las compañías de gentilhombres de lanzas y arcabuces de la guarda del virreinato del Perú.' *Anuario de Estudios Americanos*, no. 13 (1956): 141–215.

Lohmann Villena, Guillermo. *Juan de Matienzo, Autor del 'Gobierno del Perú' (su Personalidad, su Obra)*. Sevilla: Escuela de Estudios Hispano-Americanos, 1966.

Lopetegui, León. *El padre José de Acosta S.I. y las misiones*. Madrid: Consejo Superior de Investigaciones Científicas. Instituto Gonzalo Fernández de Oviedo, 1942.

Lorandi, Ana María. 'La resistencia y rebeliones de los diaguito-calchaqui en los siglos XVI–XVII.' *Cuadernos de Historia* 8 (1988): 99–122.

Lorandi, Ana María. *Ni ley, ni rey, ni hombre virtuoso: Guerra y sociedad en el virreinato del Perú, siglos XVI y XVII*. Buenos Aires, Barcelona: Universidad de Buenos Aires, Facultad de Filosofía y Letras; Gedisa Editorial, 2002.

Lorandi, Ana María, and Roxana Boixados. 'Etnohistoria de los valles calchaquíes en los siglos XVI y XVII.' *Runa* XVII–XIX (1987, 1988): 263–419.

MacCormack, Sabine. *Religion in the Andes: Vision and Imagination in Early Colonial Peru*. Princeton, NJ: Princeton University Press, 1991.

MacLachlan, Colin M. *Spain's Empire in the New World: The Role of Ideas in Institutional and Social Change*. Berkeley: University of California Press, 1991.

Mangan, Jane E. *Trading Roles: Gender, Ethnicity, and the Urban Economy in Colonial Potosí*. Durham, NC: Duke University Press, 2005.

Martín Marcos, David. *People of the Iberian Borderlands: Community and Conflict between Spain and Portugal, 1640–1715*. Early Modern Iberian History in Global Contexts. New York, London: Routledge, 2023.

Martínez Cereceda, José Luis. *Gente de la tierra de guerra: Los lipes en las tradiciones andinas y el imaginario colonial*. Colección Estudios Andinos 7. Lima, Santiago, Chile: Fondo Editorial, Pontificia Universidad Católica del Perú; Dirección de Bibliotecas, Archivos y Museos de Chile, 2011.

Masters, Adrian. *We, the King: Creating Royal Legislation in the Sixteenth-Century Spanish New World*. Cambridge: Cambridge University Press, 2023.

Matthew, Laura E. *Memorias de conquista: De conquistadores indigenas a mexicanos en la Guatemala colonial*. Wellfleet, MA: CIRMA, 2017.

Mazín Gómez, Oscar. 'Architect of the New World: Juan Solórzano Pereyra and the Status of the Americas.' In Pedro Cardim, Tamar Herzog, José Ibáñez, and Gaetano Sabatini, eds. *Polycentric Monarchies: How Did Early Modern Spain and Portugal Achieve and Maintain a Global Hegemony?* 27–42. Eastbourne: Sussex Academic Press, 2012.

McLeod, Murdo. 'Self-Promotion: The *Relaciones de Méritos y Servicios* and Their Historical and Political Interpretation.' *Colonial Latin American Historial Review* 7, no. 1 (1998): 25–42.

Medina, José Toribio. *Historia del Santo Oficio de la Inquisición de Lima (1569–1820)*. Vol. I. Santiago de Chile: Imprenta Gutenberg, 1887.

Medina, José Toribio. *Diccionario biográfico colonial de Chile*. Santiago de Chile: Imprenta Elzeviriana, 1906.

Medinaceli, Ximena. 'La ambigüedad del discurso político de las autoridades étnicas en el siglo XVI. Una propuesta de lectura de la probanza de los Colque Guarachi de Quillacas.' *Revista Andina* 38 (2004): 87–104.

Mendoza Loza, Gunnar, *Obras completas*, Vol. 1. Sucre: Fundación Cultural del Banco Central de Bolivia/Archivo y Biblioteca Nacionales de Bolivia, 2005.

Merluzzi, Manfredi. *Politica e governo nel Nuovo Mondo: Francisco de Toledo viceré del Perù (1569–1581)*. Rome: Carocci, 2003.

Merluzzi, Manfredi. *Gobernando los Andes: Francisco de Toledo virrey del Perú (1569–1581)*. Trans. Patricia Unzain. Lima: Fondo Editorial, Pontificia Universidad Católica del Perú, 2014.

Millones, Luis. *El Retorno de las huacas. Estudios y documentos del siglo XVI*. Lima: IEP, 1990.

Miskimmon, Alister, Ben O'Loughlin, and Laura Roselle. *Strategic Narratives: Communication Power and the New World Order*. New York, London: Routledge, 2013.

Montoya Guzmán, Juan David. 'La fabricación del enemigo: Los indios pijaos en el Nuevo Reino de Granada, 1562–1611.' *TRASHUMANTE. Revista Americana de Historia Social* 19 (2022): 96–117.

Morong Reyes, Germán. *Saberes hegemónicos y dominio colonial. Los indios en el Gobierno del Perú de Juan de Matienzo (1567)*. Rosario [Santa Fe], Argentina: Prohistoria Ediciones, 2016.

Morris, Craig, and Adriana Von Hagen. *The Incas: Lords of the Four Quarters*. London: Thames & Hudson, 2011.

Mumford, Jeremy Ravi. *Vertical Empire: The General Resettlement of Indians in the Colonial Andes*. Durham, NC: Duke University Press, 2012.

Muñoz Arbeláez, Santiago. *Costumbres en disputa: Los Muiscas y el Imperio Español en Ubaque, Siglo XVI*. Bogotá: Universidad de los Andes, Facultad de Ciencias Sociales, Departamento de Historia, 2015.

Murra, John V. *La organización económica del estado inca*. Trans. Daniel R. Wagner. México: Siglo Veintiuno, 1978.

Murray, B. P., B. K. Horton, R. Matos, and M. T. Heizler. 'Oligocene-Miocene Basin Evolution in the Northern Altiplano, Bolivia: Implications for Evolution of the Central Andean Backthrust Belt and High Plateau.' *Geological Society of America Bulletin* 122, nos 9–10 (2010): 1443–62.

Nakashima, Roxana, and Lia Guillermina Oliveto. 'Las informaciones de méritos y servicios y el imperio global de Felipe II a través de la trayectoria de Francisco Arias de Herrera.' *Revista Electrónica de Fuentes y Archivos*, no. 5 (2014): 120–28.

Nesvig, Martin Austin. *Promiscuous Power: An Unorthodox History of New Spain*. Austin: University of Texas Press, 2018.

Newson, Linda. 'Indian Population Patterns in Colonial Spanish America.' *Latin American Research Review* 20, no. 3 (1985): 41–74.

Newson, Linda. *Life and Death in Early Colonial Ecuador*. The Civilization of the American Indian Series, Vol. 214. Norman: University of Oklahoma Press, 1995.

Newson, Linda. *Supervivencia indígena en la Nicaragua colonial*. London: University of London Press, 2021.

Nolasco Pérez, Fray Pedro. *Religiosos de la merced que pasaron a la América española*. Sevilla: Tipografía Zarzuela, 1924.

Nordenskiold, Erland. 'The Guarani Invasion of the Inca Empire in the Sixteenth Century: An Historical Indian Migration.' *Geographical Review* 4, no. 2 (1917): 103–21.

Nowell, Charles. 'Aleixo García and the White King.' *The Hispanic American Historical Review* 26, no. 4 (1946): 450–66.

Oliveto, Lia Guillermina. 'Chiriguanos: La construcción de un estereotipo en la política colonizadora del sur andino.' *Memoria Americana* 18, no. 1 (2010): 47–73.

Oliveto, Lia Guillermina. 'Ocupación territorial y relaciones interétnicas en los Andes Meridionales. Tarija, entre los desafíos prehispánicos y temprano coloniales.' Universidad de Buenos Aires, 2010.

Oliveto, Lia Guillermina. 'De mitmaqkuna incaicos en Tarija a reducidos en La Plata. Tras las huellas de los moyos moyos y su derrotero colonial.' *Anuario de Estudios Bolivianos. Archivisticos y Bibliográficos* 17 (2011): 463–90.

Oliveto, Lia Guillermina. 'Piezas, presos, indios habidos en buena guerra, cimarrones y fugitivos. Notas sobre el cautiverio indígena en la frontera oriental de Tarija en el siglo XVI.' In Gerardo Pérez and Diana Roselly, eds. *Vivir en los márgenes. Fronteras en América colonial: Sujetos, prácticas e identidades, siglos XVI–XVIII*, 29–66. México: Instituto de Investigaciones Históricas, UNAM, 2021.

Oliveto, Lia Guillermina, and Paula Zagalsky. 'De nominaciones y estereotipos: Los chiriguanos y los moyos moyos, Dos casos de la frontera oriental de Charcas en el siglo XVI.' *Bibliographica Americana*, no. 6 (2010).

Ots Capdequi, José María. *El estado español en las Indias*. México: El Colegio de México, 1941.

Owens, John B. *'By My Absolute Royal Authority': Justice and the Castilian Commonwealth at the Beginning of the First Global Age*. Rochester, NY: University of Rochester Press, 2005.

Palomeque, Silvia. 'Casabindos, cochinocas y chichas en el siglo XVI. Avances de investigación.' In María Ester Albeck, Marta Ruiz, and María Beatriz Cremonte, eds. *Las tierras altas del área Centro Sur Andina entre el 1000 y el 1600 D.C.*, 233–63. Jujuy: EDIUNJU, 2013.

Palomeque, Silvia. 'Los chicha y las visitas toledanas. Las tierras de los chicha de Talina (1573–1595).' In Ana M. Presta, ed. *Aportes multidisciplinarios al estudio de los colectivos étnicos surandinos reflexiones sobre Qaraqara-Charka tres años después*, 117–89. La Paz: Plural-IFEA, 2013.

Pärssinen, Martti. *Tawantinsuyu: The Inca State and Its Political Organization*. Helsinki: Societas Historicas Finlandiae, 1992.

Paz, Gustavo, and Gabriela Sica. 'La frontera oriental del Tucumán en el Río de la Plata (siglos XVI-XVIII).' In S. Truchuelo and E. Reitano, eds. *Las fronteras en el mundo atlántico (Siglos XVI–XVIII)*, 293–330. La Plata: Universidad Nacional de La Plata. Facultad de Humanidades y Ciencias de la Educación, 2017.

Pietschmann, Horst. *El estado y su evolución al principio de la colonización española de América*. México: Fondo de Cultura Económica, 1989.

Pifarré, Francisco. *Historia de un pueblo*. Vol. 2. *Los guaraní-chiriguano*. La Paz: CIPCA, 1989.

Platt, Tristán, and Pablo Quisbert. 'Tras las huellas del silencio: Potosí, los incas y Toledo.' *Runa* XXXI, no. 2 (2010): 115–52.

Ponce Leiva, Pilar, and Alexander Ponsen. 'Administration and Government of the Iberian Empires.' In Fernando Bouza, Pedro Cardim, and Antonio Feros, eds. *The Iberian World, 1450–1820*, 300–319. London, New York: Routledge, 2020.

Powell, Philip. '*Presidios* and Towns on the Silver Frontier of New Spain. 1550–1580.' *The Hispanic American Historical Review* 24, no. 2 (1944): 179–200.

Powell, Philip. 'Portrait of an American Viceroy: Martín Enríquez, 1568–1583.' *The Americas* 14, no. 1 (1957): 1–24.

Prado, Fabricio. 'The Fringes of Empires: Recent Scholarship on Colonial Frontiers and Borderlands in Latin America.' *History Compass* 10, no. 4 (2012): 318–33.

Presta, Ana María. *Espacio, etnias, frontera. Atenuaciones políticas en el sur del Tawantinsuyu. Siglos XV–XVIII*. Sucre: ASUR, 1995.

Presta, Ana María. *Encomienda, familia y negocios en Charcas colonial: Los encomenderos de La Plata, 1550–1600*. Lima: IEP, Instituto de Estudios Peruanos: Banco Central de Reserva del Perú, 2000.

Presta, Ana María. 'Portraits of Four Women: Traditional Female Roles and Transgressions in Colonial Elite Families in Charcas, 1550–1600.' *Colonial Latin American Review* 9, no. 2 (2000): 237–62.

Presta, Ana María. 'Hermosos, fértiles y abundantes. Los valles de Tarija y su población en el siglo XVI.' In Stephan Beck, Narel Paniagua, and David A. Preston, eds. *Historia, Ambiente y Sociedad en Tarija, Bolivia*, 25–39. La Paz: Instituto de Ecología, Universidad Mayor de San Andrés—School of Geography, University of Leeds, 2001.

Presta, Ana María. 'Los valles mesotérmicos de Chuquisaca entre la fragment-ación territorial yampara y la ocupación de los migrantes qaraqara y charka en la temprana colonia.' In Presta, ed. *Aportes multidisciplinarios al estudio de los colectivos étnicos surandinos, reflexiones sobre Qaraqara-Charka tres años después*, 27–60. La Paz: Plural-IFEA, 2013.

Presta, Ana María, and María de las Mercedes del Rio. 'Un estudio etnohistórico en los corregimientos de Tomina Yamparaes: Casos de multietnicidad'.

Quondam, Amedeo, and Eduardo Torres Corominas. *El discurso cortesano*. Trans. Cattedra di Spagnolo del Dipartimento di Scienze Documentarie, Linguistico-filologiche e Geografiche dell'Univ. Roma 'La Sapienza'. Madrid: Ed. Polifemo, 2013.

Rabasa, José. *Writing Violence on the Northern Frontier: The Historiography of Sixteenth Century New Mexico and Florida and the Legacy of Conquest*. Latin America Otherwise. Durham, NC: Duke University Press, 2000.

Radding Murrieta, Cynthia. *Wandering Peoples: Colonialism, Ethnic Spaces, and Ecological Frontiers in Northwestern Mexico, 1700–1850*. Latin America Otherwise. Durham, NC: Duke University Press, 1997.

Raffino, Rodolfo, Christian Vitty, and Diego Gobbo. 'Inkas y chichas: Identidad, transformación y una cuestión fronteriza.' *Boletín de Arqueología PUCP*, no. 8 (2004): 247–65.

Raffino, Rodolfo, Diego Gobbo, and Anahí Iácona. 'De Potosí y Tarija a la frontera chiriguana.' *Folia Histórica del Nordeste*, no. 16 (2006): 83–129.

Rama, Angel, and John Charles Chasteen. *The Lettered City*. Post-Contemporary Interventions. Durham, NC: Duke University Press, 1996.

Ramírez Barrios, Julio Alberto. *El sello real en el Perú Colonial: poder y representación en la distancia*. Lima, Sevilla: Fondo Editorial, Pontificia Universidad Católica de Perú, Editorial Universidad de Sevilla, 2020.

Ramírez Barrios, Julio Alberto. 'En defensa de la autoridad real: Oficiales de la pluma de la Real Audiencia de Lima durante la rebelión de Gonzalo Pizarro (1544–1548).' *Revista de Historia Del Derecho* 63 (2022): 61–91.

Ramos, Gabriela. 'Política eclesiástica y extirpación de idolatrías: Discursos y silencios en torno al Taqui Onkoy.' In Gabriela Ramos and Henrique Urbano, *Catolicismo y extirpación de idolatrías. Siglos XVI–XVIII. Charcas. Chile. México. Perú*, Vol. 5, 137–68. Cusco: Centro de Estudios Andinos 'Fray Bartolomé de las Casas', 1993.

Ramos, Gabriela. 'El Rastro de la discriminación. Litigios y probanzas de caciques en el Perú colonial temprano.' *Fronteras de La Historia* 21, no. 1 (2016): 66–90.

Ramos Pérez, Demetrio. 'La crisis indiana y la Junta Magna de 1568.' *Jahrbuch für Geschichte Lateinamerikas*, no. 23 (1986): 1–61.

Rappaport, Joanne. *The Disappearing Mestizo: Configuring Difference in the Colonial New Kingdom of Granada*. Durham, NC: Duke University Press, 2014.

Renard-Casevitz, France Marie, Thierry Saignes, Anne Christine Taylor, and Institut français d'études andines. *Al este de los Andes: relaciones entre las sociedades amazónicas y andinas entre los siglos XV y XVII*. Quito: Abya-Yala, 1988.

Reséndez, Andrés. *The Other Slavery: The Uncovered Story of Indian Enslavement in America*. First Mariner Books edn. Boston, MA, New York: Mariner Books, Houghton Mifflin Harcourt, 2017.

Restall, Matthew. *Seven Myths of the Spanish Conquest*. New York: Oxford University Press, 2003.

Revilla Orías, Paola A. *Entangled Coercion: African and Indigenous Labour in Charcas (16th–17th Century)*. Work in Global and Historical Perspective 9. Boston, MA: De Gruyter Oldenbourg, 2020.

Ross, Richard, and Philip Stern. 'Reconstructing Early Modern Notions of Legal Pluralism.' In Richard J. Ross and Lauren Benton, eds. *Legal Pluralism and Empires, 1500–1850*, 109–43. New York, London: New York University Press, 2013.

Rostworowski de Diez Canseco, María. *History of the Inca Realm*. Trans. Harry B. Iceland. Cambridge, New York: Cambridge University Press, 1999.

Ruan, Felipe. 'The *Probanza* and Shaping a Contesting *Mestizo* Record in Early Colonial Peru.' *Bulletin of Spanish Studies* 94, no. 5 (2017): 843–69.

Ruiz, Teofilo. *A King Travels: Festive Traditions in Late Medieval and Early Modern Spain*. Princeton, NJ: Princeton University Press, 2012.

Ruiz Ibáñez, José Javier. *Las dos caras de Jano: Monarquía, ciudad e individuo. Murcia, 1588–1648*. Murcia: Universidad de Murcia, 1995.

Ruiz Ibáñez, José Javier, and Gaetano Sabatini. 'Monarchy as Conquest: Violence, Social Opportunity, and Political Stability in the Establishment of the Hispanic Monarchy.' *The Journal of Modern History* 81, no. 3 (2009): 501–36.

Saignes, Thierry. 'Une frontière fossile: La cordillera Chiriguano au XVIe siècle.' PhD dissertation, Université de Paris, 1974.

Saignes, Thierry. 'Andaluces en el poblamiento del Oriente Boliviano. En torno a unas figuras controvertidas. El fundador de Tarija y sus herederos.' In Consejo Superior de Investigaciones Científicas, *Actas de Las II Jornadas de Andalucía y América. Universidad Santa María de La Rábida. Marzo 1982*, Vol. 2: pp. 173–206, 1983.

Saignes, Thierry. 'Las zonas conflictivas: Fronteras iniciales de guerra.' In Franklin Pease and Frank Moya Pons, eds, *El primer contacto y la formación de nuevas sociedades*, Vol. II, 269–99. Madrid: Ediciones UNESCO, Ediciones Trotta, 2007.

Saignes, Thierry, and Isabelle Combès. *Historia del pueblo chiriguano*. Lima, La Paz: Instituto Francés de Estudios Andinos; Embajada de Francia en Bolivia: Plural Editores, 2007.

Salinero, Gregorio. *Hombres de mala corte. Desobediencias, procesos políticos y gobierno de Indias en la segunda mitad del siglo XVI*. Madrid: Difusora Larousse – Ediciones Cátedra, 2018.

Sanabria, Hernando. *Cronica sumaria de los gobernadores de Santa Cruz (1560–1810)*. Santa Cruz de la Sierra: Publicaciones de la Universidad Boliviana Gabriel René Moreno, 1975.

Sanchez Concha Barrios, Rafael. 'Las expediciones descubridoras: La entrada desde Larecaja hasta Tarija (1539–1540).' *Boletin del Instituto Riva Aguero* 16 (1989).

Santos-Granero, Fernando. *Vital Enemies: Slavery, Predation, and the Amerindian Political Economy of Life*. Austin: University of Texas Press, 2009.

Scholl, Jonathan. 'At the Limits of Empire: Incas, Spaniards, and the Ava-Guarani (Chiriguanaes) on the Charcas-Chiriguana Frontier, Southeastern Andes (1450s–1620s).' PhD dissertation, University of Florida, 2015.

Scott, Heidi V. *Contested Territory: Mapping Peru in the Sixteenth and Seventeenth Centuries*. History, Languages, and Cultures of the Spanish and Portuguese Worlds. South Bend, IN: University of Notre Dame Press, 2009.

Seed, Patricia. *Ceremonies of Possession in Europe's Conquest of the New World, 1492–1640*. Cambridge, New York: Cambridge University Press, 1995.

Seed, Patricia. *American Pentimento: The Invention of Indians and the Pursuit of Riches*. Minneapolis: University of Minnesota Press, 2001.

Silva Lezaeta, Luis. *El conquistador Francisco de Aguirre*. Santiago de Chile: Imprenta de la Revista Católica, 1904.

Smietniansky, Silvia. 'El uso motivado del lenguaje: Escritura y oralidad en los rituales de toma de posesión. El caso de Hispanoamérica colonial.' *Revista de Antropología* 59, no. 2 (2016): 131–54.

Stern, Steve J. *Peru's Indian Peoples and the Challenge of Spanish Conquest: Huamanga to 1640.* Madison: University of Wisconsin Press, 1986.

Tantaleán Arbulú, Javier. *El virrey Francisco de Toledo y su tiempo: Proyecto de gobernabilidad, el imperio hispano, la plata peruana en la economía-mundo y el mercado colonial.* 2 vols. Lima: Universidad de San Martín de Porres, Fondo Editorial, 2011.

Trelles Arestegui, Efraín. *Lucas Martínez de Vegazo: Funcionamiento de una encomienda temprana inicial.* Lima: Pontificia Universidad Católica del Perú, Fondo Editorial, 1991.

Truchuelo, Susana, and Emir Reitano. *Fronteras en el mundo atlántico (siglos XVI–XIX).* La Plata: Universidad Nacional de La Plata. Facultad de Humanidades y Ciencias de la Educación, 2017.

Turner Bushell, Amy. 'Gates, Patterns, and Peripheries: The Field of Frontier Latin America.' In Christine Daniels and Michael V. Kennedy, eds. *Negotiated Empires: Centers and Peripheries in the Americas*, 15–28. London: Routledge, 2002.

Urquidi, José Macedonio. *El origen de la noble villa de Oropesa. La fundación de Cochabamba en 1571 por Gerónimo Osorio.* Cochabamba: Editorial Canelas, 1970.

Valcárcel, Luis E. *El virrey Toledo, gran tirano del Perú: Una revisión histórica.* Lima: Universidad Garcilaso de la Vega, 2015.

Valenzuela Márquez, Jaime. 'Los indios cautivos en la frontera de guerra chilena: entre la abolición de la esclavitud y la recomposición de la servidumbre esclavista.' In Carmen Alveal and Thiago Dias, eds. *Espaços Coloniais: Domínios, Poderes e Representações*, 229–61. São Paulo: Alameda Casa Editorial, 2019.

Vallejo, Jesús. 'Power Hierarchies in Medieval Juridical Thought: An Essay in Reinterpretation.' *Ius Commune* 19 (1992): 1–29.

Vallejo, Jesús. 'Concepción de La Policía.' In Marta Lorente, ed. *La jurisdicción contencioso-administrativa en España. Una historia de sus orígenes*, 117–44. Madrid: Consejo General del Poder Judicial, 2010.

Van Deusen, Nancy E. 'Why Indigenous Slavery Continued in Spanish America after the New Laws of 1542.' *The Americas* 80, no. 3 (2023): 395–432.

Varón Gabai, Rafael. *La ilusión del poder: Apogeo y decadencia de los Pizarro en la conquista del Perú.* Lima: Instituto de Estudios Peruanos: Instituto Francés de Estudios Andinos, 1996.

Wachtel, Nathan. *Los vencidos. Los indios del Perú frente a la conquista española (1530–1570).* Trans. Antonio Escohotado. Madrid: Alianza Editorial, 1976.

Wachtel, Nathan. 'Los mitimaes del valle de Cochabamba: La política colonizadora de Wayna Capac.' *Historia Boliviana* 1, no. 1 (1981): 21–57.

Wachtel, Nathan. 'The Indian and the Spanish Conquest.' In Leslie Bethell, ed. *The Cambridge History of Latin America*, Vol. I, 207–37. Cambridge: Cambridge University Press, 1984.

Weaver Olson, Nathan. 'A Republic of Lost Peoples: Race, Status, and Community in the Eastern Andes of Charcas at the Turn of the Seventeenth Century.' PhD dissertation, University of Minnesota, 2017.

Williams, Caroline. 'Opening New Frontiers in Colonial Spanish American History: New Perspectives on Indigenous-Spanish Interactions on the Margins of Empire.' *History Compass* 6, no. 4 (2008): 1121–39.

Yun-Casalilla, Bartolomé. *Iberian World Empires and the Globalization of Europe 1415–1668*. Palgrave Studies in Comparative Global History. Puchong, Selangor: Springer Singapore, 2018.

Zamora, Romina. *Casa poblada y buen gobierno. Oeconomia católica y servicio personal en San Miguel de Tucumán., Siglo XVIII*. Buenos Aires: Prometeo Libros, 2017.

Zanolli, Carlos. 'Los chichas como mitimaes del inca.' *Relaciones de la Sociedad Argentina de Antropología* XXVIII (2003): 45–60.

Zanolli, Carlos Eduardo. 'Tierra, encomienda e identidad: Omaguaca (1540–1638).' Colección tesis doctorales. Buenos Aires: Sociedad Argentina de Antropología, 2005.

Zimmerman, Arthur Franklin. *Francisco de Toledo: Fifth Viceroy of Peru, 1569–1581*. New York: Greenwood Press, 1938.

Voices of the Expeditions

Archives constitute the backbone of this book and this brief appendix's purpose is to bring a flavour of that to its readers. The selection of materials that have been included are as representative as possible of the cacophony of voices that speak to us through the archive. But archives are not innocent. As Kathryn Burns recently suggested, they are 'less like mirrors and more like chessboards'.[1] They have their own pasts and were shaped by choices that formed them, sometimes by sheer luck. Intermediaries of various sorts, including notaries, lawyers, petitioners, and various authorities contributed to what we find today.[2] With a growing number of documents now digitised, it is easy to lose perspective of this dimension of the archive. In the 'physical' archive, documents are generally grouped together, and it is sometimes possible to interpret the logic behind their organisation, although sometimes this might be random. The choice here includes unpublished materials and documents that have been transcribed and published in Spanish before, but never translated into English. There are also complete documents and sections of documents that are relevant to the expeditions. Each has a brief introduction to bring some context, followed by a Spanish transcription and an approximate English translation of the transcription.

1. Martín de Almendras' expeditions 1564–1565

Document 1

In the aftermath of the expedition by Peru's viceroy don Francisco de Toledo (1574), Quillaca lord don Juan Colque Guarache drafted his first report of merits and services to the Crown, with the help of notaries, lawyers, and, more importantly, distinguished witnesses. They were able to remember

---

1 Kathryn Burns, *Into the Archive: Writing and Power in Colonial Peru* (Durham, NC: Duke University Press, 2010), p. 124.
2 Adrian Masters, *We, the King: Creating Royal Legislation in the Sixteenth-Century Spanish New World* (Cambridge: Cambridge University Press, 2023), pp. 180–221.

Colque Guarache's participation in Martín de Almendras' earlier expeditions of 1564–1565. This *probanza* has been previously published by Waldemar Espinoza Soriano; twice, in 1981 and 2003.[3] The materials have been used in academic publications over the years.[4] Here are some excerpts from the report, taken from the original in the Archivo General de Indias in Seville, Spain.

AGI, Charcas, 53, [1574–1576], Información de méritos y servicios de don Juan Colque Guarache

Excerpt 1

[fol. 3r]

[pregunta número 3 del segundo cuestionario]

Yten si saben que quando el capitan Martin de Almendras fue a la jornada de los chichas contra los yndios de la dicha provincia estavan rrevelados por no pagar tasa a su magestad el dicho don Juan Colque fue nombrado por la rreal audiencia por capitan general de todos los yndios que fueron en la dicha jornada y los sustento a su costa sin que le diese socorro ninguno lo qual gasto mas de doze mill pesos de sus propios bienes y haziendas y que mediante los ardiles y medios que tubo los yndios se rreduxeron al servicio de su magestad que de entonces pagan tasa sin que despues aca se ayan alterado digan

Translation:

[Question 3, second questionnaire]

---

3 Waldemar Espinoza Soriano, 'El Reino Aymara de Quillaca-Asanaque, Siglos XV y XVI', *Revista del Museo Nacional de Lima* XLV (1981): pp. 175–274; Waldemar Espinoza Soriano, 'La Confederación Quillaca-Asanaque. Siglos XV y XVI', in *Temas de Etnohistoria Boliviana* (La Paz: Producciones CIMA, 2003).

4 Thomas Alan Abercrombie, 'The Politics of Sacrifice: An Aymara Society in Action', PhD dissertation, The University of Chicago, 1986; Thomas A. Abercrombie, *Pathways of Memory and Power: Ethnography and History among an Andean People* (Madison: University of Wisconsin Press, 1998); Graña, 'Autoridad y memoria'; Mario Julio Graña, '"Bastardo, mañoso, sagaz y ladino." Caciques, pleitos y agravios en el sur andino. Don Fernando Ayavire y Velasco contra Don Juan Colque Guarache. Charcas, Siglo XVI', *Anuario 2000*, 2001, pp. 541–77; Ximena Medinaceli, 'La ambigüedad del discurso político de las autoridades étnicas en el siglo XVI. Una propuesta de lectura de la probanza de los Colque Guarachi de Quillacas', *Revista Andina* 38 (2004): pp. 87–104; María Carolina Jurado, 'Autoridades étnicas menores y territorios. El impacto de la fragmentación colonial en las bases del poder en Macha (Norte de Potosí) S.XVI-XVII', PhD dissertation, Universidad de Buenos Aires, 2010; Platt, Bouysse-Cassagne, and Harris, eds, *Qaraqara–Charka*.

Idem, if they know that when Captain Martín de Almendras went on the expedition to the Chichas against the Indians of that province, who had rebelled because they were not paying tribute to His Majesty, the Real Audiencia appointed don Juan Colque captain of all the Indians who went along; and that he fed them and kept them from his own resources, without any help, in which he may have spent his own goods worth 12,000 pesos; and thanks to his manners and means these Indians submitted to the service of His Majesty and ever since have been paying tribute and have not rebelled again.

Excerpt 2

[fol. 9v]

[Declaración de Antonio de Robles]

18   a la diez y ocho preguntas dixo que este testigo vio que el dicho don juan colque fue en servicio de su magestad e acompañamiento del capitan Martin de Almendras a la jornada de los chichas e que el dicho don juan como cacique e señor principal yva por capitan general de todos los yndios amigos que fueron aquella jornada e vio este testigo que el dicho don Juan como tal capitan general sirvio en la dicha jornada con sus armas muy bien como buen capitan e por su yndustria e buena diligencia vio este testigo que el dicho capitan Martin de Almendras ovo a las manos al cacique e capitan principal de los yndios chichas e fue caussa con tomar el dicho capitan para que sesaren como cesaron los delitos e muertes que los dichos yndios chichas conmetian e los pacificaron y quedaron de paz como lo an estado desde entonces asta han tributado y servido a su magestad como yndios que estan en su rreal corona con lo qual el dicho don juan colque hizo servicio notable a su magestad de mas de que vide este testigo que el dicho don juan gasto en lo susodicho mucha cantidad de hazienda por que llevo mas de trezientos carneros cargados de comida para sustentar como sustentava a los yndios amigos que fueron a la dicha jornada de que el hera capitan general y esto rresponde a la pregunta

[Statement by Antonio de Robles]

To the eighteenth question this witness replied that don Juan Colque went in the service of His Majesty in the company of Captain Martín de Almendras on the expedition to the Chichas, and that don Juan, as *cacique* and lord went as captain of all the Friendly Indians that served in that expedition, and this witness saw that in that role don Juan served with his weapons as a good captain and this witness saw how, because of his industriousness and diligence, Captain Martín de Almendras held the hands of the *cacique* and main captain of the Chichas Indians, and because of his submission all the unrest and murders that these Indians had been committing ceased and they were pacified, remained peaceful and are still that way, paying tribute and serving His Majesty as Indians under his royal crown, demonstrating that don Juan Colque did a notable service to His Majesty, and this witness saw don Juan spent much of his wealth on these tasks: he took 300 llamas loaded with food for the upkeep of friendly Indians that went on the expedition in which he was main captain, and this is his response to the question.

Excerpt 3

[fol. 59r]

[Declaración de don Juan Marca, cacique de los Incas que residen en Potosí]

A la sesta pregunta dixo que este testigo vio como el capitan Martin de Almendras fue al allanamiento e pacificacion de los yndios chichas que se avian rrevelado y el dicho don Juan Colque fue con el e fue con dicho copia de muchos yndios suyos e se allano e pacifico aquella provincia e despues aca es publico que pagan tasa e venidos que fueron de la jornada oyo este testigo dezir a caciques e yndios chichas que el dicho don Juan Colque fue mucha parte para que se pacificasen los yndios chichas porque los halago mucho y tuvo con elllos tales tratos que los hizo benir de paz e que este testigo entiende e tiene por cierto que el dicho don Juan Colque hizo las dichas jornadas a su propia costa y que hasta agora no a oydo dezir ni sabe que se le aya dado gratificacion alguna y esto responde

[Statement by don Juan Marca, *cacique* of the Incas in Potosí]

To the sixth question, this witness replied that he saw Captain Martín de Almendras go to pacify the Chicha Indians that had rebelled and don Juan Colque accompanied him, taking many of his Indians, and pacified that province, and it is public knowledge here that they are now paying tribute; and after they returned from the expedition, this witness heard from *caciques* and Chicha Indians that don Juan Colque had played a major part in their pacification because he praised them and treated them in a manner that convinced them to surrender; and this witness understands and believes it to be truth that don Juan Colque funded the expeditions from his own resources and until now he has not heard from anyone, nor does he know, that the don received any recompense; and this is his response.

Document 2

On his death Martín de Almendras left a widow, doña Constanza Holguin de Orellana, and five young children, including the heir to his Tarabuco *encomienda* and future governor of Santa Cruz de la Sierra, Martín de

Almendras Holguín. Following her husband's wishes, doña Constanza became their tutor, and hired administrators to run the family assets that were burdened by the hefty debts that Martín de Almendras had contracted for his expeditions.[5] With support from the Real Audiencia de Charcas, immediately after his death doña Constanza and her children drafted a report of her husband's merits and services, and a second report in 1580. For the first report, many witnesses were still alive at the time and the claims in the second report drew on the witness testimony recorded in the first. This second report reflects the difficulties that the second generation of *encomenderos* faced, when a decline in indigenous populations affected the value of their grants.

AGI, Patronato, 124, R9, [1565, 1580] Informaciones de méritos y servicios de Pedro Alvarez Holguin y Martín de Almendras
Available in PARES: https://pares.mcu.es/ParesBusquedas20/catalogo/description/123863, accessed 27 May 2024.

Excerpt 1

[Cuestionario numero dos]

18 si saben que aviendo los yndios chiriguanaes quemado el valle de tarija y muerto a algunos españoles y muchos esclavos que el capitan Juan Ortiz de çarate alli tenia y desbaratadole las haziendas y ganado que el dicho valle avia y tenyendose noticia que los dichos yndios chiriguanaes tenian cercado al dicho capitan Juan Ortiz de çarate con quinze españoles que con el estavan el dicho capitan martyn de almendras por mandado de la rreal audiencia con quarenta hombres de guerra fue al socorro del dicho cerco y por su yda y nueva que della tubieron los dichos yndios chiriguanaes y otros muchos que con ellos estavan no executasen el proposito que tenian y en la dicha jornada el dicho general Martyn de Almendras sin hazer daño alguno a los naturales traxo de paz algunas provincias de yndios especialmente la de los chichas lo qual paso avra nuebe meses poco mas o menos en todo lo qual gasto gran suma de pesos de oro sin le ser dada ayuda de costa alguna

19 si saben que luego que vino de la jornada contenyda en la pregunta antes dicha el dicho capitan Martyn de Almendras que avia siete meses poco mas o menos y abiendose alcado y rrebelado las provincias de omaguaca casabindo apatamas diaguitas y juries y calchaqui y aviendo muerto muchos españoles que en ellas estavan poblados y teniendo nueva que asimysmo avian muerto al capitan Francisco de Aguirre que estava en santiago del estero en la provincia de

5 Presta, *Encomienda, familia y negocios en Charcas colonial*, p. 82.

tucuman el dicho capitan Martyn de Almendras por horden desta rreal audiencia fue proveydo por governadorr y capitan general para el castigo y poblacion de las dichas provincias para la qual jornada hizo y adereco ciento y veynte hombres y compro mas de trezientos cavallos y muchas municiones y pertrechos de guerra a su costa sin le ser hecha merced alguna ayuda de costa antes enpenandose y dejando adeudados su muger e hijos y haziendas y gastando de su propia hazienda mas cantidad de quarenta mill pesos que ffue uno de los mas notables servicios e ynportantes que a su magestad se a ffecho en este rreyno por quedar esta provincia quieta y pacifica con solo aver ffecho las dicha jornadas el dicho general martyn de almendras que antes estavan ynquietas y desasosegadas.

20   si saven que andando el dicho capitan Martyn de Almendras con la dicha gente conquistando las dichas provincias y abiendo conquistado y pacificado a los apatamas y llegado al valle de jujuy donde padesci-eron grandes travajos de hambre vino a hazer la guerra y a traer de paz a los yndios/omaguacas y andando y peleando con los dichos yndios y llevandoles de vencida e yendo en el alcance dellos con zelo de servir a dios y a su magestad de adelanto de los suyos a llamarlos en nombre de su magestad vinyesen de paz porque los soldados no los matasen ny hiziesen mal daño fue avido a manos de los dichos yndios donde le mataron avra dos meses poco mas o menos

21   si saben que toda la gente que el dicho general Martyn de Almendras hizo a su costa e llevo consigo a la dicha jornada e tenya quando murio fue en socorro del capitan Francisco de Aguirre governador de la provincia de tucuman e conquista de las dichas provincias rrebeladas

22   si saven que de mas de los gastos que el dicho general -image 29- Martyn de Almendras hizo con la dicha gente al tienpo que murio dexo cantidad de ocho mill pesos de hazienda en armas cavallos y peltrechos de guerra plata labrada y otras cosas todo lo qual rrepar-tieron y tomaron para si los soldados de la dicha jornada sin que se enbiase cosa alguna ny traxese a su muger e hijos."

[Questionnaire 2]

18   If they know that, after the Chiriguana Indians burnt the valley of Tarija and murdered some Spaniards and many slaves that Captain Juan Ortiz de Zárate held there, destroying his farms and cattle that he ranched in that valley, and receiving news that the Chiriguana Indians had put Captain Juan Ortiz de Zárate under siege along with fifteen Spaniards who were with him, by mandate of the Real Audiencia with forty men Captain Martín de Almendras travelled to raise that

siege and because of his journey and news that he was coming, the Chiriguana Indians and many others that were with them failed to achieve their objective; in the expedition, without harming any Indians, Captain Martín de Almendras brought them to peace, mainly those in the Chichas; this all happened within nine months, more or less, and during that time he spent a large sum of gold pesos without receiving any financial help.

19   Also, if they know that around seven months more or less after Captain Martín de Almendras returned from the expedition addressed in question 18, news came that the provinces of Omaguaca, Casabindo, Apatamas, Diaguitas, Juries, and Calchaqui had all fallen into rebellion and many Spaniards who were living there had been murdered; news of the murder of Captain Francisco de Aguirre in Santiago del Estero in the province of Tucuman had arrived; and Captain Martin de Almendras was commissioned by the Real Audiencia, and given the titles Governor and Chief Captain, to punish the populations in these provinces, which he did, equipping 120 men and buying more than 300 horses along with ammunition and military equipment, all at his own expense without any recompense, borrowing and leaving his wife and children in debt, spending from his wealth the sum of more than 40,000 pesos, which was one of the most notable and important services ever performed for His Majesty in this Kingdom because such expeditions as general Martín de Almendras led have left the province peaceful, where before the [Indians] were rioting and rebellious.

20   If they know that, during his expedition, Captain Martín de Almendras and his followers conquered these provinces and, having defeated the Apatamas, reached the Jujuy valley, where the population were starving; waged war and brought peace to the Omaguaca/ Indians, fighting and almost defeating them; tried to bring them to serve God and His Majesty, and in doing so moved ahead of his men, trying to call on the Indians to surrender, so his soldiers would not kill or injure them, but was taken by the Indians and murdered, two months ago.

21   If they know that all the people that general Martín de Almendras took at his own expense on the said expedition, who were with him when he passed away, continued to advance to help Captain Francisco de Aguirre, governor of the province of Tucuman, and to conquer these rebellious provinces.

22   If they know that, as well as the expenses that general Martín de Almendras incurred on feeding and equipping his people, when he

passed away he left weapons, horses, and war materials, silver and other items, worth 8,000 pesos, that were seized by the soldiers of the expedition and distributed, without sending anything back to his wife and children.

Don Francisco de Toledo's expedition in 1574.

Document 1

Many of the official documents of this expedition, that can be found in the Patronato 235 files at the AGI in Spain, were published by Ricardo Mujía early in the twentieth century in connection with a border dispute between Bolivia and Paraguay.[6] Others were probably lost in a fire at the Biblioteca Nacional del Perú in 1943, as not all of Viceroy Toledo's papers were carried to Spain and some of those left behind were held by Juan de Yturrieta, Toledo's agent in Lima. This first document is unique: it is the authorisation given to don Juan Colque Guarache to recruit indigenous people from *encomiendas* in the frontier region to accompany him and Viceroy Toledo on their expedition. As captain and leader of the Indians that accompanied Toledo, this was one of the perquisites afforded to don Juan.

AGI, Charcas 57, [1622] Información de méritos y servicios de don Diego Copatete Guarache

[fol. 1r]

Don Francisco de Toledo Capitan general en estos rreynos y provincias del piru digo por quanto e mandado que de los yndios mas sercanos a esta ciudad se saquen cien yndios para el servicio de esta guerra de los chiriguanaes y se saque sobre repartimiento de los que cada pueblo a de dar como pareze por una memoria su tenor es la qual es esta que se sigue

Los yamparaes de su magestad

Veynte y quatro yndios   24 Yos

Tarabuco de la encomienda de Martin de Almendras

Veynte y quatro yndios   24 Yndios

Condes de la corona real y ualparocas

6 Mujía, *Bolivia–Paraguay.*

Veynte y un yndios   21 Yndios

Churumatas y los moyos lacaxa y siuire <sueres>

De diferentes encomiendas de muchos encomenderos

Veynte yndios   20 Yndios

Pacha de la encomienda de Hernando Sedano

onze yndios   11 Yndios

por ende de la pressente por la que mando a por los caciques y principales
de los dichos pueblos y rrepartimientos que luego [f 1v] sin otra delacion
traiga cada unos los yndios que se les esten rrepartidos por las dichas
memorias so pena de cada quinientos pesos para los gastos de las dichas
guerras y la privacion de sus cacicazgos y mando y doy comission a don
juan colque que assi lo haga cumplir y executar so la dicha pena. Hecha
en la plata a quinze dias del mes de mayo de mill y quinientos y setenta y
quatro años don Francisco de Toledo por mandato de su magestad alvaro
rruiz de navamuel.

I, Don Francisco de Toledo, Captain of the Kingdoms and Provinces of Peru,
say that, as I have commanded that 100 men be drawn from the Indians
nearest to this city [La Plata] to serve in this War against the Chiriguanaes,
and be drafted from each *repartimiento*, each Indian town will provide as
instructed in this report as follows:

The Yamparaes under His Majesty

Twenty-four Indians   24 Ind[ian]s

Martín de Almendras' encomienda in Tarabuco

Twenty-four Indians   24 Indians

Condes Indians under His Majesty, and Gualparocas

Twenty-one Indians   21 Indians

Churumatas, Moyo-Moyos, Lacaxa, and Sueres

Distributed among various *encomiendas* assigned to various *encomenderos*

Twenty Indians   20 Indians

Hernando Sedano's encomienda in Pacha

Eleven Indians   11 Indians

Accordingly, via this report I command that the *caciques* and chiefs of these towns and *repartimientos* [fol. 1v] without delay bring these Indians from their *encomiendas* on pain of subjection to a fine of 500 pesos towards the expenses of these wars and the loss of their *cacique* positions; I instruct don Juan Colque to enforce this and execute the punishment if needed. Drafted in La Plata, 15 May 1574. Don Francisco de Toledo. By mandate of His Majesty. Alvaro Ruiz de Navamuel.

Document 2

The next document is a strange glimpse into the preparations for the expedition. Don Juan Colque Guarache is given permission, at his option, to carry an arquebus on the expedition, despite restrictions on arming indigenous people. This would highlight his status on the battlefield and is clearly an indication of his privileges as a member of the Indian nobility.

AGI, Charcas 57, [1622] Información de méritos y servicios de don Diego Copatete Guarache

[fol. 1r]

Se de a don Juan Colque un arcarbuz para la guerra

Joan Porcel capitan de las municiones e Cristoval de Ambers dad a don juan colque que ba a servir a su magestad en esta jornada un arcabus de los de municion de aquellos que en la ciudad de la plata por mi mandado el capitan las aveo e hizo encureñar y tomad su carta de rrecivo que con ella y esta mi libranca sera bien dado fecho en este campo de su magestad en la cordillera a diez y ocho de jullio de mill y quinientos y setenta y quatro años don Francisco de Toledo

Don Juan Colque should be given an arquebus for the war.

Juan Porcel, in charge of ammunition, and Cristobal de Amberes, should give don Juan Colque, who will serve His Majesty in the expedition, an arquebus and the ammunition required drawn from the weapons that, on my instruction, the captain secured and prepared in La Plata, and receive this letter as a receipt and a token of my written approval that this will be permitted, written in the camp of His Majesty in the Cordillera, on 18 July 1574. Don Francisco de Toledo.

Document 3

Although Appendix 2 contains a list of those who accompanied each of the expeditions analysed in this book, that list is the product of years of work, and not a transcription of any complete list of expedition members found in the archives. The AGI in Seville holds a list prepared by Captain Diego Moreno of the farm owners or *chacareros* that were supposed to be recruited to accompany him to the Chiriguanaes. The *chacareros* had recently been the beneficiaries of a series of ordinances issued by Viceroy Toledo concerning the Indians that they kept on their farms (*yanaconas*). The ordinances were intended to make the *chacareros* aware of their obligations and privileges as grantees of that workforce. This document gives us a glimpse of the world of the *chacareros* on the frontier at the time of Toledo's expedition. This document also shows the challenges that captains faced in recruiting men to fight in remote lands. As it shows, it was not uncommon to send substitutes. The pages are not numbered.

AGI, Charcas, 58, [1656] Información de servicios de Diego Moreno Contreras, hijo legitimo del Capitan Diego Moreno.

Conduta de capitan dado en La Plata a 12 de mayo de 1574

Don Francisco de Toledo capitan general [fol. sig reverso] en estos en estos rreynos y provincias del Piru & por quanto entre las otras personas y gente que se a combocado y llamado para hazer la guerra a los yndios chiriguanaes y para allanar estas fronteras an sido los senores de chacaras de esta provincia por tocarles tan particularmente la dicha guerra para el siguro de sus personas y haziendas que en tanto peligro an estado y porque para que esto se cumpla se a hecho memoria particular de las dichas personas que es la siguiente

Alonso de Dueñas – Juan de Pendones – Joan de Ortega – Francisco Comarin – Sebastian Herrador – Joan de Bega portero – Andres Gonzalez – Joan Clavijo – Francisco Garcia de Leaños – Francisco Goncalez Picon y sus companeros – Alonso Gomez – el hijo de Francisco Sanchez Hinojosa con ssu padre – Francisco Vazquez – Nicolas Nuñez – Ascensio Martin – Diego de Ocampo – el licenciado Gorbalan – Martin Ximenez – el desterrado Pedro Bexarano – Melchor Pardo – Joan de Xaen – Pedro de la Torre – Diego de Molina – el gallego chiquito – Joan Griego

por ende acorde de car y di la presente por la qual mando a todas las dichas personas que luego sin otra delacion alguna se apercivan y bengan armados y aderecados para yr a la dicha guerra y parescan ante mi para fin del mes [folio siguiente verso] de mayo sin poner en ello escussa ni delacion alguna y porque podria ser que algunos dellos estuviesen ympedidos para no poder yr a la dicha guerra mando que sean compelidos y apremiados a que vengan con sus armas y cavallos para el dicho tiempo

los que parecieron

Alonso de Dueñas un hombre aderecado de armas y cavallos

Francisco Gonzales Picon y sus companeros que den luego el hombre que a de yr por ellos aderecado de armas y caballo

Joan de Pendones un hombre aderecado de armas y cavallo o las armas de arcabuces y cotas que pareciere a senoria el senor presidente

Alonso Gomez un hombre con sus armas y cavallo

Francisco Vazquez vaya con sus armas y cavallo

el hijo de Francisco Vazquez Hinojosa y su padre sean traidos ante su senoria para que ordene lo que an de dar para la dicha guerra

Joan de Ortega que de una cota y un arcabuz

Nicolas Nuñez que de una cota y un arcabuz

Francisco Martin que preste el arcabuz y vallesta

el licenciado Gorbalan una cota y un arcabuz

Sebastian Herrador quatrocientos pesos o que vaya en persona a la guerra armado y aderecado

Martin Ximenez el desterrado que de un arcabuz y un cavallo Pedro Vejarano [sig fol reverso] Joan de Vega portero quede una cota o un arcabuz

Martin Pardo un caballo herrado

Juan de Xaen una cota o un arcabuz

Pedro de la Torre una cota y un arcabuz

Diego de Molina un cavallo herrado

Joan Clavijo que de una cota y un arcabuz

el gallego chuquito una cota y un arcabuz

Joan Griego un arcabuz

Francisco Garcia de Llanos una cota

la hija de Joan de Rribamartin un cavallo herrado

todo lo qual mando que los sussodichos y cada uno dellos guarden y cumplan sin poner en ello escusa ni dilacion alguna para el dicho dia quatro de mayo so pena de caer en mal caso y de perdimento de sus haziendas a costa de los quales cumplira todo lo susodicho por combenir assi al servicio de su magestad y que no combiene que aya otra dilacion y mando a diego cavallero de la fuente alguacil mayor de esta ciudad y a sus lugares tenientes que con las personas de los susodichos que estan en esta ciudad cumplan y executen esta mi provision en todo y por todo e como en ella se contiene y con las personas que estan ausentes la baya a executar Pasqual Xuarez compeliendo y apremiando a los que an de benir en persona a que sin otra dilacion alguna vengan aderecados para el dicho dia ante su senoria [fol sig verso] del senor presidente como esta dicho y a los que an de dar los dichos hombres en su lugar y armas y cavallos como esta rreferido antes de este y los dineros que les estan rrepartidos a que luego, en La Plata a 28 de abril de 1574.

Certificate of Conduct given in La Plata 12 May 1574

Don Francisco de Toledo, Captain General [following fol. verso] in this Kingdom and Provinces of Peru, etc., among the people who have been called to wage war against the Chiriguanaes and to pacify these frontiers, are several who are farm owners in this province because that war pertains to their affairs and the safety of themselves and farms that have been in peril; to make this happen, a list of these people has been drafted:

Alonso de Dueñas – Juan de Pendones – Joan de Ortega – Francisco Comarin – Sebastian Herrador – Joan de Bega – Andres Gonzalez – Joan Clavijo – Francisco Garcia de Leaños – Francisco Goncalez Picon and companions – Alonso Gomez – the son of Francisco Sanchez Hinojosa with his father – Francisco Vazquez – Nicolas Nuñez – Ascensio Martin – Diego de Ocampo – *licenciado* Gorbalan – Martin Ximenez – the exiled Pedro Bexarano – Melchor Pardo – Joan de Xaen – Pedro de la Torre – Diego de Molina – the Little Galician – Joan Griego

and accordingly I agreed to draft and have drafted the present document whereby I command that all these people, without delay, attend my call and present themselves with their weapons, ready to go to war, and do so before the end of the month [next fol. verso] of May without excuse or delay; because some might put forward some impediment to their going, I command that they be coerced to turn up with their weapons and horses at the said time.

Those who turned up:

[instead of] Alonso de Dueñas: a man with weapons and horses

[instead of] Francisco Gonzales Picón and his companions: they will provide a man who will travel in their stead, with weapons and horse [instead of] Juan de Pendones: a man with weapons and horse, or arquebuses and armour, whichever the president of the Audiencia finds more suitable

[instead of] Alonso Gómez: a man with weapons and a horse

Francisco Vázquez will travel with his weapons and horse

Francisco Vázquez Hinojosa and his son will be brought before his lordship to be told what they should provide for the war effort

Joan de Ortega will be asked to provide armour and an arquebus

Nicolás de Nuñez will be asked to provide armour and an arquebus

Francisco Martín will be asked to provide an arquebus and a crossbow

Licenciado Gorbalán will be asked to provide a suit of armour and an arquebus

Sebastián Herrador, to provide 400 pesos or travel in person with weapons and supplies

Martín Ximenez, who has been forcibly exiled, will have to provide an arquebus and a horse

Pedro Vejarano [next fol. verso] and Juan de Vega will be asked to provide a suit of armour or an arquebus

Martín Pardo, [to provide] a horse with its shoes

Juan de Jaén, [to provide] a suit of armour or an arquebus

Pedro de la Torre, [to provide] a suit of armour and an arquebus

Diego de Molina, a horse with its shoes

Joan Clavijo, a suit of armour and an arquebus

the little Galician, a suit of armour and an arquebus

Joan Griego, an arquebus

Francisco García de Llanos, a suit of armour

The daughter of Joan de Ribarmartín, a horse with its shoes

All that I command must be delivered with no excuse or delay by 4 May or else [defaulters will] face a punishment of the loss of their farms. This must be accomplished to serve His Majesty and without delay, and I command Diego Caballero de la Fuente, Main Sheriff of this city [La Plata], and his lieutenants to obey this and carry out my provision in its entirety, naming Pascual Juarez responsible for those who are absent, to coerce them to turn up without delay and on the following date before his lordship [next fol. verso] the president [of the Audiencia] as commanded, and those who are to provide substitutes as listed, and the cash that will be distributed, in La Plata on 28 April 1574.

Juan Lozano Machuca's expedition in 1584–1585

Document 1

Of the *capitulaciones* for the expeditions discussed in this book, only a part of one signed by Juan Lozano Machuca has been found. It is included in the report of merits and services submitted by Captain Pedro de Cuellar Torremocha, who allegedly founded the town that Lozano Machuca was supposed to establish, and this is the reason why he added the material to his own *probanza*. The document is only the 'auto' (*provision* of the Real Audiencia) and gives an idea of the ceremonial side of these documents and the theatricality of power.

AGI, Patronato, 126, R17, [1582], Información de Pedro de Cuéllar Torremocha

Available in PARES: https://pares.mcu.es/ParesBusquedas20/catalogo/descrip-tion/123895, accessed 27 May 2024.

[fols 73r–75v]

Auto

en la ciudad de La Plata a quinze dias del mes de junio de mill y quinientos e ochenta e quatro años los senores presidente e oydores de la audiencia y chancilleria rreal de su magestad a quien por fallecimiento del virrey don Martin Enrriquez yncunbe de govierno de su distrito dixeron que aviendose apregonado por orden y mandado de los dichos (f155) señores guerra a fuego e sangre contra los yndios chiriguanaes para rrepemir y castigar los danos muertes e rrobos que tan de hordinario an fecho e hacen en los vasallos de su magestad que estan en sus fronteras y tienen sus haziendas en ellas el fator Juan Loçano machuca se ofrecio a hacerla dicha guerra y jornada a su costa y meter en la cordillera hasta ducientos o ducientos y cinquenta hombres para el dicho efeto como se contiene en el ofrecimiento que hizo y capitulacionnes que con el fueron tomadas e asentadas por los dichos señores y se le dio titulo de capitan general de la dicha jornada y de governador y capitan general de lo que poblare el qual a nonbrado capitanes y los demas oficiales de guerra y entre los que asi a nombrado an sido al capitan Arias de Herrera por su teniente general e al capitan Pedro de Cuellar por maese de canpo personas de la prudencia e partes que ser rrequiere e abien ose mirado e adbertido por los dichos señores con maduro acuerdo y deliberacion lo que conbiene proveer para que la dicha jornadase haga con toda quietud les a parecido que lo que el dicho general oviere de hacer y deter inar en qualquier caso y hevento cevil o criminalmente lo aya de hacer e haga con consejo consulta e parecer de los dichos capitan Arias de Herrera y Pedro de Cuellar y no el solo ni con el uno de llos sino todos tres juntos y lo que se acordare (f156) por la

mayor parte de los tres aquello se cumpla y execute e porque los demas
capitanes e oficiales de guerra no se sientan de que no se comunica con
ellos lo tocante a la dicha guerra y jornada mandaron que quando al dicho
general le pareciere convenir llamar a consulta lo haga y todos puedan
tener botos consultibos y los disicisbos para qualquier efeto y negocio cevil
o criminal ayan de ser y sean los de los dichos capitanes Arias de Herrera
y Pedro de Cuellar y para mejor efeto man aron que este proveymyento
no se de quenta ni lo ayan de saver mas que el dicho general y los dichos
capitanes Arias de Herrera y Pedro de Cuellar los quales y cada uno de
los guarden el secreto de el y executen lo que conbiene y contiene este
auto so pena de caer en mal caso contra el servicio de su magestad y que
como tal se procederá contra el que lo contrario hiziere o de lo cubriere
el secreto y mandaron que cada uno dellos haga en manos se su señoria
de presidente pleito menaje de que asi lo cumplira el licenciado cepeda el
licenciado Francisco de Vera proveyeron este auto los señores presidente e
oydores el día mes e año en el contenido juan de losa e aviendo se notifi-
cado a los dichos nuestro general y capitanes en su cumplimyento cada uno
dellos hizo juramento y pleito menaje de lo guardar cumplir con todo (f157)
secreto e rretitud como dellos consta e parece que son del tenor siguiente=

en la ciudad de La Plata el dicho dia quinze de junio de mil quinientos e
ochenta e quatro años por mandado de los dichos señores vino a la sala del
acuerdo el dicho general Juan Loçano Machuca y por los dichos señores le
fue dado a entender el efeto deste auto y lo que en el se contiene el qual
lo aceto e hincado de rrodillas ante su señoría el eselentisimo presidente
quitado el bonete puestas anbas manos se las tomo se señoría entre las
suyas y segun fuero de castilla juro e prometió una e dos e tres vezes e
hizo pleito mejane como cavallero hijodalgo de guardar lo contenido en el
dicho auto e cada una cosa e parte del y de guardar asimesmo el secreto
so pena de caer e yncurrir en mal caso con tra el servicio de su magestad
el qual pleito menaje hizo estando también presente el senor licenciado don
francisco de bera del consejo de su magestad oydor desta rreal audiencia y
el señor licenciado Rruano Telles fiscal della e dello doy fee el licenciado
Cepeda el licenciado Francisco de Bera ante mi juan de losa

en la dicha ciudad de La Plata a diez y seis dias de mes de junio de
mill y quinientos e ochenta y quatro años estando su señoría del señor
presidente en su aposento solo entro en el dicho capitan Arias de Herrera
y en presencia de mi el presente secretario su senoria le tomo asímismo
pleitomenaje abiendo primero dadole a entender el efeto del dicho auto
(f158) el qual prometio guardarlo e cumplirlo asi e hincado de rrodillas
ante su señoria y sin bonete puestas anbas sus manos entre las de su
señoría juro en forma e hizo pleitomenaje como cavallero hijodalgo según
fuero de castilla una e dos y tres vezes de que asi lo guardava e cumplira
sin exceder dello en manera alguna e guardara secreto so pena de caer

e yncurrir en mal caso contra el servicio de su magestad el licenciado
Cepeda ante mi juan de losa-

en la ciudad de la plata a seis dias del mes de jullio de mill e quinientos
y ochenta y quatro años estando su señoria de señor presidente en su
aposento solo entro en el el dicho capitan Pedro de Cuellar y en presencia
de mi el presente secretario su señoria le tomo así mesmo pleito menaje
abiendo primero dadole a entender el efeto de el dicho auto el qual
prometio guardarlo e cumplirlo asi e hincado de rrodillas ante su señoria
e sin bonete y puestas anbas sus manos en tre las de su señoria juro en
forma e hizo pleito menaje como cavallero hijodalgo segun fuero de castilla
una y dos y tres vezes que asi lo guardara e cumplira sin exceder delos en
manera alguna y guardara el secreto so pena de caer en mal caso contra el
servicio de su magestad el licenciado cepeda ante mi Juan de Losa

In the city of La Plata on 15 June 1584, the President and Judges of the Royal
Audiencia and Chancilleria of His Majesty who, owing to the passing of
viceroy don Martín Enriquez are in charge of the government of his district,
announced through a town-crier the order and mandate for [fol. 155] a war of
blood and fire against the Chiriguanaes to punish them for the damage to and
thefts from His Majesty's vassals who reside along His Kingdom's frontiers
and have farms in those regions, that they have regularly been committing
and still commit; the factor Juan Lozano Machuca has put forward an offer
to wage that war and carry out the expedition at his own expense, taking up
to 250 men to the *cordillera* based on his offer and *capitulaciones*; and he has
been given the title of captain of the expedition and governor and captain of
any town that he should found, having appointed captains and other officers
of war, including Captain Arias de Herrera as his lieutenant and Captain
Pedro de Cuellar as Maese de Campo, both people with the prudence and
quality required; and after revising what it is practical to do, it was decided
that the said general [Lozano Machuca] should only make decisions after
securing advice from captains Arias de Herrera and Pedro de Cuellar and not
by himself, or after consulting each of them separately; all three will decide
and agree [fol. 156] based on a majority, and to keep all other officials in the
loop it was decided that whenever a broader consultation is needed it will be
convened and captains Arias de Herrera and Pedro de Cuellar will have a
decisive vote; and all three should know what they plan to vote but should not
let others know, so they do not disservice His Majesty; and all three were asked
to take an oath before the President and so it will be done. *Licenciados* Cepeda
and Francisco de Vera drafted this decree. [Present were] The President and
Judges on the day, month, and year indicated. Juan de Losa.

After being notified of its accomplishment, each of [the captains] took the
oath to observe all these conditions [fol. 157] as they are supposed to, and
the procedures were as follows:

In the city of La Plata on the said day 15 June 1584 by mandate from their lordships, the said general Juan Lozano Machuca attended the agreement chamber and through their lordships he received an explanation of this decree, which he accepted and, on his knees before the President, having removed his hat, and with both hands clasped together, the President held them between his own hands and according to the Customs of Castile the general swore and promised once, twice, and three times, and took the oath as an *hidalgo* and a gentleman to uphold what was explained to him and keep these instructions secret, or do a disservice to His Majesty; in presence of *Licenciado* don Francisco de Vera, judge of this Audiencia and *Licenciado* Ruano Telles, attorney of the Audiencia. In witness of this, *Licenciado* Cepeda, *Licenciado* Francisco de Vera in my presence, Juan de Losa.

In the said city of La Plata on 17 June 1584 in the presence of the President, Captain Arias de Herrera walked in and in my presence and in the presence of our secretary took an oath after having the decree explained to him, [fol. 158] which he promised to keep and follow, and on his knees before his lordship and without his hat, with both hands together between his lordship's hands he pledged, as the *hijodalgo* and gentleman that he is, in line with the Customs of Castile, once, twice, and three times, that he will keep it and abide by it, keeping it secret or disservice His Majesty otherwise. *Licenciado* Cepeda in my presence, Juan de Losa.

In the city of La Plata on 6 July 1584 in the presence of the President, Captain Pedro de Cuellar walked in and in the presence of his secretary took the oath and pledge, after having the decree explained to him, which he promised to abide by, and on his knees before the President and without his hat and with both hands between the President's hands, he pledged and took the oath as a gentleman and *hijodalgo* according to the Customs of Castile, once, twice, and three times, saying that he will keep it and keep it secret or disservice His Majesty. *Licenciado* Cepeda in my presence, Juan de Losa.

Document 2

The following document is a notarial record drafted after the expedition of Juan Lozano Machuca. It records the sale of eight indigenous men and women by Juan de Valero or Balero, a Spanish captain who had been in Chile before settling in Charcas, to the *encomendero* of Quillacas, Antonio Pantoja de Chávez. They may have been seized during the expedition of Juan Lozano Machuca or perhaps before it. The clerk that drafted the document made some involuntary mistakes which may indicate that he followed the formula normally used for documents for the sale of black slaves. Despite prohibitions and decrees clearly banning the sale of indigenous people, this record shows that such transactions continued. However, it is worth noting that this is not reflected in the volume of paperwork in the archives, which might mean that many of these transactions were carried out informally or were recorded by notaries in settlements and towns across the border. Only a handful of these notaries' records have survived.

Archivo y Biblioteca Nacionales de Bolivia (ABNB), Venta de ocho piezas de indios, cinco varones y tres mujeres, sacados de la jornada de los chiriguanaes, que hace el capitán Juan Valero, residente en la ciudad de La Plata, a favor de Antonio Pantoja de Chávez, los cuales, por auto de la audiencia de La Plata, tiene por esclavos y yanaconas perpetuos y se los vende al precio de novecientos cincuenta pesos de plata ensayada y marcada. Escribanía pública de Blas López de Solórzano, 25 de noviembre de 1585, La Plata. EP 48.

[fols 400r–401r]

[fol. 400r] Sepan quantos esta carta de benta bieren como yo el capitán Juan Balero residente en esta cibdad de La Plata otorgo y conozco por esta presente carta que bendydos en benta rreal y verdadera a vos Antonio Pantoja conviene a saber ocho piezas de yndios los cinco yndios barones chicos y grandes y los tres hembras que los nombres de los tres son el uno /mata/ y el otro /satiri/ y el otro /ay/ y los otros que son xrianos se llaman el uno clemente y el otro francisco/ y las tres yndias hembras se llaman la una /myto/ y la otra /sumpe/ y la otra que es xriana se llama /juana/ los quales dichos yndios yo hube y saque de la jornada de los chiriguanaes los quales por auto de esta rreal audiencia estan dados por esclavos y por yanaconas perpetuos que los hube de los en buena guerra y dellos conprados en benta los quales dichos [la palabra esclavos esta tachada en el original] yndios son de los que estan dados por yanaconas perpetuos como consta paresce por un testimonyo que los doy y entrego con los dichos [la palabra negros esta tachada en el original] yndios que son los de los mesmos contenydos en el dicho testimonyo los quales digo que le bendo y traspaso toda la dacion y derecho que dellos tengo por precio y quenta de nobecientos y cinquenta [la palabra seiscientos esta tachada en el original] pesos de plata ensayada y rrubricada que por ello me abeys dado y pagado e yo de vos he rrecebido de que me doy por bien contento y entregado a my boluntad por quanto los rrecebi de vos y pase a my parte y poder rrealmente y con efecto y en rrazon [fol. 400v] de la entrega que de pressente no paresce rreñida ni mera sujeción propia y paga como en ella se contiene y no me hobligo a la seguridad de los dichos yndios ny a otra cosa alguna ny de que yo ny otro en my nombre no pediremos los dichos yndios en tiempo alguno aunque su magestad los de por esclavos perpetuos y aunque los den por libres porque /ora los den por esclavos/ora no yo no tengo de quedar obligado a cosa alguna mas de a solamente no los tomar o pedir yo ny otro por my e yo el dicho Antonyo Pantoja digo que me doy por entregado de los dichos ocho yndios susodichos y los rrescato con las dichas condiciones y a my rriesgo segun y de la manera que esta dicho y declarado y me obligo de no me llamar a engaño aunque los dichos

yndios se an dados por libres y me los saquen luego y ambos todos para
lo cumplir obligamos nuestras personas y bienes muebles y rraizes abidos
e por aber e damos poder cumplido a todas y qualequyer justicias de su
magestad a la jurisdicion de las quales y de cada una dellas nos sometemos
con las dichas nuestras personas y bienes y rrenunciamos nuestro propio
fuero y prebilejios jurisdicion y domicilio y la ley sit conbenerit jurisdicción e omnyum judicum para [fol. 401r] que por todo rrigor de derecho
nos conpelan y apremyen a lo ansi cumplir y guardar y aber por firme por
bien executabasen otra qualquyer manera que aya cumplido efeto como
si lo hubiesemos llevado por avyda ynstancia de juez competente dada y
procesada en cosa juzgada y por nos consertada y rrenunciamos todas
y qualesquyer leyes fueros derechos y por demás mandamientos fechos
en nuestro fabor e todas en general y cada una en especial y la ley del
derecho en que diz que general rrenunciacion de leyes ffecha non bala y
lo otorgamos ansi ante el presente escribano y testigos de sus escriptos
que fuesse en la dicha ciudad de la plata a veynte y cinco dias del mes de
nobienbre de myll y quinientos y ochenta y cinco años siendo pressentes
por testigos a lo que dicho es Juan Ladron de Leyba y Martyn Alonso
de los Rrios y el padre Antonio Nabarro Ordoñez clerigo presbitero y los
dichos otorgantes el presente testimonio doy fee que conozco lo firmaron
de sus nombres en este rregistro va entre rrenglones de los// bala// y testado/
esclavos/negros noba/ va entre rrenglones y en la margen la novecientos y
cinquenta y bala/seyscientos y nobenta.

Antonio Pantoja de Chaves   Johan Valero

Ante my Blas Lopez de Solorzano

[fol. 400r] Let it be known to whoever shall see this letter that I, Captain
Juan Balero, resident in the city of La Plata, acknowledge and accept for this
letter sold in royal sale to you Antonio Pantoja, eight pieces of [sic] Indians,
five male Indians small and big, and three female Indians, named as follows:
of the three, one is /mata/ and the second /satiri/ and the third /ay/ and the
others are Christian and are called, one Clemente, and the other Francisco/
and the three females are called, one /myto/, and the second /sumpe/ and the
other who is a Christian is called /Juana/ all of which I had and took from the
expedition to the Chiriguanaes who by royal decree of this Real Audiencia
are given as slaves and perpetual *yanaconas* and as such I had them and got
them in Just War and purchased through a sale of them as enslaved [this word
is crossed out in the original] Indians given as perpetual *yanaconas*; as it is
stated in a deposition that I am handing all the said negroes [the word negroes
is crossed out in the original] Indians that are the same as those contained
in the same deposition and are those who I am selling and transferring with
all my rights for the price of nine hundred and fifty [the words six hundred
are crossed out in the original] assayed silver pesos that you have paid me

and have received from you and I am pleased about this and have agreed to relinquish all my rights [fol. 400v] when I handed them over and I am not obliged to keep them safe, neither of any other thing, nor when His Majesty decides to give them the status of perpetual slaves, or even if they are declared free, because whatever the circumstances I am no longer obliged to anything as I am no longer allowed to ask for them back and I agree that all eight Indians have been handed over and that I rescued them in the set conditions and at my risk and I have no other thing to declare and should not be obliged to, even when these Indians are set free and taken from me, and to confirm this we both place our goods and property as guarantee before any Justice of His Majesty in whatever jurisdiction and in all of them, and in each of them, we are liable with our goods and ourselves, and surrender our own privileges, jurisdiction, and *sit conbenerit jurisdicción e omnyum judicum* law [fol. 401r] enforce this; in presence of the notary in La Plata on 25 November 1585. Witnesses Juan Ladron de Leyba and Martin Alonso de los Rios, and Father Antonio Navarro Ordoñez, priest. They signed their names in this register.

Antonio Pantoja de Chavez and Juan Valero, in my presence, Blas López de Solorzano

Chronology of Charcas, 1438–1585

Government	Events
Inca Pachacuti (1438–1471)	Tahuantinsuyu expansion into Charcas
Inca Topac Inca Yupanqui (1471–1493)	Chiriguanaes arrive on the southeastern border of Charcas. Unrest following the Inca succession. Siege of Oroncota.
Huayna Capac (1493–1525)	Unrest along the southeastern border. More fortifications. Chichas play a more significant role in border control.
Atahualpa and Inca Huascar (1532–1537)	War of Inca Succession (1525–1532). Aleixo García reportedly arrived on the border in 1526. Collapse of Inca fortifications and chaos along the frontier. Collapse of Tahuantinsuyu.
Francisco Pizarro (1532–1541), and Paulo Inca Vaca de Castro (1541–1544) Blasco Nuñez Vela, first viceroy of Peru (1544–1546) Gonzalo Pizarro (1546–1548)	First round of *encomiendas* in Jauja in 1534 and second round in Cusco on 1 August 1535. Expedition of Diego de Almagro into Chile (15 September 1535–1537). Civil wars (1537–1548). Gonzalo and Hernando Pizarro enter Charcas with Paulo Inca and, after a fierce battle in Cochabamba, negotiate the extension of Crown jurisdiction over the district with the *naciones de Charcas* (August–November 1538). 'Discovery of Porco' (1538). New round of *encomiendas* in Charcas, Francisco de Almendras receives Tarabuco and Presto Indians (1539). Foundation of Villa Plata (1539–1540). New Laws of 1542. Expedition of Diego de Rojas/Francisco de Mendoza (1543). Francisco de Almendras executed by Diego Centeno (1545). 'Discovery of Potosí' (1548).

Government	Events
Pedro de La Gasca (1548–1550)	New *encomiendas* in Guaynarima (1548). Spanish colonists settle in valleys in the east of Charcas. Chiriguanaes largely in control of the border.
Antonio de Mendoza, second viceroy of Peru (1551–1552) Andrés Hurtado de Mendoza, Marquis of Cañete, third viceroy of Peru (1556–1560)	Rebellion of Hernández Girón (1553). Martín de Almendras takes on Tarabuco and Presto *encomienda* (1554). Establishment of Londres (1558), Córdoba del Calchaquí (1559), and Cañete (1560) by Juan Pérez de Zurita in Tucumán. Establishment of Santo Domingo de la Nueva Rioja by Captain Andrés Manso and of La Barranca or Condorillo by Captain Ñuflo de Chaves (1559).
Diego López de Zúñiga y Velasco, Count of Nieva, fourth viceroy of Peru (1560–1564)	Establishment of the Real Audiencia de Charcas (1561). Establishment of Nieva in Tucumán (1562). Rebellion of Juan Calchaquí in Tucumán. Appointment of Francisco de Aguirre as governor of Tucumán (1563). Destruction of Santo Domingo de la Nueva Rioja and Condorillo by the Chiriguanaes (1564).
Real Audiencia de Charcas in charge of the district (1564)	Expedition to the Chiriguanaes by Pedro de Castro (1564).
Lope García de Castro, Governor of Peru (1564–1567)	Martín de Almendras expeditions to the Chichas and Tucumán (1564–1565). Charcas is divided into eleven *corregimientos* (1565).

Government	Events
Francisco de Toledo, fifth viceroy of Peru (1569–1581)	Visita General (23 October 1570–1575). Punitive expedition to the Chiriguanaes by Hernando Díaz (1570). Toledo receives the attorney of Santa Cruz de la Sierra and other notables in Cusco (1571). Toledo arrives in Potosí (December 1572). Toledo arranges the Potosi *mita* mining work shift and the resettlement of Indians (1573). Journeys of García Mosquera to the border (1573). Rebellion of don Diego de Mendoza in Santa Cruz de la Sierra (1573–1575). *Capitulación* for the foundation of Tarija with Luis de Fuentes y Vargas (January 1574). Toledo decides to mount a large-scale expedition and wage war against the Chiriguanaes (April 1574). Expedition to the Chiriguanaes (June–August 1574). Establishment of Tarija and Tomina (1574).
Martín Enríquez de Almanza y Ulloa, sixth viceroy of Peru (1581–1583)	Waves of raids and attacks by the Chiriguanaes.
Real Audiencia de Charcas in charge of the district (1583–1585)	The Real Audiencia declares war on the Chiriguanaes (December 1583). Campaign on three fronts, one headed by Juan Lozano Machuca (1584–1585). Death of Machuca (February 1585).

List of Participants in the Expeditions

List of members of the 1564–1565 expeditions

Name	Position in the expedition	Documentary evidence	Social position
Gerónimo González de Alanís	Maese de Campo	AGI, Patronato, 132, N2, R8, [1590] Información Juan Mejia Miraval, fols 15v and 84r.	Soldier. Mineral mill owner.
Don Martín Alata		AGNA, Sala XIII, 18.6.4, fol. 15r.	Andean chief.
Antonio Alderete Riomayor		AGI, Charcas, 78, N34, [1585] Probanza Antonio Alderete Riomayor, fol. 2r.	Soldier.
Gaspar de Almendras		AGI, Patronato, 124, R9, [1580] Información Pedro Alvarez Holguín y Martín de Almendras, image 571.	Soldier; Martín de Almendras' nephew.
Martín de Almendras	Leader		*Encomendero.*
Don Fernando Ayavire Cuysara		Platt et al., eds. *Qaraqara–Charka*, p. 871.	*Cacique Principal* of Charcas.

Name	Position in the expedition	Documentary evidence	Social position
Friar Gonzalo Ballesteros		Fray Pedro Nolasco Pérez, *Religiosos de la merced que pasaron a la América española*, p. 294.	Mercedarian priest.
Don Juan Calpa		AGI, Charcas, 53, [1574–1576] Probanza de don Juan Colque Guarache, fol. 64v.	*Cacique Principal* of Hatun Colla.
Alonso de Carrión		AGI, Patronato, 132, N2, R8, [1590] Informacion Juan Mejia Miraval, image 54v.	Soldier.
Castroverde		Julien, *Desde el oriente*, p. 231.	Soldier.
Gaspar Centeno		AGI, Charcas, 53, [1574–1576] Probanza de don Juan Colque Guarache, fol. 38r.	Soldier.
Juan de Cianca		Acuerdos de Charcas VI.	*Encomendero.*
Don Juan Colque Guarache		AGI, Charcas, 53, [1574–1576] Probanza de don Juan Colque Guarache.	*Cacique Principal* of Quillacas, Asanaques, Sivaroyos, and Haracapis.
Juan Bautista Gallinato		AGI, Lima, 213, N9, [1601] Probanza Juan Bautista Gallinato, fol. 2r.	Soldier.
Tomás Gonzalez		AGI, Patronato, 132, N2, R8, [1590] Informacion Juan Mejia Miraval, fol. 87v.	Soldier.
Andrés de Herrera		AGI, Patronato, 132, N2, R8, [1590] Informacion Juan Mejia Miraval, fol. 52r.	Soldier.

Name	Position in the expedition	Documentary evidence	Social position
Gerónimo de Holguín	(Named captain by those who took Aguirre prisoner after Almendras' death)	Levillier, *Audiencia de Charcas*, VI, p. 208.	Soldier.
Melian de Leguizamo		AGI, Patronato, 132, N2, R8, [1590] Informacion Juan Mejia Miraval, image 174.	Soldier.
Andrés López		AGI, Patronato, 124, R9, [1580] Información Pedro Alvarez Holguín y Martín de Almendras, image 548. AGI, Patronato, 132, N2, R8, [1590] Informacion Juan Mejia Miraval, fol. 84r.	Soldier.
Diego López de Aguilera		AGI, Patronato, 124, R9, [1580] Información Pedro Alvarez Holguín y Martín de Almendras, image 590.	Soldier.
Juan Mejía Miraval		AGI, Patronato, 132, N2, R8, [1590] Informacion Juan Mejia Miraval, image 1r.	Soldier.
Pero Mendez		AGI, Patronato, 124, R9, [1580] Información Pedro Alvarez Holguín y Martín de Almendras, image 21.	Soldier.

Name	Position in the expedition	Documentary evidence	Social position
Martín Monje		López Villalva (dir.), *Acuerdos de Charcas* VI.	*Encomendero,* Martín de Almendras' brother-in-law.
Sebastián Pérez		AGI, Patronato, 124, R9, [1580] Información Pedro Alvarez Holguín y Martín de Almendras, image 562.	Soldier.
Rodrigo Prieto		AGI, Charcas, 53, [1574–1576] Probanza de don Juan Colque Guarache, fol. 38a.	Soldier.
Lope de Quevedo		AGI, Patronato, 132, N2, R8, [1590] Informacion Juan Mejia Miraval, image 15v.	Soldier.
Leonis Ramírez		AGI, Patronato, 132, N2, R8, [1590] Informacion Juan Mejia Miraval, fol. 45v.	Soldier.
Antonio de Robles		AGI, Charcas, 53, [1574–1576] Probanza de don Juan Colque Guarache, fol. 12r.	Soldier.
Juan Rodríguez		AGI, Patronato, 124, R9, [1580] Información Pedro Alvarez Holguín y Martín de Almendras, image 581.	Soldier, owner of a mineral deposit in Potosi.
Don Diego Soto		AGNA, Sala XIII, 18.6.4, fol. 15r.	Andean chief.

List of members of the 1574 expedition

Name	Position in the expedition	Source	Social position
Father Joseph de Acosta	Only travelled to the actual border; did not venture into Chiriguana territory	Acosta, Jose de, *Historia Natural y Moral de Las Indias* (Sevilla: Casa de Juan Leon, 1590), p. 162.	Jesuit.
Diego de Aguilar	Gentilhombre de la Compañía de Lanzas	AGI, Lima, 208, N24, [1589], Diego de Aguilar, images 39 and 40. AGI, Lima, 208, N24, Probanza de Diego de Aguilar, image 15.	Soldier, accompanied Juan Ortiz de Zárate.
Agustín de Ahumada		AGI, Patronato, 149, N1, R1, [1627] Méritos y Servicios Lorenzo de Cepeda y Hermanos, image 23.	*Visitador* in La Plata.
Pedro de Albuquerque		AGI, Patronato, 137, N1, R4, [1598] Luis Hernandez Barja, image 85.	Soldier.
Francisco Aliaga de los Rios		AGI, Lima, 209, N1, [1589] Probanza Rodrigo Campuzano de Sotomayor, image 5.	Soldier.
Juan de Amor		AGI, Patronato, 189, R26, [1579] Mercedes concedidas por Toledo, fol. 4r.	Soldier.
Juan Arias		AGI, Patronato, 132, N2, R7, [1590] Alonso de Paredes, fol. 24v.	Soldier.

Name	Position in the expedition	Source	Social position
Rodrigo Arias		AGI, Lima, 218, N2, [1611] Antonio Zapata, fol. 27r.	Soldier.
Agustín de Arze Quirós		AGI, Lima, 214, N5, [1602] Probanza de Gaspar Flores, image 6; AGI, Patronato, 127, N1, R17, [1583] Toribio Bernaldo y Rodrigo de Arce, image 1.	Soldier, served with Captain Barrasa and others.
León de Ayance		ABNB, EP20, Poder a Diego de Zárate para compra de Ganado para la Expedición de Toledo, fols 319r–320r.	Soldier.
Don Fernando Ayavire Cuysara		AGI, Charcas, 45, Memorial de los caciques principales de la provincia de los Charcas, fol. 14v.	Charcas lord.
Don Francisco Aymoro	Official supplier to the *entrada*	AGI, Charcas, 79, N22, [1592] Probanza de méritos y servicios de don Francisco Aymoro, fol. 13.	Yampara *cacique*.
Don Francisco de Ayra		AGI, Charcas, 56, in Platt et al., *Qaraqara–Charka*, p. 722.	*Cacique* of Pocoata, Urinsaya.
Diego Barrantes Perero		AGI, Patronato, 127, N1, R17, [1583] Toribio Bernaldo y Rodrigo de Arce, image 55.	Soldier; joined the expedition late.

Name	Position in the expedition	Source	Social position
Francisco Barrasa	Captain of the viceroy's guard and 'Campero' – military camp organiser		*Criado* of Toledo – Camarero de su Excelencia.
Antonio Bello Gayoso		Biblioteca Nacional del Perú, Mss 511. 378–381 in Sarabia Viejo and Lohmann Villena, *Francisco de Toledo*, V2, p. 60.	Soldier.
Pedro Benitez		AGI, Patronato, 131, N2, R3, [1588] Rodrigo de Orellana, image 31.	Soldier.
Captain Francisco de Cáceres	Organised food supply logistics	AGI, Lima, 207, N25, [1575], Pedro Gutiérrez de Flores, image 460.	Soldier.
Captain Francisco Camargo		AGI, Lima, 218, N2, [1611] Antonio Zapata, fol. 23r.	Soldier.
Rodrigo de Campuzano Sotomayor		AGI, Lima, 213, N4, [1600] Alvaro Ruiz de Navamuel, fol. 61v.	Soldier.
Alonso de Carvajal		*Revista de Archivos y Bibliotecas Nacionales*, V1 Y1, 108.	Soldier.
Fray Francisco de Carvajal		AGI, Lima, 213, N4, [1600] Alvaro Ruiz de Navamuel, fol. 107r.	Franciscan.
Juan de Castro		AGI, Charcas, 53, [1574–1576], Probanza de don Juan Colque Guarache, fol. 51a.	Soldier.

Name	Position in the expedition	Source	Social position
Hernando de Cazorla	One of don Gabriel Paniagua de Loaysa's captains	AGI, Patronato, 131, N1, R3, [1587] Informacion de Hernando de Cazorla.	Soldier.
Gaspar Centeno		AGI, Patronato, 132, N1, R4, [1589] Informacion de Juan Gutierrez de Beas, fol. 13v.	Soldier.
Don Juan Colque Guarache	Captain of all Indians who went on the expedition	AGI, Charcas, 53, [1574–1576] Informacion de don Juan Colque Guarache.	*Cacique* of Quillaca, Asanaque, Sivaroyo, and Aracapi.
Fray Francisco del Corral		Antonio de la Calancha, *Chronica moralizada del orden de San Augustin en el Perú con sucesos exemplares vistos en esta monarchia* (Barcelona: Pedro Lacaballeria, 1638), p. 464.	Augustinian.
Francisco de la Cuba		AGI, Charcas, 79, N25, [1593] Francisco de la Cuba, image 9.	Soldier.
Captain Pedro de Cuellar Torremocha		AGI, Patronato, 126, R18, [1582] Roque de Cuellar e hijo, image 20.	Soldier, accompanied Juan Ortiz de Zárate.
Alonso Díaz		ABNB, Tierras e indios, 1579, N 46, fol. 10r.	Soldier.
Alonso Dominguez	Gentilhombre de la Compañía de los Lanzas	AGI, Lima, 213, N4, [1600] Alvaro Ruiz de Navamuel, fol. 36r.	Soldier.

Name	Position in the expedition	Source	Social position
Ambrosio Fernandez Azeituno		AGI, Lima, 209, N1, [1589] Probanza Rodrigo Campuzano de Sotomayor, image 6.	Soldier.
Sancho de Figueroa		AGI, Patronato, 133, R5, [1591] Francisco de Guzmán, image 217.	Soldier.
Gaspar Flores	Gentilhombre de la Compañía de Arcabuceros	AGI, Lima, 214, N5, [1602] Probanza de Gaspar Flores, image 3.	Soldier.
Diego de Frias Trejo	Alferez General	AGI, Panama, 61, N67, [1578] Diego de Frias Trejo.	Soldier.
Juan de Gallegos		Levillier, *Gobernacion del Tucuman*, V2, p. 581.	Soldier.
Captain Pablo de Gamboa		AGI, Lima, 218, N2, [1611] Antonio Zapata, fol. 27r.	Soldier.
García de Grijalva		AGI, Charcas, 46, quoted in Hanke, *Los Virreyes Españoles en America*, p. 73.	Soldier.
Felipe Godoy		AGI, Patronato, 137, N1, R4, [1598] Luis Hernandez Barja, image 142.	Soldier.
Gaspar de Grijalva		AGI, Patronato, 137, N1, R4, [1598] Luis Hernandez Barja.	Soldier.
Francisco Guana	Llama caravan shepherd (*fletero*)	AGI, Contaduria, 1805, [1575] Gastos de la Guerra de los Chiriguanaes, pl. 293.	Soldier.

Name	Position in the expedition	Source	Social position
Juan Gutiérrez de Beas	Accompanied Captain Alonso de Vera carrying food supplies to the returning expedition	AGI, Charcas, 79, N12, [1589] Probanza de Juan Gutiérrez de Beas, fol. 14v; AGI, Patronato, 132, N1, R4, [1589] Informacion de Juan Gutierrez de Beas, fol. 1v.	Soldier.
Fray Pedro Gutiérrez Flores		AGI, Lima, 207, N25, [1575] Pedro Gutiérrez Flores, fol. 10v.	Viceroy Toledo's chaplain.
Francisco Guzmán	Proveedor General	AGI, Charcas, 78, N20, [1583] Probanza de Cristóbal Ramirez de Montalvo, fol. 31r; AGI, Patronato 133, R5, [1591] Francisco de Guzmán.	Soldier.
Lope Hernández		AGI, Charcas, 53, [1574–1576] Probanza de don Juan Colque Guarache, fol. 52r.	Soldier.
Luis Hernandez Barja		AGI, Patronato, 137, N1, R4, [1598] Luis Hernandez Barja.	Soldier.
Gerónimo de Hinojosa		AGI, Patronato 131, N2, R3, [1588] Rodrigo de Orellana, image 24.	Soldier.
Pedro Jimenez del Castillo		AGI, Patronato, 137, N1, R4, [1598] Luis Hernandez Barja, image 117.	Soldier.

Name	Position in the expedition	Source	Social position
Pascual Juárez		ABNB, EP20, Declaración de Gómez Coton sobre fanegas que García Mosquera dejó cuando fue con la expedición de Toledo, fols 345r–346r.	Soldier.
Captain Francisco de Lasarte y Molina		AGI, Patronato, 134, R1, Diego de Peralta, Información de Servicios de Diego de Peralta, image 45.	Soldier.
Captain Gutierre Laso de la Vega		AGI, Lima, 218, N2, [1611] Antonio Zapata, fol. 52r.	Soldier.
Felipe de León		AGI, Lima, 207, N25, [1575] Pedro Gutiérrez Flores, image 585.	Notary in Potosí.
Gaspar López	Escribano real – royal notary	AGI, Contaduría, 1805, [1575] Gastos de la Guerra de los Chiriguanaes, pl. 294.	
Pero López de Armesto	Lieutenant to the captain of ammunition	AGI, Contaduría, 1805, [1575] Gastos de la Guerra de los Chiriguanaes, pl. 294.	Soldier.
Iñigo de Luyando	Member of Compañía de Lanzas	AGI, Lima, 207, N13, [1581] Juan Ortiz de Zarate, fol. 51r.	Soldier.
Carlos de Malvenda		AGI, Patronato, 189, R26, [1579] Mercedes concedidas por Toledo, fol. 4r.	Soldier.

Name	Position in the expedition	Source	Social position
Miguel Martín		AGI, Patronato, 235, R7, [1582] Justicia de Santiago de la Frontera, image 109.	Soldier.
Juan Martínez de Ribera		*Revista de Archivos y Bibliotecas Nacionales*, Year 1 Vol. 1, 49.	Soldier.
Francisco de Matienzo		Lohmann Villena, *Matienzo*, p. 84.	Soldier, Juan de Matienzo's son.
Hernando de Maturana		AGI, Charcas, 93, N1, [1646] Francisco de Maturana Trascapo, fol. 46v.	Soldier, accompanied don Gabriel Paniagua de Loaysa and Juan de la Reinaga Salazar.
Don Juan de Mendoza	Assisted with the withdrawal of the expedition	AGI, Patronato, 144, R1, [1608] Luis de Mendoza y Rivera, image 1.	Soldier.
Don Antonio de Meneses		AGI, Lima, 207, N13, [1581] Juan Ortiz de Zarate, fol. 45r.	Soldier.
Pedro de Mieres		AGI, Lima, 214, N5, [1602] Probanza de Gaspar Flores, image 11.	Soldier.
Juan de Montoya		AGI, Indiferente, 1086, L6, [1577], images 132, 128.	Soldier.
Manuel de Morales	Llama caravan shepherd (*fletero*)	AGI, Contaduría, 1805, [1575] Gastos de la Guerra de los Chiriguanaes, pl. 291.	

Name	Position in the expedition	Source	Social position
Diego Moreno	Captain	AGI, Patronato, 131, N2, R3, [1588] Rodrigo de Orellana, image 27.	Soldier.
Juan Bautista Morisco		ABNB, EP18, Poder a Catalina Ñusta viuda de Juan Bautista Morisco para cobrar de Fray Pedro Gutiérrez por el tiempo que sirvió en la entrada de los Chiriguanaes, fols 399r–399v.	Soldier.
García Mosquera	Guide	AGI, Patronato, 235, R4, [1574] Relacion de lo que se hizo en la jornada que el excelentisimo señor virrey del piru don Francisco de Toledo hizo por su persona entrando a hazer Guerra a los chiriguanaes de las fronteras y cordill-eras desta provincial en el año de setenta y quatro, n/d. 8.	
Diego Nuñez Bazán		José Macedonio Urquidi, *El Origen de la Noble Villa de Oropesa. La fundación de Cochabamba en 1571 por Gerónimo Osorio* (Cochabamba: Editorial Canelas, 1970), p. 335.	Soldier.

Name	Position in the expedition	Source	Social position
Antonio de Obregón	Gentilhombre de la Compañía de Arcabuceros	AGI, Lima 213, N4, [1600] Alvaro Ruiz de Navamuel, fol. 28v.	Soldier.
Gallo de Ocampo		AGI, Lima, 207, N8, [1578] Francisco de Valenzuela, fol. 5r.	Soldier.
Francisco Ochoa de Uralde		AGI, Patronato, 235, R7, [1582] Justicia de Santiago de la Frontera, image 115.	Soldier.
Francisco de Orellana			Tiquipaya *encomendero*, accompanied don Gabriel Paniagua de Loaysa.
Juan Ortiz de Zárate	Captain for Potosí	AGI, Charcas, 85, N5, [1606] Juan Alonso de Vera y Zárate.	*Criado* of Toledo.
Hernando Remón de Oviedo	Gentilhombre de la Compañía de Lanzas	AGI, Lima, 214, N5, [1602] Probanza de Gaspar Flores, fol. 10v.	Soldier.
Don Gabriel Paniagua de Loaysa	Captain General	AGI, Charcas, 87, N19, [1618] Informaciones Gabriel Paniagua de Loaisa.	*Encomendero.*
Antonio Pantoja y Chaves		AGI, Patronato, 126, R6, [1582] Méritos y Servicios Diego Pantoja de Chaves, image 7.	Son of Quillaca *encomendero* Diego Pantoja.
Alonso de Paredes		AGI, Patronato, 132, N2, R7, [1590] Alonso de Paredes, fol. 2r.	Soldier, accompanied don Gabriel Paniagua de Loaysa.

Name	Position in the expedition	Source	Social position
Juan Pavón		AGI, Patronato, 131, N2, R3, [1588] Rodrigo de Orellana, image 27.	Soldier, under Captain Diego Moreno.
Juan Pedrero de Trejo		Levillier, *Gobernación de Tucumán*, V2, p. 560.	Soldier.
Alonso de Peñafiel		AGI, Patronato, 126, R11, [1582] Alonso de Peñafiel, image 3.	Soldier.
Diego Peralta Cabeza de Vaca		AGI, Patronato, 134, R1, Diego de Peralta, image 9.	Soldier.
Martín Pérez de Recalde	Justicia Mayor del Campo	Reginaldo de Lizárraga, *Descripción Colonial* (Buenos Aires: Librería de la Facultad, 1916 [1605]), V2, p. 139.	*Licenciado.*
Juan Perez de Valenzuela		AGI, Patronato, 124, R10, [1580] Garci Martin de Castaneda, image 21.	Soldier, accompanied Juan Ortiz de Zárate.
Alonso Pérez Negral		*Revista de Archivos y Bibliotecas Nacionales*, Year 1 Vol. 1, p. 424.	Soldier.
Juan Pinto	Llama caravan shepherd (*fletero*)	AGI, Contaduría, 1805, [1575] Gastos de la Guerra de los Chiriguanaes, pl. 293.	

Name	Position in the expedition	Source	Social position
Balthasar Ramírez	Priest	'Descripcion del Reyno del Piru', in Victor Maurtua, *Juicio de límites entre el Perú y Bolivia. Prueba peruana presentada al gobierno de la República Argentina* (Barcelona: Imprenta de Henrich y Cia, 1906), VI, p. 361.	
Cristóbal Ramírez de Montalvo		AGI, Charcas, 78, N20, [1583] Probanza de Cristóbal Ramirez de Montalvo, fol. 31r; AGI, Patronato, 132, N1, R4, [1589] Informacion de Juan Gutierrez de Beas, fol. 37v.	Soldier.
Juan de la Reinaga Salazar	Captain	AGI, Patronato, 131, N2, R3, [1588] Rodrigo de Orellana, image 21; AGI, Patronato, 146, N3, R1, [1613] Juan de la Reinaga Salazar, fol. 1v.	Soldier, accompanied Francisco de Orellana – they shared the same tent and company of men. His *probanza* states he accompanied don Gabriel Paniagua de Loaysa.

Name	Position in the expedition	Source	Social position
Juan de Reinoso	*Paje de guion* – was carrying Toledo's weapons and armour	AGI, Lima, 212, N19, [1599] Juan de Reinoso, image 15.	
Melchor de Rodas	Sargento Mayor del Campo	AGI, Patronato, 131, N1, R3, [1587] Méritos y Servicios Hernando de Cazorla, image 19.	Soldier.
Juan Rodriguez de Heredia		Victor M. Barriga, *Los mercedarios en el Perú en el siglo XVI. Documentos del Archivo General de Indias. 1518–1600* (Arequipa: Establecimientos Graficos La Colmena SA, 1942), V3, p. 89.	Soldier, accompanied don Gabriel Paniagua de Loaysa.
Alvaro Ruiz de Navamuel	Secretary	AGI, Lima, 213, N4, [1600] Alvaro Ruiz de Navamuel, fol. 4r.	
Pedro de Saavedra		AGI, Panama, 61, N67, [1578] Diego de Frias Trejo, image 9.	Soldier.
Francisco de Saavedra Ulloa		AGI, Patronato, 126, R18, [1582] Roque de Cuellar e hijo, image 30.	Soldier, accompanied Juan Ortiz de Zárate.
Antonio Bautista de Salazar	Secretary to the viceroy	AGI, Lima, 208, N24, [1589] Diego de Aguilar, images 39 and 40.	Soldier.
Hernando de Salazar		AGI, Charcas, 94, N19, [1589] Probanza de Hernando de Salazar, fol. 245v.	Soldier.

Name	Position in the expedition	Source	Social position
Fray Gerónimo de Salcedo		AGI, Lima, 213, N4, [1600] Alvaro Ruiz de Navamuel, fol. 70r.	Franciscan.
Pedro Sande		AGI, Charcas, 53, [1574–1576] Probanza de don Juan Colque Guarache, fol. 24r.	Soldier.
Fray Miguel de Santo Domingo	Secretary	Fray Ivan Melendez, *Tesoros verdaderos de las Yndias en la historia de la gran provincia de San Juan Bautista del Peru* (Rome: Imprenta de Nicolas Angel Tinassio, 1681), V3, p. 351.	
Pedro Sarmiento de Gamboa			Cosmographer.
Captain Pedro Sotelo Narbaez		Antonio de Egaña (ed.), *Monumenta Peruana (1586–1591)* (Rome: Monumenta Historica Societatis Iesu, 1954), V3, p. 113.	Soldier.
Don Francisco de Toledo	Viceroy and Governor General		Viceroy of Peru
Fernando de Toledo Pimentel		AGI, Charcas, 84, N10, [1605] Fernando de Toledo Pimentel, fol. 2r.	
Don Luis de Toledo Pimentel	Maese de Campo	AGI, Lima, 207, N25, [1575] Pedro Gutierrez Flores, fol. 77r.	Viceroy Toledo's uncle

Name	Position in the expedition	Source	Social position
Ginés de Torres		*Revista de Archivos y Bibliotecas Nacionales*, Year I Vol. I, p. 235.	Soldier.
Gasión Torres de Mendoza		AGI, Lima, 207, N25, [1575] Pedro Gutiérrez de Flores, image 266.	Soldier, went as *vecino* of La Paz.
Don Francisco de Valenzuela	Arrived too late from Los Reyes. Went to help Toledo with Ramirez de Quiñones	AGI, Lima, 207, N8, [1578] Francisco de Valenzuela, fol. 8v.	Soldier.
Diego de Valera		AGI, Patronato, 120, N2, R6, [1575] Diego de Valera, image 1.	Soldier.
Dr Tomás Vazquez		AGI, Contaduría, 1805, [1575] Gastos de la Guerra de los Chiriguanaes, pl. 294.	One of Toledo's physicians.
Lope Vázquez Pestana		AGI, Charcas, 79, N11, [1592] Lope Vazquez Pestana, image 3.	Soldier.
Gutierre Velazquez de Ovando		Levillier, *Gobernación de Tucumán*, V2, p. 568.	Soldier.
Captain Alonso de Vera		AGI, Patronato, 132, N1, R4, [11589] Informacion de Juan Gutierrez de Beas, fol. 1v.	Soldier.

Name	Position in the expedition	Source	Social position
Gerónimo de Villarreal		AGI, Patronato, 147, N4, R3, [1618] Probanza de don Pedro de Portugal y Navarra, image 14.	Soldier, accompanied don Gabriel Paniagua de Loaysa.
Juan de Villegas		AGI, Patronato, 141, R1, [1603] Juan de Villegas, image 3.	Soldier.
Juan de Yllanes		AGI, Charcas, 94, N19, [1589] Probanza de Hernando de Salazar, image 545.	Soldier.
Antonio Zapata	Gentilhombre de la Compañía de Lanzas. Responsible for arranging tents and setting up camp	AGI, Lima 218, N2, [1611] Probanza de Antonio Zapata, fol. 2r.	Soldier, *criado* of Toledo.
Diego de Zárate		AGI, Charcas, 86, N17, [1610] Probanza de Diego de Zárate Irarrazábal y Andía, fols 44v–45r.	Polo de Ondegardo's youngest brother.
Fernando/ Hernando de Zárate	Captain for La Plata	AGI, Charcas, 86, N17, [1610] Probanza de Diego de Zárate Irarrazábal y Andía, fols 44v–45r.	Juan Ortiz de Zárate's cousin.

List of members of the 1584 expedition

Name	Position in the expedition	Source	Social position
Francisco Arias de Herrera	Teniente General	AGI, Patronato, 127, N2, R4, [1584–1590] Probanza de Francisco Arias de Herrera, image 12.	Soldier.
Rodrigo de Bustamante		AGI, Patronato, 127, N2, R4, [1584–1590] Probanza de Francisco Arias de Herrera, images 129 and 130.	Soldier.
Antonio Carreño		AGI, Panama, 237, Registro de Partes: Tierra firme, L12, fols 113r–114r.	Soldier.
Don Juan Colque (El Mozo)		Capoche, *Relación General de la Villa Imperial de Potosí*, pp. 142–43.	*Cacique* of Quillacas, Asanaques, Sivaroyos, and Aracapis.
Pedro de Cuellar Torremocha	Maese de Campo	AGI, Patronato, 126, R17, [1606] Información de los méritos y servicios de Pedro de Cuéllar Torremocha, fol. 147.	
Captain Juan Dávalos de Oñate		AGI, Charcas, 80, N17, [1598] Pedro de Mendoza Quesada, image 22.	Soldier.
Antonio Diez Matamoroso		AGI, Charcas, 80, N17, [1598] Pedro de Mendoza Quesada, image 71.	Soldier.
Diego García de Paredes	Captain and Sargento Mayor	AGI, Patronato, 255, N4, G3, R1, [1591] Diego Garcia de Paredes, fol. 2r.	Soldier.

Name	Position in the expedition	Source	Social position
Captain Alonso González de Chamorro		AGI, Patronato, 127, N2, R4, [1584–1590] Probanza de Francisco Arias de Herrera, image 234.	Soldier.
Juan Lozano Machuca	Leader and organiser	AGI, Charcas 79, N14, [1590] Probanza Nuñez Maldonado.	*Factor* and *veedor* in Potosí.
Alonso Fernández de Tamargo		Luis Torres de Mendoza, *Colección de documentos inéditos relativos al descubrim- iento, conquista y organización de las antiguas posesiones españolas de América y Oceanía sacados de los archivos del reino y muy especial- mente del de Indias* (Madrid: Imprenta de Frias y Cia, 1865), V16, p. 31.	Soldier.
Juan Valero or Balero		ABNB, EP 48, fols 400r–401r.	Soldier.
Francisco Mendez		ABNB, EP39, [1586] fols 77r–78r.	Soldier.
Pedro Mendoza de Quezada	Alferez	AGI, Patronato, 127, N2, R4, [1584–1590] Probanza de Francisco Arias de Herrera, image 234; AGI, Charcas, 80, N17, [1598] Pedro de Mendoza Quesada, image 10.	Soldier.

Name	Position in the expedition	Source	Social position
Fray Diego de Reynoso		AGI, Charcas, 80, N17, 1, [1598] Pedro de Mendoza Quesada, image 32.	Mercedarian friar.
Don Fernando de Toledo Pimentel		Levillier, *Biografías de los Conquistadores de Argentina*, p. 226.	Viceroy Toledo's nephew.

Index

www.ingramcontent.com/pod-product-compliance
Lightning Source LLC
Chambersburg PA
CBHW070411100426
42812CB00005B/1704